Table o

Dedicated to all those who helped me to grow-up
and to my wife, Stephanie; my sons, Chris and Steve;
and my grandchildren, Brie, Ryan and Mya.

Introduction

Sadly, I did not become interested in my family history until late in life, by which time too many stories had died with those who had lived them. Neither my parents nor grandparents kept any journals as far as I know. The only letters I have are those written by my father to my mother during World War II. Unfortunately, these don't provide much information, as they were heavily censored at that time due to war time security. What I have recorded are incidents that are engraved on my memory. While I have very little to corroborate their accuracy, it is these memories, even if they are inaccurate, which influenced me to become who I am.

Deciding on an appropriate title for a book is a daunting task. After much searching my son, Steve, suggested *Mrefu*—my thanks.

Prologue

At long last, Kenya was my home. For eighteen months I had been living in England, with my eighty-year-old grandmother, dreaming the wild and dramatic dreams of a twelve and thirteen-year-old boy's idea of living in Africa. Now I was standing on the veranda of the little oblong box of a house, which my mother had built with the help of two Indian *fundis*.

"That is just one of the many new words you are going to have of learn, Anthony," Ma said. "*Fundi* means a skilled tradesman."

I gazed towards some hills, over the flat grasslands that had been burnt brown by the blazing sun and shimmered in the afternoon heat.

"Those are the Ngong Hills," Ma told me. "Look at the four peaks, about equal in height, and then the fifth peak to the right, which is lower and further apart than the others. Do they look like anything special to you?"

"Well, they're hills I guess," I replied, concerned that I didn't have a proper answer.

"The Africans have a myth about those hills. In the days when giants were a hundred-miles tall, one tripped over Donyasabuk—that's a round hill that sticks out of the plains far away to the east. When he stood up, the giant pulled back the earth with his left hand and the Great Rift Valley fell down behind. Look at the hills again and you'll see the imprint of the giant's left hand."

The more I looked at the hills, the clearer the imprint of the giant's hand became. That image burned into my memory.

"One day we'll drive around the hills and see what the giant created."

How different and how much more mysterious this desolate landscape seemed from the lush, green, rolling hills of the English countryside. And my new home appeared more like a large garden shed, compared to the comfortable country house that had been our home in Sussex. Was I apprehensive? Disappointed? Perhaps, but what I remember is the excitement of starting my new life in Africa.

"Tea's here," Ma said. I walked back into the living room where Kamau, the houseboy, was placing a silver tea pot—which had been a part of Ma's tea service for as long as I could remember—on a table, along with cups and saucers, a plate of sandwiches, and a chocolate cake.

Ma said something to Kamau in Swahili, which was interrupted by the English phrase "chocolate cake" and included something that sounded like 'bwana kidogo'.

Kamau replied in Swahili. I heard the word "kidogo" again. As a grin spread across his face, Kamau held his hand at chest height. Suddenly his hand shot above his head. He looked up, his eyes wide, and said something that sounded like 'rayfu' to me, and then chuckled.

Ma laughed, "Kamau says we can't call you "bwana kidogo", which means little bwana, because you are so tall. He says that you will have to be bwana Mrefu, which means the tall bwana."

At thirteen I was not far off six feet, and was taller than all the African staff whom I had met when I'd arrived earlier that afternoon.

Chapter 1

I'm strutting up and down the terrace in the bright sunlight, bursting with pride. When I pass the open French doors, I can see up the stairs to where my friend Peter is standing on a stool. He is bent over a pedestal sink, while my mother and his mother wash blood and sand out of his hair. I have just hit him over the head with my "sugar teaser"—the fender off a tricycle—with which I was playing in the sandbox next to the house. Peter, who is almost two years older than me, had bossed me about once too often.

This is my earliest memory—from the summer of 1939, the year I turned three.

Here is what I have learnt about my earliest days. I was born on June 4, 1936, in Yelverton—a village close to Plymouth in South Devon, England—seven months after my parents were married. Ma told me that officers in the Royal Marines were not allowed to marry until they reached the rank of captain. As my father, who was twenty-two, was only a lieutenant, he had to obtain permission to marry from his commanding officer. Marines served aboard ships so, for the first four years of their marriage, my parents lived wherever my father's ship was based. Soon after I was born, they moved from Plymouth to Portsmouth, where I was christened in the Royal Marine Barracks and (Ma told me) was fed champagne in my bottle to celebrate. Subsequently, we moved to Chatham, which is where we were living when I hit Peter over the head.

I have a vague recollection of playing marines with my father. In it, I'm standing to attention with a toy gun on my shoulder while my father, wearing his uniform, salutes—but this memory is probably more from a photograph than from real life.

My father was born in Natal, South Africa, in 1913. He was christened Paddy, because he was born on St. Patrick's Day, March 17. Apparently, this caused much consternation among minor officials, as it was not considered proper in those days to christen someone with what was considered to be a nickname. Paddy boarded at a prep school in Natal—an experience he later described as the most miserable time of his life.

His father, Norman Sheridan, had been born in 1874, the youngest son of William Sheridan—the harbour master at Seaham in Durham, England—and his wife Annie. Norman became a doctor and joined the Royal Army Medical Corps in England. He went to South Africa for the Boer War, where he met my grandmother, Winifrede Kendall, who was serving as a nurse. The only family story I remember hearing about my grandfather, whom I never met, is that he was more interested in racehorses and diamonds than in medicine. I don't know how correct the story is, but for me it created an air of glamour and intrigue that made him a fascinating character.

My grandmother's family had a military background: Her father was the surgeon-general of the Indian Army; her grandfather was a general in the same army; and her brother was an army officer. However, she was apparently disowned by her family for going to nurse in South Africa, rather than staying home and pursuing activities more properly suited to a young lady of the times—seeking a suitable husband, I assume.

Besides my father, Norman and Winifrede had two other children: Terrence and Noreen. My grandparents divorced, which was an event that was considered shameful at the time, and after Paddy had finished prep school, Winifrede and he moved to Kenya. My grandmother changed her last name from Sheridan to Brind-Sheridan—Brind being her third given name, as well as the name of her maternal grandfather. As schooling in Kenya was very limited at the time, my father was sent to Bedford Grammar School in England. I doubt that he went back to Africa during his schooling in England, as it was a three-week trip by ship each way. I believe he enjoyed Bedford, where he rowed. Ma told me that rowing was a sport he chose because rowers received a pint of stout after each workout. He wanted to join the navy, but was rejected because he had a deformed breastbone—the result of having been kicked by a horse as a child. However, in 1931, directly out of school, he was accepted as an officer cadet in the Royal Marines.

My mother's parents lived in Enfield, in the north of London. They were cousins who married in their late twenties, but did not have any children until my grandmother was about forty. My maternal grandfather, Percival Pickford, was a prosperous jeweller and goldsmith who had a business in the City of London, but also invested in property. He was also a pawnbroker, but that part of his business was never mentioned to me by my mother or grandmother; a cousin who took over the business told me about it many years later. Percy was handsome, athletic, and according to my mother, great fun. He made a good living and he and my grandmother were, at the time, considered "comfortably off". I have only vague memories of him, as he died when I was four. Staplehurst, their house in Enfield, was fairly large—huge to my childhood eyes. It was staffed by three servants, and had a large garden, a tennis court, and a barn at the foot of a meadow, which was home to a small flock of Rhode Island Red chickens.

My maternal grandmother, Helen Grover, was a formidable woman, and an ardent member of the British Women's Total Abstinence Union. I never saw her wear a dress without a White Ribbon brooch, which was the union's badge. As a young woman, she was active in lecturing on the evils of alcohol, and trying to close down pubs in the working-class areas of London. She must have been an awesome figure: almost six-feet tall with an upright stance, dressed in straight-laced clothing, probably with a hat perched on the top of her head, staring through her *pince-nez* and waving her cane for emphasis.

Her temperance activities were the butt of much family humour behind her back, particularly as Percy always had a bottle of Scotch in the sideboard. When, many years later, I heard a radio program about Nellie McClung—an ardent Canadian temperance activist—I came to realize that not only did Granny's work require considerable courage but also that her motivation was to protect women and children. At that time many working men, who were paid in cash at lunchtime on Saturday, would go straight to the pub on payday. They spent too much of their meagre pay on drink, and then returned home to abuse their families and leave them insufficient money for rent and food. I have come to admire what Granny did, instead of laughing about it.

My mother, Wendy, was the vibrant and good-looking younger sister of Joan, who was homely and overweight throughout her life. Wendy went to private schools. I don't know how she did academically, but her strengths were more social and athletic. Her favourite sport was riding, particularly fox-hunting. She played lacrosse, but this was curtailed when she tore a ligament in her knee, which was operated on but not well repaired. From the few stories she told me, and from her photographs, it is clear that my mother had been a rather wild young woman. She was attractive, stylish, popular with men, and liked to party.

Soon after my mother left school, the family went to visit relatives in Australia and New Zealand, a trip that took about six months. I often wondered if the reason for the trip was to provide closer supervision for Wendy and Joan. On the voyage home, a young woman named Babs boarded the ship when it stopped in India. She and my mother were to become lifelong best friends. Babs, who had grown up in India, invited Wendy to come and stay with her when she returned there a few months later. Perhaps my grandparents agreed when they learned that Babs' father, an engineer, lived in the jungle far away from civilization. However, her stay in India was anything but dull. She and Babs had many friends, particularly among the young army officers who were stationed nearby. The highlight of her trip was an invitation to a maharajah's wedding—a celebration that lasted for a week—with long parades of important guests riding on elephants and sumptuous feasts eaten with gold cutlery off of gold plates.

Wendy met Paddy at a dance. Shortly afterwards, Babs wrote about an escapade when she and Wendy went to meet Paddy and a friend, who were cruising on a small sailboat on the Norfolk Broads. They missed their rendezvous, so Wendy and Babs spent the first night sleeping in Babs' car. When they met up the next day, the two men suggested that the girls sail the boat to the next pub, while they drove the car. It turned out that the boat didn't have a keel and wouldn't sail upwind, so the two girls ended up pulling the boat by hand from the tow path. Despite this, they had "a splendid few days." Babs said that Wendy became convinced that Paddy was the man for her. Babs' strongest memories of Paddy were his good temper and sense of humour.

Paddy was serving on the battleship HMS Rodney in 1935, when he and my mother married. The following year he was seconded to the Royal Marines Small Arms School to be an instructor. Charles Shand, one of the recruits at the school, recalled my father's approach to training: "For the first time in our service we were encouraged to think, to plan, to be resourceful, and to use initiative and common sense. Your father set the scene. His quiet, friendly manner put us at ease immediately. He had chosen his instructors very carefully and they followed his example. He was absolutely on top of his job and we could not have wished for better instruction or instructors … I look back on those weeks as probably the happiest time in my thirty-three years' service."

When the war broke out, we were living in Chatham—a large naval base in Kent, in southeast England. My father was at sea aboard the HMS Ajax. He wrote to Ma and told her to move to North Devon as quickly as possible, as Chatham was a sure target for bombing. Soon after we left, Chatham was bombed and the area where we had lived was severely damaged.

Chapter 2

"Wakey, wakey, we're here!" My mother's voice dragged me from a deep sleep. I was curled up in the back seat of the Hillman, covered by a blanket. We'd arrived in Westward Ho, a village near Bideford in North Devon, late at night, in the autumn of 1939.

We had rooms in 4A Kingsley Terrace, a row of four-storey, attached houses that overlooked the sea, though my memory suggests that our rooms overlooked the parking area at the rear. The building had housed the school attended by Rudyard Kipling, some seventy years before, and was also the setting for the fictional school in his controversial novel, *Stalky and Co*. In his memoirs, he described it as being 'twelve bleak houses by the shore'.

Soon after our arrival, at the same time that HMS *Ajax*—along with two other British cruisers, *Exeter* and *Achilles*—was involved in the Battle of the River Plate, I came down with measles. Patients with measles were kept in the dark to protect their eyes. I remember crying in a darkened room, in a combination of misery and frustration, because my mother was paying more attention to the radio, which was reporting on the battle, than to me. The three British ships, with the commodore aboard *Ajax*, were attacking the German pocket battleship *Admiral Graf Spee*. My father was in command of a turret on the foredeck of *Ajax*. It must have been terrifying, as the *Graf Spee*'s big guns had a much longer range than that of any of the smaller British ships. In a letter to his brother Terrence, Paddy wrote that they were bracketed by the *Graf Spee*'s shells and "God only knows how we weren't blown out of the water." He didn't mention that his turret had been hit and that one of the marine gunners had been killed.

After being severely damaged, *Exeter* dropped out of the battle, but *Ajax* and *Achilles* inflicted enough damage on the bigger ship that her captain decided to seek refuge in Montevideo, a neutral harbour. International law required the *Graf Spee* to leave a neutral harbour after a specified time. Based on intelligence that he was facing a greatly reinforced and superior British fleet, the *Graf Spee*'s captain, Hans Langsdorff, decided to scuttle his ship outside the harbour rather than have his crew face certain death. However, the information he received was based on misinformation created by British Intelligence. A merchant fleet sailing down the South American coast made a lot of smoke, while fabricated British radio messages reported the arrival of a naval squadron. In reality, *Ajax* and *Achilles* had only been reinforced by HMS *Cumberland*, another cruiser that was also outgunned by the *Graf Spee*. Langsdorff, who had disobeyed Hitler's orders to fight to the death, committed suicide three days after scuttling his ship.

During the battle, the *Graf Spee* had a large number of Allied merchant seamen aboard, as it had been Langsdorff's practice to put a shot across a merchant ship's bow and evacuate the crew before sinking it. The captured merchant seamen were freed in Montevideo.

Among Paddy's effects was a photograph of the *Graf Spee*, inscribed: "Thank you very much, Werner Kolb, Ltu.po Sec. 1938." This was probably a memento from a meeting of the two ships before the war.

In 1939, a large munitions factory was being built east of Toronto. As the sinking of the *Graf Spee* was the first good news of the war for the Allies, the new town that was growing up around a munitions factory was named Ajax, in recognition of that vessel's role as the lead ship in the victory. Every member of the crew has a street in Ajax named after him, and as a result one street in Ajax is named Brind-Sheridan Court.

My one other memory of our short stay at Westward Ho is of leaning out a high window to watch a workman mix mortar in the parking area below. He mixed cement and sand together on the asphalt, turning it over and over with his shovel until the dry ingredients were well mixed and piled into a neat hill. He dug a hole in the middle of the hill so that it resembled a volcano, filled the hole with water, and then carefully shovelled the sides into the water before slicing his shovel into the mixture. He repeated the process until the mixture attained the correct consistency. I follow this procedure each time I make pancakes.

We then moved to 6 Bayview Terrace, where we had a house to ourselves. The terrace was twelve attached houses, similar to what would usually be found in any town, but this terrace was situated high on a hill and surrounded by fields with no other houses close by. It may have been built by the local parish council in the mid-nineteenth century to raise funds. The house, which was about twenty-four feet wide, had three storeys with an open courtyard in the centre, with passageways connecting the front and rear parts of the house. The kitchen and a play room were on the ground floor, the living room and dining room on the second floor, and the bedrooms on the third.

In front of the house, a small yard was enclosed by walls. Behind, the garden was divided by a rear lane. In the small garden next to the house was a rockery, which I converted into a miniature battlefield for my toy soldiers and Dinky toys. Beyond the lane was the continuation of the garden, which contained a lawn with a hammock and a small orchard.

To the northeast, the back rooms of the terrace looked down on surf pounding onto a long sandy beach that led to the mouth of the Bideford River, with a golf course in the dunes behind. Except for a small area at the near end, next to the rocks, most of the beach was cut off by barbwire fencing and covered with metal objects designed to hinder an enemy landing. The dunes were mined. To the northwest, the rocks gradually climbed to high cliffs that stretched to the horizon. Out at sea, usually shrouded in mist, was the Isle of Lundy, which was home to about thirty people and millions of birds, and issued its own postage stamps.

With the blitz in London in full swing, we were assigned a family of evacuees to board with us, a mother with three or four children. I was fascinated with the oldest girl, Angela, who was about ten. She created a bomber out of the playroom furniture, made goggles out of wooden curtain rings, assumed the role of pilot, assigned the rest of us kids to crew positions, and ordered us to bomb the hell out of Berlin.

Relations between our mothers were not so good. Ma complained that Angela's mother whined about missing London and didn't appreciate the opportunity she had been given, for her children to be safe and experience the wonders of country life. Their different perspectives were also aggravated by class differences. After a short stay, Angela's family returned to London. Rather than take in more evacuees, which was required if you had a house with vacant rooms, Ma looked for a more compatible family to share the house. Soon Bar Mitchell and her two sons—Michael, who was a month younger than I, and Peter, one year younger—came to live with us.

Michael, Peter, and I found another friend—with whom I shared a first name—Anthony Seagrave, who lived about a mile up the road. I think Anthony was a bit older than I was. He was the leader of our gang and the perpetrator of at least one prank that got us into trouble. Anthony found an old hunting rifle with a long, silver-coloured barrel (and fortunately no ammunition) in his attic. We decided that this gave us a great opportunity to play a game of robbers. We found a perfect ambush spot in some bushes beside a lane and hid, waiting for our first victim. Soon we heard a bicycle coming, its rider puffing as he pedalled up the hill. All four of us jumped out, with Anthony waving the rifle.

"Your money or your life!"

It was the village Bobby.

"Now then, sonny, you best hand that gun over," said the Bobby.

We meekly handed over our treasured weapon and, after giving our names and addresses, scuttled off home to await the constable's visit to our mothers. I don't remember any dire punishment and suspect the whole affair was treated as a bit of a joke, at least by my mother. Most of the time our gang simply explored the acres of farmland and woods that surrounded our homes, living in the wonderful fantasy world of young boys left to their own devices.

After a year or so, Anthony's family departed. From the adults, I gathered there was some sort of scandal, but I never learned what it was.

One afternoon, during the summer I turned four, I was sailing a toy boat in the saltwater swimming pool that had been carved out of the dense mass of rocks to the west of the sandy beach. The boat ran out of wind and bobbed helplessly about three feet from the edge of the pool. I leant over, trying to reach the mast, and fell in. I surfaced out of my depth, with the edge of the pool appearing far out of reach. Adrenalin must have given me enough strength to strike out and cover the three or four feet between myself and the rope that was hanging from the side of the pool. It was the first time I had swum. That must have given me confidence, for I soon learnt to swim properly and have always loved the water. The following year, I learned to surf on the small portion of the beach that was still open to the public, on a plywood equivalent of today's boogie board. I must have had a relatively high level of tolerance for cold water, as I started swimming and surfing during the Easter holidays.

Horses were a big part of our life. In my father's letters to Ma, during our time at Bayview Terrace, he often mentioned how he wished he could be with his wife on the many horseback rides she enjoyed. Once he referred to having a wonderful ride in the desert when *Ajax* was docked, probably near Alexandria, but due to censorship he could not identify the location. My beginnings on horseback were not so happy. The main thrust of my lessons was being continually instructed to sit up straight and grip with my knees, as I steered the pony between the broken white lines on the road—due to petrol rationing, there was virtually no traffic on the roads. To add insult to injury, I was not properly dressed. I rode in shorts and Wellington boots, though later I did have a pair of jodhpurs.

Ma must have wanted me to be an all-rounder, as she enrolled me in dance lessons as well. I was less than enthusiastic when I discovered I was the only boy, but I was enrolled so was expected to finish. At the end of the classes, the teacher organized a show for the parents. At the beginning, we were all asked who we were. According to Ma, all the smiling girls, who were dressed in frilly skirts, said that they were fairies. Apparently, I said nothing until pressured, when I reluctantly admitted: "I'm a elf."

As our car was on blocks due to the petrol rationing, Ma's transportation was a bicycle. At first, I was perched on a seat that was attached to the frame of her bike, immediately behind the handle bars, but I soon had my own bike. In summer, we often rode down to the beach. The hill down was very steep and, when I first started to ride, I used to walk my bike down it. The first time I rode down I was terrified. I gripped the brakes as hard as I could, but still seemed to go faster and faster. Near the bottom of the hill, the road took a ninety-degree turn to the right, to meet a road that went along the bottom of the hill. To go to the rock swimming pool, our frequent haunt, meant turning almost a hundred and eighty degrees to the left, shortly after the first turn. With my heart in my throat, my body rigid with fear, and my bike wobbling, I made the first turn. Still proceeding at what seemed a fearsome speed, I approached the hairpin bend. I made it halfway around before I froze. I went straight ahead, hit a gate, and flew over the handlebars and the gate to land in a field of cabbages. My bruised ego overshadowed my scrapes and scratches.

Unfortunately, Ma left no diaries or letters, so all I know of her from that time is through my eyes as a child and some comments in my father's letters to her. To me, she was a mixture of strict expectations, encouragement, and laissez-faire: I was going to ride and dance, regardless of what I thought. I soon realized there was no point in protesting, so I put up with it. I loved wearing anything that indicated I was a marine, and I suspect that greatly helped in discipline, as marines were expected to obey orders. Ma told me that, as Daddy was away at war, I was the man in the house and, as such, I had to behave like a man. This made me feel grown-up and responsible.

To me, Ma always seemed competent and in control, but in several of my father's letters he gave her advice on how to handle me: "If he misbehaves he should spend the afternoon in the nursery—but that is easy for me to say." From his comments, I gather I was not the easiest child to handle. However, there was not much in his letters about me; I got the impression that fatherhood was something rather obscure for him, having had so little contact with me.

Ma was also battling guilt. I'd had a brother, David, who had been born in 1938 and died in his crib when he was six weeks old—an unexplained death. Ma continued to grieve David's death. In one letter in particular, dated June 1941, Paddy urged her not to brood over it.

When nothing was scheduled, I was free to explore with friends, on my own or with James, our bull terrier, who was always referred to as Daddy's dog. James, like many dogs, loved chasing anything that was thrown for him. The one time he tolerated strangers was when he could persuade them to throw a stick or stone for him. According to Ma, he also had an adventurous side. Apparently, he sometimes went down to the bus stop by himself, hopped on the double-decker bus, went upstairs, and lay down under the back seat. He would get off in the village of Appledore—the story is that he had a girlfriend there—and return home by the same means later in the day, in time for his evening meal.

James's strongest characteristic was his protectiveness of the family. Ma's story about this is that once, when she was ill, she called the doctor. He said he would come around and was told that Ma was in bed upstairs at the back of the house, but that the front door was open so he could come in. He walked up the front path and was met by James, whom he knew from previous visits. James growled. The doctor told him it was okay and continued towards the door. James took hold of his ankle. If the doctor tried to move, either back or forward, James bit it. If he stayed still, James just held his ankle firmly in his jaws. Beating a bull terrier has no effect; the doctor stood with James's jaw locked around on his ankle for about an hour, until Bar Mitchell returned.

One day in the spring of 1941, Ma decided to visit Plymouth to see some of her old marine and navy friends. We stayed in a house in Yelverton, the village where I was born, a few miles out of town. One night when Ma went out to a pub near Plymouth, the city was heavily bombed and she was unable to get back to the house. When the air raid sirens sounded, our landlady, who had agreed to look after me, went up to our room to take me down to the shelter, but James would not let her touch me. As a result, I slept through the only air raid of my life in an upstairs room protected by a bull terrier. In one of his letters, my father begged Ma never to visit Plymouth again.

When I turned six, I went to school. Highgate School had been evacuated from London to an estate nearby and I attended there, as one of the few day boys, for one term. I don't recall if I was happy there or not, but my one clear memory of the school is that during one morning break, the older boys were having a competition to see how far they could throw a dart. I was walking across the playing field when they yelled at me. I looked up to see a dart coming straight for me. I backed up, lifting my shoulder to protect myself. The dart struck me in the shoulder, sinking up to the hilt. Another school story that Ma revelled in telling was that one day I had come home and said that all the other boys had been beaten, but I hadn't because I was too young. Whereupon Ma, hugely pregnant, marched the two miles up to the school to demand that her son be treated the same as everyone else. If they were beaten, I was to be beaten too, regardless of my age.

My father's visits to Bayview Terrace were few and often unexpected, as he could not divulge his whereabouts or plans in his letters and mail delivery was often long-delayed and unreliable. He sent a telegram after the Battle of the River Plate that simply said: "All's well. Happy Christmas, All love Paddy." A letter that arrived a couple of weeks later said, "I'm sorry our little scrap scared you," but revealed nothing about his whereabouts or destination, in that or his other letters. A telegram we received five weeks after the battle read: "Arrived England this morning. Will phone you about 1900. All love Paddy." He visited us at least three times, maybe more. At other times, Ma went to see him where his ship had docked or where he was stationed. When he was in barracks while *Ajax* was being repaired, he kept writing to say, "Plans are so uncertain it's not worth you coming ..." though they did sometimes get together for a week or so. When arrangements were finally made, we would rush to London on the train; I would go and stay with my grandmother and Ma would travel on to Liverpool or Portsmouth or Chatham, wherever the ship had docked.

Paddy's letters to Ma, written every two or three days during that time, tended to be repetitious and contained very little information. One letter started: "There is so much I want to tell you, if I was allowed to, but I can't so I don't have much to write about." By 1940 all letters were censored and some had sentences either cut out or blacked out. All too often, they included news about friends and acquaintances who had been killed. At times Paddy was desperately lonely, continually expressing frustration at being apart from the woman he adored. But he was not averse to taking out women, or "popsies," as he referred to them, for a meal or a dance in some of the many ports he visited. He said he was "a tiny bit jealous" when Ma told him about "boyfriends," but I never read any criticism of her. His life, when in port, had much to commend it: playing squash and tennis, partying with friends—he mentioned many hangovers—eating out and visiting new places like Athens.

From 1940 to 1942, *Ajax* was based in the Mediterranean and on October 12, 1940, she was attacked in the middle of the night by Italian destroyers and torpedo boats. Unbeknownst to the Italians, *Ajax* had just been outfitted with radar, a new gimmick then, and she sank a destroyer and two torpedo boats, "leaving the Italians defeated and bewildered." Later, *Ajax* was part of the British fleet that routed the Italian fleet at the battle of Cape Matapan. After the battle, as British ships were picking up survivors from the sunken Italian ships, they were attacked by the Luftwaffe and had to abandon many Italians in the water. However, the British admiral contacted the Italian HQ and gave them the coordinates for the remaining survivors, some of whom were later rescued by an Italian hospital ship. What was left of the Italian fleet after the battle went back into port and didn't come out again until 1944, when Italy surrendered.

One of my father's fellow sailors on *Ajax* in 1941 wrote of him: "He had a terrific sense of humour and fun, indeed some of the shore times in *Ajax* were amongst some of the best in the war." He said that his favourite memory was of the time he and Paddy were on a pub crawl in Alexandria. There was an air raid, so they had to get back to their ship. They could not find a taxi, so they "borrowed" a steamroller to get back to the dock, where they managed to persuade an Arab sailor to take them out to their ship in spite of the air raid.

Staplehurst was my second home at this time. We visited as a family—I remember at least two Christmases there, including one with my father—and I often stayed on my own. Granny, who was in her mid-seventies, was austere in appearance. Her typical dress was high-necked, long-sleeved, and long-skirted, in sombre, dark colours, and she had a strong scent of lavender about her. She clearly adored me. Though she was not demonstrative, I always felt loved; but I didn't like kissing her because she had whiskers on her chin. Her style was rather formal. We usually ate lunch in the dining room, table properly set and meals beautifully prepared by the house-keeper, Mrs Watson. Often it was just the two of us, Granny and me, sitting in splendid isolation at a table large enough to seat twelve. Supper was a less formal meal, often served on trays in the lounge and prepared by Mrs Watson before she left for the day.

I must have once said I loved custard, for at every meal there was a large bowl of custard "especially for Anthony." Depending on how many were dining, there might be two or three other desserts—often much more appetizing than custard—but I was never offered a choice and didn't dare ask for a change. Mrs Watson was kind and let me help her in the kitchen, while my interest lasted or there was the prospect of a bowl of cake mix to lick clean. Her husband was the chauffeur/gardener. I would often hang around with him, even though he forbade me to play in the blue Rover, which he kept polished and immaculate despite the lack of petrol.

The lounge at Staplehurst, a large comfortable room with a deep blue carpet and blue leather furniture, was more like today's family room. The drawing room was kept for formal entertaining that did not include children.

I spent a lot of time in the garden. A raised terrace overlooked a lawn that was sometimes used for croquet. It had an herbaceous border on the left and a vegetable garden, which included rows of black and red currants, behind a hedge at the far end. One of my favourite pastimes was hanging over the fence behind the vegetable garden and watching the action in the railway shunting yard next to the property. To the right of the lawn was a paved path that passed three fish pools on the way to a grass tennis court. Below that was a meadow with a barn for chickens. When I was playing alone, I turned the garden into an imaginary battlefield and won battle after battle, as Granny fell asleep, her mouth open, rocking gently in the swing set. But there was one battle I was very glad I lost. I was playing with my father, who was pretending he couldn't find my hiding place. After he passed me, I jumped out of the bushes, aimed my bow and arrow at his back and let fly. Thankfully, the arrow shot straight up in the air.

My most frequent companions then were Laddie, a golden retriever, and Bruin, a cairn terrier. But occasionally my second cousin, Michael Grover, who was about two years older than me, was shanghaied into coming over to play with me. I suspect that he saw me as a nuisance when I was very young, but as I grew older we became close friends. Aunt Joan, who was single, would visit on occasion, but never more than that as she was busy working as an ambulance driver, and was seldom around.

In September 1942, my father was posted as captain of marines to the HMS Victorious, an aircraft carrier. Soon after, I visited the ship. Left alone in his cabin for a while, I went through his drawers and, much to my delight, found an automatic pistol. Here, fantasy gets mixed up with reality. I know I upset the marine sentry at the gangway by sneaking up behind him, but I don't think I stuck the pistol in his back, as I sometimes imagine. Either way, my father was mad. He pointed out to me, in no uncertain terms, that not only was I never to touch a pistol again, but it was wrong to go through other people's drawers.

As the Americans were short of aircraft carriers in the Pacific, *Victorious* was seconded to the U.S. Navy and temporarily renamed the USS *Robin* or, as the American sailors called her, the "Limey flat top". With my father aboard, she set sail for Norfolk, Virginia, where she was refitted. My father's time in Norfolk appears to have been one long party. In almost every letter he wrote, he seemed to be suffering from a hangover. The U.S. Marines, and others ashore, entertained him and his colleagues lavishly, so Paddy and his fellow officers felt obliged to return the hospitality on board, which was costly as they had to pay for everything served to guests. Paddy became quite melancholy at times, fearing that his future was to end up "as a gin-soaked old major." He was also spending a lot of money, as the cost of living was so much higher in the United States.

In the longest letter he wrote to Ma, he described a visit to New York, where he had been the guest of a wealthy couple who were relatives of his winger, or lieutenant. He was amazed by the large size of the rooms in their downtown Manhattan apartment, and that the spare room in which he stayed had an en suite bathroom—his experience in England had been mainly of small rooms, with one bathroom per house. He went to clubs, dances, and shows, ate steaks larger than he had ever seen before, and increased his bank overdraft. *Victorious* eventually sailed to Pearl Harbor via the Panama Canal and Los Angeles, where Paddy and the other crew were entertained by some of the British Hollywood stars. He went shopping for Ma and, after much hesitation, finally plucked up the courage to buy her some "scanties."

But it was not all fun and games. *Victorious* was involved in several actions against the Japanese around the Solomon Islands. I know Ma had some good times too, but some of Paddy's letters indicate that she was having a tough time financially. I suspect that his stories of his adventures must have been hard for her to read.

Ma gave birth to my sister, Penelope, on January 15, 1943, while Paddy was at sea in the Pacific. Ma's way of establishing my relationship with the new arrival to our family was to say that, as Penelope's father was away at war, I would have to play that role. This made me feel important and responsible. I was always very protective of Penelope, and don't ever remember being jealous.

May of 1943 brought a major change in my life. I went away to board at Fernden School, near Haslemere in Surrey, shortly before my seventh birthday.

Chapter 3

The rendezvous for boys travelling to Fernden was a platform at Waterloo Station in London. Like the other boys, aged from six to thirteen, I wore a blue raincoat over a grey sweater, a grey shirt with a red and green tie, grey shorts, and grey knee-socks. A red and green cap sat on my head, probably askew, with a mop of blond hair falling over my forehead. The group slowly coalesced in the middle of the platform. Older boys greeted friends, while the new boys stood apprehensively on the periphery, some clinging to their parents while others tried to assert their independence. I can't remember how I reacted or how I felt on that first, of several firsts, day of term. I must have been afraid to leave Ma, but I knew that I had to go away to school ... just as I knew my father had to go away to war. I was determined not to cry. Mr Charles, the headmaster, was there to greet students and reassure apprehensive parents of new boys. Soon we were herded into compartments, while trunks—filled with clothing that had been specified on the school's clothing list—were stowed in the guard's van. I don't know if I kissed Ma goodbye. If I did, it would have been one of the last times, as kissing parents in front of other boys was a ritual that was soon to be abandoned.

Fernden was a private school in the true sense of the word. The school and its property were owned by the headmaster and school fees were the primary source of income for the school. Mr Brownrigg, the headmaster's father, had bought the property in 1907 and started the school. When he passed it on to his son in 1936, he left several loans, which Mr Charles decided to pay off through belt tightening. Mr Charles, while I was a student, must have run the school himself, for I can find no record of a Board of Governors. School Inspectors visited Fernden in 1938, but did not return until 1955—at which time they wrote a glowing report complimenting the headmaster for both his teaching and administration, and his wife for managing all the household responsibilities. Fernden was selected for me as Ma knew Jane Charles and knew that the school focused on families whose sons were destined for the military. During and immediately after the war, there were enough students to run a quality school, but by the 1980s competition for students was tight, costs increased, and the school closed down rather than go into debt.

The approach to the school was up a long winding driveway, to a court-yard in front of a red brick building with a tiled roof that seemed immense to me. On the left of the courtyard, there were steps leading up to some classrooms, the gym, and the chapel. To the right, the windows on the far side of the main building looked over the tops of trees to the rolling, wooded countryside with only a few other houses in sight. A steep path down the hill, through majestic beech trees, led to the playing fields, which were large enough for five soccer pitches. Behind a hedge in the far left-hand corner was a swimming pool.

I was assigned to New Dormitory, a long room with about twenty iron bedsteads. Each was covered with a dark-grey blanket, had a towel folded over the foot rail, and had a small wooden locker at its side. As this was the beginning of the summer term, the temperature was pleasant, but the following winter I learnt that the few radiators were little if any defence against the outside temperature. If there was a frost outside, there was ice on the inside of the windows. Stairs, which were open to the elements at the bottom, led down to a door that opened onto a semi-circle of washba-sins—with a row of toilets opposite the basins. If that room was heated, I don't remember it. Baths (showers were virtually unknown then) were in a warmer room in the main school building and were taken every few days, but with only four inches of water so as to save fuel for the war effort.

Though being away from home, sleeping in a dormitory, and eating with a hundred and forty others in the same dining hall must have been frightening, I have no memory of misery or homesickness. I must have adapted to school life well, for when I look back on the six years I spent at Fernden, my overall sense is that it was a good time with only moments of unhappiness or frustration or disappointment. In a letter to my mother, Paddy wrote that he was glad to hear I was adjusting well to school.

My first term teachers were Miss Randall, who was short, dark, and plump, and Miss Godbold, who was thin, bent, and bleached blonde. The two form-one classes had about eight boys in each. The one lesson I remember was weekly letter-writing home, in which we copied off the board: "Dear Mummy, I hope you are well. I am happy. I like school ..." I remember feeling annoyed that I couldn't write what I wanted, but since I couldn't compose a letter, I was stuck.

On my seventh birthday, celebrated about a month after I had arrived at school, I received a large parcel from Granny. I opened it eagerly. It was a toy carpentry set. I was mortified, for at school I had started working in a proper carpentry shop with proper tools. Unfortunately, it was a skill I never developed.

The dining hall was a hub of social life. Twelve boys, six aside, sat at a table with a master at the head. Table-mates became friends and meals were a constant burble of excited chatter and exuberance, which some times got out of hand. Punishment for activities, such as flicking peas across the table, was standing on the bench. The first time it happened to me, I felt mortified. It seemed as if the whole world was looking at me and snickering, when in reality it was probably only my immediate friends who were smirking behind their hands. To hide my embarrassment, I pretended I was working on complicated arithmetical problems, like adding two numbers, in my head. I was reminded of this many years later, when I had a student placement at the Provincial Mental Hospital in Coquitlam and saw a patient who counted all the windowpanes of the barred windows every morning. What games a mind can play to try to show it is in control. At any rate, standing on the bench earned one a certain status and only curtailed my exuberance for a short while. It was not the only time I ended up being made a spectacle.

Mrs Charles, the headmaster's wife, though the mother of three small children, often had to prepare breakfast for the entire school and fill in for staff shortages. It was a struggle to create healthy meals in a time of strict rationing and great shortage of food. Hers must have been a Herculean task, for which she received far too little recognition and too much criticism. The food was not very good, but it was certainly sufficient. My only real complaint was the semolina and sago puddings, neither of which I have eaten since. My favourite breakfast, a preference shared by many boys, was Marmite on bread fried in bacon fat. The best tuck (extras brought from home) was Tate and Lyle's Golden Syrup, which could be dribbled on porridge or smeared over bread.

In the summer term we played cricket. One afternoon during my first term, I was playing on the lower field when it started to rain and the master-in-charge told the fielding team to run in and put on their sweaters. I ran past one of the batsmen, an older boy named Gurney (everyone was called by their surname). I did not notice that he was swinging his bat, which came up and hit me under my chin. My scream, I was later told, could be heard across the whole field, loud enough to stop a match several hundred yards away. I was carted off to hospital, where I developed a crush on the nurse who held my hand while the doc stitched up my chin without anaesthetic.

When I returned home after my first term, I walked upstairs to the dining room ahead of Ma. I looked up at a painting of trees in the mist, which I had never liked, rested my hand on the oak dining table and said, as casually as I could: "I'm bored at home. When do I go back to school?"

Then I learnt about my birthday present: an air rifle. I was only allowed to use it under strict supervision, but owning a real rifle was to me a symbol of great maturity. And it was summer. My time was spent at the beach, showing off the proper swimming strokes I had learnt at school or exploring along the cliffs that ran for as far as I could see to the west. The only thing missing was Walls ice cream. My craving was the result of the pre-war ads that were posted everywhere. Due to food rationing, ice cream was not available during the war—or for some time thereafter.

In the fall term we played soccer. I desperately wanted to be a good athlete and the biggest disappointment of my school years was that, when it came to sports, I was mediocre at best and sometimes plain ungainly. I did play goalie for the school in the under-ten soccer team, at least once. Our school had an away match against St. Edmunds School, whose shirts had blue and white, vertical stripes, matched with white shorts. Their uniforms seemed so much smarter than our red and green shirts with blue shorts. Their centre-forward (striker) kicked a rising ball straight at me. I raised my arms above my head to catch it, only to watch the ball go between my hands and into the goal. We lost one to nil. The following term we played rugby and my only notable achievement in that sport was to be the muddiest boy on the team. To clean up after the game the whole team climbed into a large communal bath of tepid water, which was soon thick with mud and the source of great water fights. We also played field hockey during the winter and track and field in the summer, but my success in these two sports was not notable.

During the summer term, before breakfast, we went up to the gym where we learnt and practised the proper strokes for swimming, by lying across wooden benches on our stomachs. The exercises were tedious, but when I got into the pool I found that my swimming had improved immensely and I could swim much farther and faster. Our instructor was Sergeant King, better known as Biffer—after his form of discipline. Instead of beating boys on the bottom with a hairbrush, as the headmaster did, he would raise one leg of a boy's shorts and whack his exposed thigh with the open palm of his hand, often leaving a clear imprint of his hand on the exposed flesh. This was called a biff, and was often administered right after the offence but sometimes, for the more heinous crimes I suspect, it was administered during tea in the dining room—in front of the whole school. It hurt like hell. The challenge was not to cry.

Biffer also taught gymnastics and boxing. I learnt to climb ropes, vault a wooden horse, do upstarts and neck flips on a floor mat in the gym with some success, but received my comeuppance in the boxing ring. In one bout, I was pitted against a nerdy boy who wore glasses, didn't like sports, and walked in an ungainly manner. I sat in my corner anticipating a glorious victory and winked at my friends watching from the side. The bell sounded. I landed a few punches, but he kept backing away from my jabs and swings so I did little damage. After encouragement from Biffer, he finally started to hit back and it was me who was backing away, desperately trying to protect myself from the hardest punches I had ever experienced. By the time the bell rang to end the fight I was in tears.

"I saw you smiling at your friends," Biffer said. "Never judge others before you see them in action."

The chapel was adjacent to the gym. We attended chapel each morning and evening for a short service—a hymn, a lesson, and some prayers—with a longer service on Sunday morning. We received no religious instruction and had to piece together what it was all about from services that were not designed for learning. I wondered why we hallowed God's name, and why we asked to be forgiven for trespassing, which I thought meant trespassing on other people's property, when there were so many other more serious sins, but I was not encouraged to ask. My favourite hymn was the one with the chorus:

> *Oh hear us when we cry to thee,*
> *For those in peril on the sea.*

I truly believed that, if I sang well enough, God would keep my father safe.

The service I enjoyed most was at Christmas. The choir, its members holding candles, marched into the chapel led by a soloist who was singing the first verse of "Once in Royal David's City". The choir sang the second verse as they reached their seats at the front of the chapel, and then the whole school joined in for the remainder of the hymn. I wanted to be in the choir, but one day in chapel a master came around to each boy and told him to sing three notes on which he gave a grade: A for choir, B for average and C, I suppose, meant you couldn't hold a tune. I was given a B. I was insulted by such a short and unfair test, as I considered myself a good singer, but there was no appeal.

Scouting was a major component of the school program and everyone was expected to participate, except for four or five boys who were excluded at their parents' request. I joined the Cubs when I was seven. Their motto was "do your best"—at being honest and respectful, working as a team, and developing leadership skills. It was quasi-military in style, with a hierarchical structure, uniforms, inspections, and outdoor activities. We learnt about camping, making fires that had to be started without paper and with only one match, reading maps, tying knots, etc.. I was fascinated. While there was a strong emphasis on group loyalty, a cub could show his individual talents by earning badges—displayed on the left arm—for a wide variety of skills, from swimming to housekeeping. The Cub Pack was organized into four Sixes: six cubs led by a Sixer, with the Senior Sixer being the leader of the Pack. My greatest success at school was being appointed Senior Sixer, and my proudest moment was marching in front of the entire Cub Pack and Scout Troop carrying the cub flag in the annual parade.

School work didn't interest me much. It was a chore that had to be done, like washing up. In my second year, I had to read David Copperfield and struggling through it turned me off reading. We started both Latin and French in second form. I was never convinced by the argument that learning Latin was important because it was the root of the English language. I was much more impressed by the school boy rhyme:

> Latin is a dead language,
> As dead as dead can be.
> First it killed the Romans,
> Now it's killing me.

Sadly, starting French when I was eight didn't result in my becoming fluent, partly because there was so much emphasis on correct grammar and very little on oral communication but also because I never had, nor later developed, a proficiency in foreign languages. I liked math the best, mainly I suspect, because it came easily. Although I can't remember what it was for, I did win a prize in my second year for some school work—a book that I never read.

As most of our time at school was spent in organized activities, there was little free time; when there was, I often tested the limits by climbing trees, reading forbidden comic books with a torch (flashlight) under the bed clothes, and seeing how much cheek I could get away with. The more serious offences resulted in a beating by the headmaster or his deputy. While they acted as a mild deterrent, they also gave the recipient status—as long as he didn't appear to have cried when he returned to the dorm.

Parents usually visited only on special days. In the summer term, which was the longest, there was a father-son cricket match, followed a few weeks later by Sports (track and field) Day. In the winter terms it was for gymnastics and boxing displays. While I looked forward to seeing Ma, like most boys, I was concerned about how my mother would be perceived by others: what car she drove; what clothes she wore; what kind of picnic she brought, and what goodies she left behind. Most of the parents were much older than mine, with most fathers too old for active service. I felt proud that my father was fighting in the war, but at the same time was slightly embarrassed that my mother was young and stylish. Most mothers wore comfortable, country-style clothes with sensible shoes, practical hairstyles, and little make-up. In the summer of 1947, Ma turned up in the 'new look'—a navy blue and white, flared skirt that reached to the middle of her calves rather than a tight skirt that stopped at the knee as had been the fashion. She was the only one, which undoubtedly pleased her, but I was so embarrassed that, at first, I didn't want to know her. The best family picnic went to the Pelham brothers, two of the four Jewish boys at the school, whose immaculately dressed parents were driven to the school by a chauffeur in a 1920s Rolls Royce. They laid out what appeared to me to be a sumptuous feast. The Pelhams, who were not popular generally, had more friends for the few days after a parents' day, until their goodies ran out. I'm proud that I never joined the scroungers.

My first term report was not good. This probably reflected my priorities of making friends, gaining recognition, having fun, and trying to be a great athlete, or perhaps it was just a reaction to having been sent away from home to school. Paddy wrote, in response to the news, that it was probably best that he didn't give me a rocket.

Paddy transferred to the Commando in February 1944. I don't know if this was at his request or a reassignment. The most senior rank a marine could hold at sea was Captain and Paddy had expressed frustration in some of his letters that some of his contemporaries, who were shore based, had been promoted above that rank. The transfer meant promotion to acting major and ten days leave, the first in over a year. I was at school so I didn't see him.

When he arrived at the Commando Training Camp in Wrexham in Northern Wales, no one was aware that he was coming and he had to take the initiative to define his role. He was sent up to Scotland for a month of basic training, where he did not like being treated like a recruit again. Then he was returned to Wrexham. I had hoped to learn more details about his training from his letters, but other than the odd comment about a twenty-five mile hike or learning to rappel down a cliff, he gave no details—probably due to censorship. In his free time he visited many of the pubs in the area. While searching the web in 2009, I came across a newspaper article on Eleanor Jones, who was reminiscing about working in her mother's pub during the war. She said the marines used to visit often and mentioned the names of three marines, one of whom was Paddy. With the help of the newspaper, I contacted Eleanor by phone. She remembered Paddy as a tall, fair man from South Africa, who was sensitive, more like an artist or a poet than the usual tough Commando.

His schedule and future plans were always uncertain, so he was never sure when he would be on an exercise out of camp or if and when he would be posted to active service. This uncertainty made it difficult for Ma to plan visits, but she did spend three weekends with him. It was difficult to find accommodation for us—or digs as he referred to it—so that we could visit as a family during the summer holidays. Eventually, he arranged for us to stay in the local vicarage, only to be told a few days before we were due to arrive that the vicar had to go away on a family emergency. So our arrival was delayed a week.

We spent about four weeks in Wrexham. I was in awe of the tall man who was my father, with his large, ginger moustache and the smart uniform. Looking back, I think he was somewhat in awe of me. I suspect his aloofness was due to his lack of experience in relating to an ebullient eight-year-old boy. I loved following him around the camp. He had become the commanding officer and so everyone saluted him, which impressed me no end. I spent one whole day with him. First he took me to the camp barber for a marine haircut. Then he said he would try and sneak me out of camp in a jeep, so we could explore the mountains, but—he told me conspiratorially—there was a problem. Only Commandos were allowed to ride in jeeps, so I would have to be disguised as one. If we were lucky, we would be able to fool the sentry into thinking I was a real Commando. I was dressed in a khaki jacket with the combined-operations insignia on the shoulder, wore a khaki, wool forage cap, and climbed into the back of the jeep behind my father and one of his friends.

"Sit up straight, look straight ahead and don't say anything, I'll do the talking," he said, as we approached the gate. The jeep came to a halt. I sat rigidly in the back, my heart pounding, and looked away from the sentry who came to check on us.

The sentry asked, "Who's that in the back?"

"A marine escort to guard the jeep."

"Very good, sir."

As the jeep pulled away, I almost burst with pride. I really believed we had fooled the sentry. We drove up narrow, rough tracks into the mountains and I revelled in bouncing around in the back, as the jeep forded streams and climbed steeper inclines than any other car could. We went for a swim in a river, then stopped for tea before returning to camp. I don't know whether we spoke much, but it didn't matter, just being near him was all I wanted.

I was enamoured with everything military. Both marines and army trained at Wrexham. I could recognize all the regiments by their badges, and learned their history. I could distinguish ranks, knew the meaning of different insignia, and the type of weapons each unit used. One evening when Paddy came to visit us at the vicarage—he had to live in camp—he said, "I've something to show you." He took off his blue beret, with the red background behind the marine badge, the regular uniform for a marine, and put on a green beret. "Now I'm a Commando," he said. To me, he was the ultimate hero.

I decided that I would wear a green beret one day.

In late August he went to Normandy. Ma told me it was just an observation trip, but he didn't return. He was assigned to 41 Commando at the request of the colonel with whom he had trained in Scotland. When I learnt that he was not coming back, my stomach hollowed and I felt very afraid. I was determined not to cry and told Ma, with a hollow laugh, "He'll be safe. The Germans will be frightened by his big moustache."

Paddy took command of X Troop, one of the four Troops that made up 41 Commando. This position was usually held by a captain or lieutenant rather than a major. Either too many captains and lieutenants had been killed or he or his colonel wanted him to have front line experience before becoming 2IC of the Commando, the usual role for a major.

Soon after Paddy went to Normandy, I returned to school and Ma and Penelope returned to Devon. Paddy fought his way through France to Belgium, where the Commando trained for two weeks in the sand dunes—in preparation for the amphibious landing on the heavily protected Island of Walcheren, in Holland, which guarded the mouth of the River Scheldt. Late at night on October 31st, 41 Commando, in full battle gear, marched the ten kilometres from De Haan—where they had been training—to Ostend to board landing craft, a move that spies undoubtedly reported to the Germans. They boarded shortly after midnight and, as dawn broke, approached the beach off Walcheren under heavy fire from the Germans. The expected air cover did not materialize, as thick fog in England had prevented the planes from taking off. Many landing craft were sunk before they reached land, but Paddy and his troop made it ashore, and charged up the beach under machine-gun fire, to join others in house-to-house fighting, in order to clear the Germans out of the village of Westkapella. General Eisenhower, the supreme Allied Commander, called the landing at Walcheren more difficult than D-Day. The four troops of 41 leapfrogged each other as they fought their way north through the sand dunes, destroying gun emplacements and taking many prisoners.

About twelve or thirteen days after the landing on Walcheren, wispy grey clouds clung to the top of the trees around Fernden, while rain streaked down the windows of the dining hall. I was just one of a hundred and forty boys talking, laughing, and eating all at the same time, when the master supervising the dining room walked down to the table where I was sitting, leaned over, and said, "Brind-Sheridan, Mr Charles wants to see you."

What had I done wrong? As I stood up, I pulled up my kneesocks, which perpetually hung around my ankles, and straightened my tie, which had, as usual, twisted to one side. I followed the master between the tables, five on one side, six on the other, to the head table, which was on a platform about eighteen inches high. I felt not only apprehensive about what I had done wrong, but embarrassed that I had been singled out in front of the whole school, and again felt sure that everyone was criticizing me. Mr Charles, who was standing at the door, put his hand on my shoulder as he guided me down the stairs to the baronial main hall, where the fireplace was never lit and the ceiling was two storeys high. We stopped at the door of his private sitting room, rather than crossing the hall to his study where he usually saw boys.

"There's someone to see you," he said gently.

He opened the door. Ma was sitting on the sofa. She didn't say anything; I knew. I ran to her and flung myself into her arms. We clung to each other and cried and cried until there were no tears left, only an aching hollow deep inside me that left me numb and drained of energy.

After about two hours, there was a knock on the door. Jane, Mr Charles' wife, asked if we were ready for some tea.

Ma nodded, "Just give me some time to straighten up."

Soon a tea tray, filled with sandwiches and cakes, was wheeled in front of the blazing fire. I sat close to Ma, eating mechanically but tasting nothing. In the background I heard the murmur of the three adults talking, not about why we were all there, but about mundane matters, like the weather and travel.

"It's time for your mother to catch her train home," Mr Charles said. "We'll leave you to say goodbye, then it will be time for you to get ready for prep."

Someone told me later that Mr Charles had told the school that my father had been killed after I had left the dining room, but I don't remember talking to anyone about it that evening. I fell into the familiar routine until it was time for bed. That night, I fell asleep struggling to understand what death meant.

I was able to stay on at Fernden as Mr Charles, knowing that my mother's income would be severely reduced, lowered my school fees.

Many years later, I met Dai Davies who, as dusk was falling on the evening of November 1st, 1944, was standing beside Paddy and a marine, checking their map, when a blast of machine-gun fire ripped the map apart. Dai fell to the ground and crawled back to cover. Paddy and the marine also fell, but both were mortally wounded. His troop tried to rescue him twice during the night, but they were driven back by heavy fire. At dawn the Germans retreated. When his troop reached Paddy, he and the marine were dead. Dai said of Paddy: "He was always a gentleman, never a bully."

My wife, Stephanie, and I first visited Walcheren fifty-seven years after Paddy was killed. He is buried at a cemetery near Bergen-op-Zoom. A low, rectangular, granite block stands at the entrance, on which is written: "Their name liveth forever more." Over 1200 identically shaped grave-stones, engraved only with a regimental badge along with personal details, are set in a peaceful, park-like setting, surrounded by trees whose golden leaves litter the well-kept lawns. I walked down the wide lawn that divided the cemetery and led to a small building at the far end, which contained the book with the location of graves, but before I reached it, as if pulled by a magnet, I veered off to my left and went straight to Paddy's grave. I sat on the damp ground in front of his simple headstone and, though he was less than half my current age when he was killed, I spoke to him as a boy would speak to his father. After a while, I wandered around looking at other headstones. All ranks and all religions are buried together. Too many were in their teens. At 31, Paddy was one of the oldest.

After leaving the cemetery, we met with two locals with whom we had made contact before leaving Canada: one a former British soldier, who had married a local Dutch woman during the war; and the other a retired Dutch teacher whose hobby was the wartime history of Walcheren. They showed us the beach, now manicured for swimmers, where the 41 had landed, took us through the village of Westkapella, where they fought the Germans street by street, and to the monument to the Commando, a World War II tank on which, ironically, some German youths were playing. We drove along the dunes, swept by a cold North Sea wind, towards the town of Domburg, which was now a vacation spot favoured by Germans. Based on his research, our Dutch guide was able to show me the area where Paddy was shot and lay dying in the sand. It was not only the cold wind that made me shiver as I stood there.

The next day, we met up with the vets who had come to commemorate the landing. Among them were Bill Wilderspin and his wife, Joyce. Bill had written to me in response to the letter I wrote to the Globe and Laurel, the Royal Marine magazine, about three years before. He had been a sergeant in X Troop and we had kept in regular contact by mail. We spent the day with the vets and their families, attending ceremonies at the monuments for four separate Commando units accompanied by a contingent of marines. Each time the bugler played the "Last Post", the traditional tribute to the fallen, tears flowed down my cheeks. That evening we attended a concert, in the church where a plaque hangs with the names of those members of 41 who were killed. The music was upbeat and I found myself tapping my feet and smiling—until it hit me that fifty-seven years ago, Paddy was lying in the sand, dying.

We returned to Walcheren for the sixtieth anniversary, when Bill arranged for me to lay the wreath on behalf of the vets of 41 Commando. Though I was deeply honoured, I felt a fraud as I had never had to fight a war. The following year a new monument to the 41 was raised, on which the names of those killed were engraved.

Chapter 4

One Sunday afternoon, shortly before the Easter holidays in 1945, Ma came to pick me and a chum up from school.

"I want you to meet someone," she said. "He's a Royal Marine officer who knew your father."

I was surprised at being taken out of school, as it was very unusual, but excited about a new experience and the possibility of a tea with a rich cake. She took us to a white Tudor cottage, framed with dark, wood beams and a thatched roof—a replica of classic sixteenth-century building, but to me (then) just a funny old house. What was far more exciting was the majestic, life-size plaster bull that peered menacingly onto the road from a barn that was on the edge of the property. I had seen the bull on several occasions during regular school walks. The bull always caused a great deal of speculation amongst the boys, and now I was going to find out all about it.

Ma introduced me to a tall, silver-haired man called Colonel Spicer. After a brief conversation between an adult who was not used to eight year olds and a boy who wasn't particularly interested in a strange adult, I asked about the bull. He knew nothing about it, as he was renting the house. I and my chum rushed off to see it. After studying the bull from underneath, which led to much school-boy humour, we explored the garden. It had a swimming pool, filled with rather grungy water, above which were several Japanese-style ornamental pools carved into the slope of the hill. While running across a wooden bridge over one pool, I slipped on the wet wood and cut my knee, resulting in a second trip to the hospital for stitches without anaesthetic.

Colonel Spicer didn't make much of an impression on me, so I gave him little if any thought over the holidays. But at the beginning of the summer term, Ma took me to his house again.

"Go upstairs," she told me, "Max has something to tell you." Colonel Spicer—I didn't think of him as Max—was lying in a steaming bathtub, his silver hair parted in the middle and neatly brushed, and his almost-white moustache neatly trimmed. After a perfunctory greeting, he said, "Your mother and I are going to get married. Now go and tell her that you are happy about it."

I was stunned. I had no inkling this was likely to happen. I was also angry at being told how to feel so I didn't really think about the implications of Ma getting married again. As I had been taught not to question my elders I only nodded to Max and went dutifully downstairs to tell Ma, in not a very convincing manner I suspect, that I was happy. I didn't see Max replacing my father, whom I knew, as a hero, could not be usurped. As I reflected on it later, I decided that getting married again was what mothers had to do, because they didn't work and needed a man to support them. I later learnt that my father's pension was meagre, though I never knew the exact amount.

Later that summer, Ma and Max were married in the garden of the house with the bull in the barn. I attended the wedding with two school chums. We were allowed a small glass of Champagne each and as much food as we liked from the plates set out on tables around the lawn. As we were not getting much attention from the adults, we slipped into the barn with the bull, stripped naked, ran across the lawn, and dove into the swimming pool—much to the amused surprise, or shock, of the guests who were standing around the pool with drinks in hand. Swimming naked was not unusual for us. All boys at school swam naked, even on visitors' days, except for those who had the beginnings of pubic hair.

That summer we moved to a new home, called Willow Green, halfway between Chichester and West Wittering, in Sussex, which was close to the sea. At the time I thought it was a mansion, but years later, when I went back to look at it, it turned out to be a cozy, two-storied, country cottage with a large lawn and herbaceous border in the front, a vegetable garden in the rear, and a large fish pool beside the house. The property was surrounded by fields, where I went hunting for rabbits with my airgun. The most exciting time was when the wheat was being harvested. As the reaper circled the field, the rabbits and other wildlife were driven into the ever decreasing central core of uncut wheat, until finally the core became too small and they had to break cover. Trying to shoot a running a rabbit, bolting for its life, with an airgun was a formidable task that I never mastered. But many of the locals waiting with their shotguns took home rabbit for supper.

As one of the few activities that Max used to enjoy was shooting birds, Ma bought him a new shotgun for his birthday. He suggested we all go out for a shoot on the evening of his birthday. Max took his old gun with hammers that had to be pulled back before it was ready to fire; Ma had the new modern gun, with no hammers and a safety catch, while I carried my airgun—though there was virtually no chance of me hitting a flying bird. We soon put up a covey of partridge. Max bought one down; I sent a pellet into the air, but nothing erupted from Ma's gun although she had clearly tried to shoot. As we walked to pick up the kill, Max asked Ma what had happened.

"I don't know," she said, "I pulled the trigger like this—" A loud explosion stunned me and left a ringing in my ear. A crater, about twelve inches across and an inch deep, appeared in the ground close to my left foot. The safety catch had been on when she tried to shoot the birds, but was off when she demonstrated why the gun had not fired. Neither Ma nor I ever went hunting with Max again and, as far as I know, he didn't hunt again either.

Max was the paymaster at the Royal Marine Barracks in Portsmouth. He drove to the station in Chichester every morning and took the train to work, returning in the early evening. He went to bed almost as soon as he returned home, and that is where he ate his supper. He suffered from a duodenal ulcer that either caused him considerable discomfort or was an excuse to play the invalid. Ma told me many years later that he had tried to persuade her to give him the family's share of dairy products. All food was rationed then and the dairy allowance was meagre. Ma refused to give him Penelope's or my share, but did give him hers.

Max's prize possession, at least in my judgement, was his 1938 SS Jaguar Saloon: black with wide, flared front fenders, with large, round, chrome headlamps mounted on them, chrome-spoked wheels, a long, narrow bonnet (hood) with air vents along its full length, and a throaty roar from its exhaust, which made it seem to me the ultimate status car. When I returned to school the following term, I casually mentioned in the dormitory, with a superior air, that we had an SS Jaguar. The boy next to me gave a snort and said in a derisive tone, "Just a cad-Bentley." Another said, "You mean a Jew's Bentley." These remarks didn't lessen my admiration for the car, I was just mad that I had been outsmarted.

It was customary for officers to have a batman—a marine servant who, in war, acted as his runner and support, and in peace time looked after his officer like a valet. Max's batman lived in a small cottage next to our house with his wife. He was a stickler for the rules or a master of self-protection. He would have little if anything to do with Ma, Penelope, or I and would only handle matters strictly related to Max and the marines, such as looking after Max's uniform. As Max was an office worker, this meant he had remarkably little to do. Ma had a nanny when Penelope was born, but now that she was older, she employed Kathleen, a local woman who cleaned house, did washing and cooking, and also looked after Penelope. She was a large, friendly woman who more than made up for the batman's coolness, and certainly made Ma's life more leisurely.

My prize possession at Willow Green was my drop-handlebar, three-speed, blue Hercules bike with aluminium fenders, to which (over time) I added a water bottle, toe clips, a dynamo light, an odometer, and a speed-ometer. It gave me the opportunity to roam far and wide. I rode the five miles up to Chichester, in the back draft of a double-decker bus, whenever I could and particularly when there was a head wind. I rode down to play on the beach at West Wittering, out to Itchenor, where yachts were moored in the estuary, or down any lane that attracted my attention. When I first went down to the beach, in 1945, it was covered with oil left over from the war. Walking on the beach meant feet stained black with tar and sorting through flotsam from wrecks. My favourite keepsake was a sailor's hat that I wore for most of that summer. The following summer the sea had cleaned up almost all the oil, while what remained had coagulated into hard, black pebbles and consequently the beaches became more crowded. The swimming was good, but I was disappointed that there was no surf.

When I came home for the summer holidays, Max had changed his batman. Webb, the new one, was a true Cockney; short and stocky with jet-black hair brushed straight back with a liberal swath of Vaseline. He was also a Commando. I thought it strange that he would choose a menial job like a batman when he was trained as one of the toughest of fighting men, but "it's a soft touch," he explained, "not much to do and no bloody sergeant to give me the gears." He was friendly to us, much more helpful around the house than the old one had been, and liked helping me with whatever I was doing. One day I was riding my bike down a country lane when a pole suddenly swung across the road in front of me. As I came to a halt, about eight village boys came out from behind the hedge. The eldest was about fourteen, four years older than me, and the youngest about six. After some verbal insults based on our class differences, two older boys held me by the arms while two of the younger ones punched me in the stomach. Shook up more than hurt, I rode home and told Webb.

"Gimme your bike," he said, and rode off.

A short while later he returned with a big grin.

"I rode down the same road," he told me. "Out came the pole. I rode straight at it, grabbed it in m'hands, broke it in half and whacked those little buggers around their ears. Off you go now, they won't bother you no more."

I rode down the same lane. Out came the pole. I slowed down. The boys appeared. They looked at me sullenly, took away the pole and I rode on, probably after a large sigh of relief, but with a big grin on my face.

When I returned to school in the summer of '45, I learnt that the Goldberg brothers, two Jewish boys in school, lived close to Willow Green. We were not, and did not become, close friends at school, but when the summer holidays came, Peter Goldberg, who was the same age as me, and his younger brother, Jeremy, became my best pals. I had much more freedom than they did, so most days I rode the three miles over to their house to play, mainly in the adjacent fields. Our favourite venue was an abandoned horse-cart surrounded by stinging nettles, which became a ship or tank or fort under siege by Germans, Indians, or many other hostile aliens. Anti-Semitism was common then. Ma described Harry Goldberg (the father) as: "a nice little Jew-boy in the rag trade." She was always polite to the Goldbergs, though never friendly. Our parents did not invite each other to their homes. I sensed Ma's disdain for the Goldbergs, but it did not impinge on my friendship for Peter and Jeremy. I was also aware that there was discrimination against Jews at school, sometimes overt and cruel, which was maybe why I was never close to them there. One day at school Jeremy came to me in tears. "Why does everyone hate Jews," he asked, "when Jesus was a Jew?" I didn't know what to say, but I thought long and hard about what he'd said, because it seemed to me that he had a good point.

Always looking for a new interest, Ma decided to breed show dogs. She bought a bull terrier bitch, Dinah, to breed show bull terriers. Poor old James was not a show dog, despite his remarkable loyalty and adventurous spirit. Bull terriers had to be sturdy, broad of head and chest, while James was lean and long legged. Dinah was bred to an expensive champion stud dog, and seven puppies were born shortly before I came home. Penelope and I watched them grow into seven very different characters: Nelson, white with a black eye patch, was all bark but not much bite; William, short, broad, and brindle, with a white collar and feet, was the tough one; Monty, brindle all over, was the clown—he got drunk at one of Ma's cocktail parties by climbing on chairs and helping himself to people's drinks. The next morning he lay in front of the kennel, looking distinctly hung over, while his brothers and sisters jumped around him barking. The others all had their foibles, right down to the runt of the litter, Prudence, who was ginger with a white collar, smaller than all the others, but always able to fight her way into the food bowls and never shy in seeking attention. Ma decided to keep William as she hoped he would be a good show dog—but his ears never stood up straight, as they should do on a bull terrier. He didn't live up to show expectations but became the family pet and an excellent watchdog. She sold the rest.

Penelope turned four in 1947, blonde and round faced, with big blue eyes and a mischievous spirit. While I was too busy to spend much time with her, I always felt very protective and often went into her room in the morning to play with her before breakfast. One morning I found her sitting in her bed, surrounded by large chunks of her hair. "Mummy's going to be cross," I said. She looked sheepish. Determined to see Ma's reaction, I made sure I was there when she came into Penelope's room. "What on earth have you done to your hair?" Ma demanded, her eyes wide with surprise. "Nothing, Mummy," Penelope replied coyly, "Peter Rabbit did it." Peter Rabbit was the mischievous hero of Penelope's favourite story books. Ma was helpless.

"Well, Peter Rabbit is a very naughty boy and when I catch him, I'll give him a jolly good spanking," she replied, trying not to grin. Penelope smiled coyly. The previous year she had gotten away with giving Ma's old Opel car mud pies for breakfast, by carefully stuffing them into the petrol tank.

Chapter 5

"Would you like to go skiing in Switzerland?" Ma asked me. It was the beginning of the Christmas holidays in 1946. I reacted with a mixture of enthusiasm and apprehension, for I had learnt early in my life that Ma expected a positive response to certain questions, and this was one of them. I was to go in a school party—not my school, but with a group from the school attended by Peter Wise, the boy whom I had hit over the head with my 'sugar teaser' when I was three. Ma, who was good friends with Peter's mother, had arranged for me to be included. I hadn't seen much of Peter, who lived in another part of England, so he wasn't a friend and being older was not likely that he would be my guardian on the trip, as Ma assured me he would be. But the lure of an adventure overcame my apprehension about going with a bunch of strangers. Just before New Year, a group of about twenty boys, aged between ten and thirteen, with the headmaster of Peter's school and his wife, took the train from London to the town of Engleberg, situated high in the Swiss Alps. After all the fun and games that a bunch of boys could create on a lengthy train journey from England to Switzerland, I felt at home with my new schoolmates. I was enthralled to find that the streets of Engleberg were covered in packed snow and the town was surrounded by snow-capped mountains. Snowball fights started as soon as we got off the train and it took some time to herd us into the hotel, where we were assigned five to a room. I was with three other ten year olds and one thirteen old, who would be the informal prefect, and who turned out to have less respect for house rules than any of us and encouraged us to break them. Towards the end of our stay, he boasted about his shoplifting success. Though I strongly disapproved, I didn't say anything. We had skiing lessons in the morning and faced the slopes and the chair lifts on our own in the afternoon, had snowball fights, and revelled in rich, chocolate and cream cakes, which were bigger and richer and creamier than anything I had ever tasted. The highlight for me was a luge (toboggan) party. A line of luges were tied together behind a horse-drawn sleigh that sped around the dark streets in the evening. We finished around a bonfire, singing campfire songs and drinking rich creamy chocolate. I went back to Switzerland with the same group two years later, and proved to be a competent skier.

As I turned eleven during the summer of 1947, I moved from cubs to scouts. This was a move from top of the pile to the bottom, but it meant a smarter uniform—especially the hat, which was similar to what the Mounties wear. It also meant the chance to go to camp. Instead of going home at the end of the summer term, many of the scouts stayed for an extra week of camp. The last weeks of term were focused on preparation. Old-fashioned army bell tents were erected on the edge of the woods and stocked with palliasses (straw mattresses) and blankets. We didn't have sleeping bags, instead we folded blankets into each other so as to create a bag that too often came undone in the middle of the night. Outside each tent was an enamel wash basin in a wooden frame, made from poles cut from trees. Water, cold only, was carried from one central tap. Trench latrines were dug and surrounded by Hessian screens, a large marquee was set up as a communal dining tent beside an open-air kitchen. Wood was cut and stacked for the traditional campfire.

The day started at 6:30 with Biffer, always immaculately turned out in his scoutmaster's uniform, blowing the traditional wake-up call of the British Army on the bugle: 'Charlie, Charlie get out of bed, get out of bed.'

Scouts had to spring out of bed, wash in cold water, prepare for inspection, and be at breakfast by 7:00. Inspection was after breakfast. Palliasses were hung out to air; blankets and clothes were neatly folded, and scout uniforms put in order. The morning was spent doing a combination of camp chores and scouting activities. The most unpopular assignment was kitchen duty, which meant peeling mountains of potatoes and was followed by washing piles of dishes in large bowls on the ground. Meals were announced with another army bugle call: 'Come to the cookhouse door boys; come to the cookhouse door.'

We learnt to use maps and compasses by going on long hikes through the country, and sometimes playing games like military manoeuvres. In one game, the younger boys had to hide in the woods from a few seniors. Most of those hiding ran off as far as possible from the searchers' base. I started by running off, but doubled back, ducked into a ditch right next to the base, and covered myself with leaves left over from the previous autumn. After the searchers left, an eerie silence descended on me and I began to wonder what it would be like if I was hiding from German soldiers. What would happen if they captured me? Would I be tortured or just stood up against a wall and shot? My imagination took hold and gradually my fantasy became so real that I felt terrified and burrowed deeper into my cocoon of damp leaves. They didn't find me, but even after the whistle was blown to announce the end of the game, it took me some time before I felt relaxed enough to come out of hiding. When I joined the group, I learnt that I was the only boy not found.

In the evenings, with blankets over our shoulders, we sat on a circle of logs, about a sixty feet in diameter, around a blazing camp fire that sent sparks shooting into the sky and created shadows that danced among the trees that surrounded us. The air was filled with the pungent smell of wood smoke. Some of the leaders, mainly older boys who returned for the camp, told ghost stories or did a skit, but the best part for me was the sing-song. Singing together gave me a great feeling of camaraderie and I soon learnt the words to many of the songs.

After my second camp, I persuaded Ma to let me ride my bike the forty miles home. It was the first time a boy had cycled home and I was cheered on by the boys waiting to go home by train or car. Biffer checked my bike, made sure I could point out my route on the map, gave me some instructions about safety and preserving my energy. As I sped down the long driveway, I felt as if I was starting on the Tour de France. My route was mainly along country roads and over the Goodwood Downs where there was little traffic. I was surprised when I got home in about three hours. I had expected to be riding all day.

Later during the holidays, Peter Wise came to stay and we were driven up to the Goodwood Downs where we set up camp on our own. There was no one and no building in sight. As night descended, accompanied by strange sounds, our two-man tent offered little comfort and I longed to be safe at home in my bedroom, while desperately trying not to appear scared. We had difficulty making a fire the next morning, so were unable to cook the breakfast that Ma had given us. I tried not to show how relieved I was when Ma arrived to fetch us home three hours ahead of schedule.

That summer sailing came into my life. Max decided, probably with encouragement from Ma, that he should do something with his stepson, so he arranged to take me sailing in one of the dinghies owned by the Royal Marine Barracks in Portsmouth. There was not much wind and I was soon bored as we wallowed in gentle swells with flapping sails. When it was finally time to go in, Max was unable to raise the centre board. He asked if I could swim ashore to get help. At last, I had something useful to do. I dove over the side, swam the fifty yards to the shore in sight of all the people on the beach, and asked the corporal who looked after the boats for help. He collected a tool bag and we carried a large aluminium kayak, the same kind as was used by the Special Boat Service, down the beach and paddled out to Max, who was sitting forlornly in the boat. I found the rescue far more exciting than the sailing.

Later that summer, Max took Ma and I, along with Michael and Peter Mitchell who were staying with us, sailing on a thirty footer that had been confiscated from the Germans at the end of the war and was now owned by the Royal Marine Barracks. We set sail for the Isle of White on another day of very light winds, with the corporal in charge of the boat. After about an hour fog came down and we were becalmed. Visibility was about two hundred yards. I looked up and saw a blue and white prow looming out of the fog high above us.

"Is that the Queen Mary?" I asked.

"I hope not," replied the corporal. He looked up to where I was pointing. "Jesus Christ, it is!"

With no engine, we wallowed in the glassy swells and looked on help-lessly as the massive, blue and white hull, as tall as a skyscraper, bore down upon us. She passed about thirty yards astern. The officer of the watch ran to the edge of the bridge and yelled, "You bloody fools." If we had been on her course, there was no way she could have avoided us.

Back at school, I was now senior enough to have a library period in my regular schedule, where we were expected to study on our own. I shared a table with two boys, called Burnett and Evershed. Our common passion was Dinky Toys (small model cars and trucks) and it was not long before a couple were produced. We organized our books into buildings—forming streets. Evershed drew a clock face on his wooden pencil box and placed it vertically in the centre of the table.

"Let's call it Big Brin," he said.

I was known as Brind-Sheridan at school, but commonly called Brin. After some discussion, we named our town Brineverburn. At the next library period we smuggled in many more Dinky Toys and spent forty-five minutes happily involved in creating urban dramas.

When I went home for the Christmas holidays, Ma told me we were going to Kenya during the next term to visit Paddy's mother, sister, and brother. I was over the moon—going to Africa and missing a whole term at school! What more could an eleven-year-old boy want? My wild fan-tasies about Africa helped me deal with the agony of waiting for the day of departure.

We had to have vaccinations and inoculations to travel and went to Chichester for our shots, which included one for cholera. The nurse told us that our arms and shoulders would soon be very sore and stiff. She tied a blue ribbon on the arm that had the shot, as a warning to others not to touch it. I didn't care how much it hurt, that blue ribbon was, to me, a true explorer's badge. We passed a woman and her son, about my age, as we left the clinic.

"What does that blue ribbon mean?" I heard him ask his mother.

"He's had an inoculation and his arm is tender," she replied.

My chest puffed with pride.

By the time Ma and I got home to Willow Green our arms were hurting. Kathleen made us some tea with hot, buttered toast served in a covered, silver dish, which had a cavity for hot water underneath to keep the toast warm. We sat in armchairs in front of a blazing fire. I lifted the lid of the silver dish with my good arm. Ma took out a piece of toast with her good arm. I replaced the lid. Ma took off the lid so I could take my piece of toast. It was a moment of magical closeness—sharing the anticipation of a great adventure together.

Kathleen looked after Penelope during the three months that we were away. She usually went to bed at half past six but insisted that, while I was away, she had to stay up until seven o'clock so she could listen to *Dick Barton Special Agent*, the radio program which came on at 6:45, for fifteen minutes every night, so that she could tell me what happened while I was away. Every night that I was home, I listened to the radio drama about the adventures of Dick, Snowy, and Jock, whose exploits make James Bond's life seem easy. Penelope did listen faithfully, but I when I returned, I was not patient enough to listen to her trying to recount some of the incredible adventures of the three agents.

We stayed at Staplehurst for a couple of days before we left. On our last night, after we had eaten supper in front of the fire in the lounge, Granny brought out the family eight millimetre movies. I had seen them many times before, but on that evening they seemed to be particularly poignant. The final reel of the evening was of a boating holiday on the Norfolk Broads before the war. The action showed my grandfather, Ma, and Joan, being towed on boards behind a motor launch. It looked like great fun and I had often hoped we would take a similar holiday. When the movie finished, I was sent up to bed. I felt sad, leaving the familiar room, which was warm and cozy and filled with many happy memories. I shivered as I entered the unheated hallway and crossed the black and white tiled floor to climb the stairs to my bedroom, which would be equally as cold. Halfway up, I stopped and gazed at the two large photos of my great grandparents that dominated the hall—the stern, old man, with a gold watch chain across his portly stomach and his sad, little wife in her lace cap. For the first time, I looked at them with affection. *If we go to live in Kenya*, I thought, *I'll never have a holiday on the Norfolk Broads.* I shivered, but not only with the cold. I didn't want to leave England.

Chapter 6

My passport photo showed a round-faced boy with protruding ears, and straw-like hair falling over his forehead. At age eleven years and six months, I was five-feet-seven-and-a-half-inches tall.

My heart was pounding with excitement as I walked across the tarmac to board the plane, a twin-engine Viking, which carried twenty-four passengers. The trip was scheduled to take three days with two overnight stops. As we sped down the runway, my face was pressed up against the window. Gradually the tail lifted, and then suddenly we were airborne and the countryside seemed to fall away, as if I was being sucked up into the heavens. I was mesmerized by how small the patchwork of fields looked, sliced by ribbons of roads and dotted by little squares that were houses. I did not leave the window until the land gave way to the grey of the English Channel. The stewardess, named Zoe, was blonde and buxom, with big, blue eyes and smiling, red lips. She was the most exotic creature I had ever seen and I fell for her immediately. As we flew over the French coast, Zoe brought round a box lunch, which contained, amongst other things, a hard-boiled egg, a rare delicacy for a boy who had grown up in wartime Britain, where only powdered eggs were readily available. I was just about to crack open my egg when the plane ran into some turbulence and bounced around like a leaf in a gale. I threw up. When the plane stabilized, I was ready to return to my egg when Zoe appeared and suggested to Ma that maybe I shouldn't eat lunch. Ma agreed and my egg, along with the rest of my lunch, disappeared. Zoe had no idea how that tested my love for her.

Our first stop was Marseille. The weather was wet, grey, and windy and the airport buildings utilitarian and uninspiring. I don't know what I had expected but certainly something exotic rather than such a dreary scene. The only novelty was hearing men talk in a language that I could hardly recognize, despite having studied it for four years. I was very disappointed. Our first overnight stop was Malta. Some marine friends of Ma's were stationed there and she, with me in tow, was invited to a cocktail party. As soon as we arrived at the Officer's Mess, Ma (with a drink in one hand and a cigarette in a long holder in the other) was lost in a crowd of chattering adults, surrounded by a blue haze of tobacco smoke, while I was plonked on a chair next to the door to the kitchen. But I enjoyed myself. Each time a steward came in with a tray of canapés, he bent down to give me first dibs and, while I gradually stuffed myself, I learnt to enjoy watching people interact—something that has stayed with me all my life. We were late to bed and woken at three o'clock for an early take off. I did not relish the kippers that we were served for breakfast.

I was excited that my first stop in Africa would be Tobruk, as I remembered the stories of the "indefatigable British Tommies" who held out there against a superior German force. Again I don't know what I expected, but it wasn't the desolate windswept airstrip, with only a few run-down buildings, that was no warmer than England. My first contact with Africa was my second disappointment. We flew on over the Sahara, an immense sea of sand that had been whipped into mountainous crests, to Khartoum. As we drove from the airport, I stared at the first palm trees I had seen, their long leaves undulating in a gentle breeze on top of slender, curved trunks. We stopped in front of a magnificent hotel overlooking the Nile, across from the statue of General Gordon, the British hero of the Sudanese wars. I gazed in awe across ornamental pools, surrounded by palm trees and shrubs, to the high, white arches topped by ornamental balustrades. I entered a spacious hall, with high ceilings, that had groups of deep, comfortable arm-chairs surrounding low tables. Ceiling fans turned lazily as waiters, black as coal and wearing long, white gowns and red fezzes, glided over polished floors on bare feet. As Ma allowed me to order, and later allowed me to sign the chit for the drinks, I felt like a budding 'Chief Pooh-Bah' reclining in a palatial palace. There were not enough rooms in the hotel for all the passengers, so Ma and I, Mary (a woman whom Ma had befriended on the flight), and Zoe had to sleep in the roofed-in area on the aft end of a river boat that was moored on the Nile, across from the hotel. Our dormitory was enclosed by mosquito netting, but the blinds had been pulled down on the river side rather than the road side, so a row of men, squatting along the quay, could see in if lights were turned on. We changed in the dark, which undoubtedly upset the three women, but all I cared about was that I was sleeping in the same room as Zoe.

En route to our next stop, Juba in Southern Sudan, the pilot saw some elephants but decided much to my embarrassment and annoyance, that he would not fly lower so we could see them better as it would likely make me sick. Juba was very hot and humid and surrounded by steaming jungle. A big waiter with a shiny, blue-black face and bare feet, wearing the ubiquitous long, white gown and a white, rimless cap, served us goat steak—very tough—in a shed with a thatched roof, no walls, and packed dirt floor. Despite the heat and intense humidity, I was bewitched. This was more my idea of Africa.

On the last leg of our journey, the land changed from green forest to desert and then back to forest, which clothed the lower slopes of Mt. Kenya. The rainy season in Kenya had just finished and so much of the country was green, though soon it would be burned brown by the endless days of sun that would scorch the earth during the four-month-long dry season. We landed in Nairobi in the early afternoon, where Noreen, my aunt, met us. She took us to stay with the head game warden of the National Park that was only a few miles outside Nairobi. As the sun began to sink, we set off in a safari wagon down a narrow track, through grass that was about two feet tall. The sun was hovering on the horizon to our right as we came to a stop. The game warden turned round—I was sitting in the back seat—and pointed to the grass to my right. Ten yards from me, a lioness was crouched in the grass, staring intently across a gulley at a herd of Impala that were bunched tightly together, their heads darting about nervously. On the other side of the wagon, three more lionesses were stalking the same herd. I watched the big cats creep stealthily through the grass—moving their big, soft paws slowly so as not to make a sound, their legs bent, their shoulders and haunches higher than their backs as they kept their profile below the grass. The game warden tapped me on the shoulder.

"Look there," he whispered, pointing to a rocky hump behind the nervous herd, "there's the old man, waiting for his dinner to be served up for him."

The head of a majestic-maned lion protruded from a rock behind the Impala.

Suddenly the herd bolted. The lionesses sprung in pursuit. As the herd, with four lionesses racing through the dust after them, fled around the crest of the hill, I saw one lioness spring on the back of a luckless buck at the back of the pack and roll out of view.

We returned to the warden's low rambling house, made of white plaster on mud and wattle walls, with a high roof thatched with papyrus grass. A fire blazed in a large fireplace—I was surprised that the evenings in Africa were cool (the altitude was about 5,500 feet). The spacious living room was furnished much the same as an English country house, except for heads of African game on the walls and skins on the floor. I was told that the loo was a thunderbox [a wooden box with a toilet seat over a deep pit] outside, and to check the surrounds carefully before I went out or came back. Once a guest had been stuck in the loo for a long time as when she came to leave there were three lions resting on the path to the house.

At the beginning of our three month visit, we stayed with my grandmother. She was frail and spent most of her time sitting in her chair. She made little impression on me, as entertaining me was delegated to Angelo, her farm manager—all he managed were some poultry on her ten-acre property a few miles west of Nairobi. Angelo had been an Italian prisoner of war interned in Kenya. Some of the Italians had been allowed out of the prison camp, during the latter part of the war, to help locals. Angelo, along with several compatriots had elected to stay on, though from what I gathered while overhearing family conversations, his motives for staying with my grandmother were very suspect.

For most of our visit, we stayed with my aunt, Noreen, and her husband, Jim, at their farm in Limuru, twenty miles northwest of Nairobi. They were the biggest race horse trainers in the country, with about twenty-four horses in training, a number of brood mares, and Kenya's most famous stud stallion of the time, Commander III. In addition, they had a large Friesian dairy herd, chickens, ducks, and geese, four Alsatians (German Shepherds), and numerous cats, a few of whom were pets, but most simply farm cats to keep down the rodents in the barns. Noreen was the antithesis of Ma. Her reddish brown hair was pulled back into a bun. She wore no make-up on her freckled and tanned face, and dressed in shirts, slacks, and flat, lace-up shoes, except in the evening when she wore a simple cotton dress and some pale lipstick. She had no children and treated me much as she treated her dogs—firmly but with great affection. Jim was a large, taciturn man with thin, grey hair and a red face, who chain-smoked. He seemed far more interested in farming than us and, though kindly, had little to do with Ma and me or, as far as I could see, with Noreen. Jim also owned a coffee plantation at Kiambu, about ten miles from Limuru, which was run by a manager. He took me there once. There were rows of bushes, about six feet high, with dark green, shiny leaves that hid the clusters of coffee beans. The bushes were planted in rows that followed the contours of the steeply sloped farmland. In 1936, Jim had bid on the farm in Ngong that had belonged to Karen von Blixen, the Danish author who wrote the novel *Out of Africa*, which was later made into a movie. Fortunately for Jim his bid was not accepted, as farmers soon learnt that Ngong was poor for coffee, while Kiambu turned out to be one of the best growing areas in Kenya.

The Limuru house was U-shaped with a small courtyard in the middle, built of grey stone, and thatched with papyrus. It was surrounded by a large lawn with flower beds in front of the fences that edged the surrounding paddocks. The inside was spacious, and furnished with chintz-covered chairs and sofas, with a liberal supply of English antiques. Ma slept in a spare room in the main house, while I slept in the Jockey's cottage, about twenty yards from the main house. As a major training stable, they contracted with an English jockey to assist in the training.

An extensive labour force helped run the farm. Each horse in training had its own *syce* (groom), while there were numerous other farm workers. Most were drawn from the Kikuyu or Wakamba tribes who came from nearby. They appeared to me to get on well enough, though they were traditional enemies. The cook and two houseboys, who worked in the house, were Luo, a tribe from the Lake Victoria area over two hundred miles away. I was particularly friendly with Owe, one of the houseboys, a man of about forty, who had a great sense of humour and a broad smile that showed off his white teeth. Our jokes were obscure, because of language and cultural differences, but that seemed to make them funnier. He taught me some words in of Ki-Swahili, the lingua-franca for all the tribes in the interior of Kenya, which had evolved from the days when the Arabs on the coast traded inland, particularly for slaves. The farm labour lived in a large compound. Nearly all were men, as their wives stayed back on the reserve lands to tend their small plots of land.

The day at the farm began at six a.m., with Owe knocking on the door.

"*Jambo Bwana,*" he said, as his bare feet, almost hidden by his white *kanzu,* slid across the polished floor to bring me a cup of tea and some biscuits. By six-thirty, I was at the stables ready for the morning exercise ride. The horses in training were saddled up, most ridden by their *syce*. I rode an elegant thoroughbred mare named W.A.A.F., who had a bay-coloured coat that glistened in the morning sun and a black mane on her arched neck. She had both a mild temperament and an excellent racing record. We set off on a five mile walk along trails. Birch, the English jockey who worked for Noreen, usually led the way, Noreen would bring up the rear, and I (and occasionally other guests) would ride in the line. I never saw Jim on a horse. There was no danger from wild animals on our ride, other than the possibility of a snake, as Limuru was a well-developed farming area for Europeans. After the walk, all the horses congregated at the Gallop, a horseshoe-shaped track where selected horses were put through their paces. Birch rode two or three, but most were ridden by the more experienced *syces* who were learning to be jockeys. I stood with the adults and listened to their chatter about each horse's speed and staying power, how breeding predicted performance, and the merits of different riders. By the time the horses were returned to the stables, groomed, fed, and watered, it was about ten o'clock. A large cooked breakfast awaited us in the dining room, where Noreen presided at the head of the table with Precious, her favourite cat, perched on the arm of her chair. When Precious wanted some food, she would slap Noreen's arm with her foreleg and was duly fed. Only one dog was allowed in the house at a time. The other three sat outside the low windows, looking in expectantly and occasionally receiving tidbits thrown to them through the windows. After breakfast, Noreen assigned me chores. One morning I was sent out with the *syces* to cut grass for W.A.A.F. I was given a *panga* (machete) and a bundling rope and set off with about ten *syces*, who were more than twice my age, to an area beyond the Gallop where the grass grew thick. One *syce* had been assigned to show me how to sharpen my *panga*, hold back the dense mass of grass with my left hand, swing the *panga* hard at the grass roots, and then collect the bundle ready for roping together. It was a back-breaking job and my lack of expertise and strength was cause for some good-natured laughing among the *syces*, who contributed some of their grass to the meagre amount I had managed to cut. I then bundled it up, slung it over my shoulder, and walked (or rather staggered) back to the stables. Noreen relented and I was not asked to cut grass again, but I did other chores around the farm

One of my favourite excursions was to the Kenya Farmers Association (KFA), a large warehouse that provided most of the food and feed that a farmer needed. Shopping was a leisurely and social affair. The main counter was also a bar, so most patrons sat on a stool, ordered a drink, and chatted among themselves, breaking off now and then to give orders to the Asian clerk—orders that might include anything from liquor, feed for a variety of animals, medicines, groceries, or food for their African staff. Though Noreen joined in the chatter about farming, she didn't drink or talk about politics. The clerk who took orders from the customers yelled instructions to an African, who then went in search of the item. Large orders, such as bags of feed or crates of beer, were stacked on the loading dock, and grocery items brought to the counter. Noreen shopped for one week's provisions at a time, but there was always a *dukka*, a shop run by an Indian, from which to buy needed grocery items in the interim.

Five o'clock was feed time. Noreen, much like an army colonel, would inspect each of the horses in training to make sure the *syce* had cleaned the stable and spread fresh hay, groomed the horse, and cleaned its hooves, and then inspected the horse for any signs of problems. After the inspection she went to the feed house. Each *syce* came with a *karie* (a metal dish like a large wok) to receive the horses' evening meal. No two horses appeared to have the same mixture of oats, barley, and bran, with a variety of tonics and medicines added. As each *syce* came in, he called the name of his horse. On instructions from Noreen, the head *syce* dished out the portions of feed, while I added the prescribed tonics. She appeared to have respect from her syces and the atmosphere at feed time was jovial. She joked with some, gave encouragement to others, and occasionally reprimanded a few—but in a kindly manner.

After the feed was over, it was bath time. Noreen's farm, unlike many others, had running water. We dressed for dinner; the women wore dresses and the men ties and jackets. We met for drinks in the living room in front of a raging fire, which took the chill off the air. The temperature could drop by as much as 20 degrees Fahrenheit after the sun went down, as Limuru was over 8,000 feet above sea level. Noreen drank very little—no more than a small glass of sherry before dinner—while Ma liked to have at least a couple of gins, a habit that was encouraged by Jim. Ma believed that I should learn to drink responsibly, so gave me a pony (a small glass) of beer and treated me more as a young adult than a child, which increased my self-confidence. I later learnt that allowing me to drink caused considerable friction, though I had no inkling of it at the time. Noreen was worried that I would become an alcoholic and, as my father's elder sister, felt she should adopt me. Ma naturally objected, but though this must have caused some difficulty at the time, it didn't prevent them from developing a good relationship that lasted for the rest of their lives.

I soon learned that Kenya was a segregated society. Europeans, predominantly British with a mix of other nationalities, ran the country—politically, and socially. They were the only ones entitled to own farmland—farm produce was the country's main export—and acted much like the country gentry of nineteenth century England. Asians, a mixture of Hindus, Sikhs,

Muslims, and Goans who were originally brought to Kenya to build the railway, could only live in designated areas of towns and, except for a few large European companies, ran business and supplied most of the technical and clerical labour. As farming was a precarious business and some farmers were inexperienced in African farming techniques, many of them found themselves heavily in debt to Indian *dukka wallas,* as the merchants were called. In this way, some of the Indian merchants amassed much of the wealth of the country. Africans were confined to Reserves, where they had small plots of land that provided only subsistence living at best. Most had a very limited education and provided the cheap menial labour for farms, industry, and government services. There were exceptions. Some Asians were professionals, such as doctors and lawyers, but their services were directed primarily to the Asian community. Some Africans had received basic education in the mission schools and held technical positions, and a few had been educated overseas and, as white Kenyans were soon to learn, had a very different vision for the country's future.

Nairobi was segregated. The buildings in the centre of town were a mixture of English style, taller buildings mostly built of stone, and false-fronted, one-storey shops, many operated by Indians. Delamare Avenue, the main street, was originally designed so a cart with sixteen oxen could turn around. With the advent of cars, it was wide enough to have four through-lanes in the middle, between grass islands with trees and a one-way road with angle parking on either side. Though the races mixed on the street, the focus was clearly European, and while hotels and restaurants were not legally segregated, by custom they were limited to whites. Most Europeans who worked in town lived in spacious suburbs set in rolling country outside of town. Asians had a residential area within city limits that included a wide range of houses, from mini-palaces to humble abodes. Africans lived in the shanty towns that surrounded the city, where basic municipal infrastructure was limited or nonexistent. While history tells of considerable unrest and crime, particularly in the African community, I was never aware of it. Being used to a class system in England, I found it natural to accept the racial divide, though I did develop a bond with some of the Africans on the farm. One day I went off with the lorry (truck) driver, and four other Africans, to pick up some feed for the horses. I chose to stand in the back of the lorry rather than sit in the cab, the normal privilege for whites, and feel the wind on my face. After loading the lorry, instead of returning to the farm, the driver went down to a local African village, a collection of corrugated iron, and mud and wattle shacks along a dirt road, with a ditch for waste water running down the middle. I received lots of attention from the locals, as I was the only white person there. People gave me a friendly greeting as we went into a tea shop, an undecorated room in a shack with an eclectic mix of old chairs and tables on a packed dirt floor. The driver bought me a cup of sweet tea. Around me there was much laughter and discussion in the Kikuyu language, so I didn't understand a word of what was said, but I felt welcome and enjoyed the relaxed, simple, and friendly environment. When I told Noreen where I had been, she came as close to losing her temper as I ever saw.

"Never, ever go down there again," she said. "It's far too dangerous."

"But, they were nice to me," I replied.

"Next time they might cut your throat."

The lorry driver must have received a rocket as, much to my dismay, he didn't talk to me again.

We met several of Noreen's friends, mainly people involved in horse racing. One Sunday, the neighbours invited us for lunch. We could see their farm across a deep ravine less than a mile away, but it was a six-mile, U-shaped drive over dirt roads to get there.

"Why don't we walk?" I asked.

"It's too steep a climb," Noreen replied.

"I bet I could get there before you if I walked."

"All right young man, but Birch (the jockey) will have to go with you."

I set off in high spirits, with Birch following behind, confident that I could win the race. The ravine was much deeper than I expected and the slope going down was much steeper, but I was not deterred. When we reached the bottom I bounded up the other side, but to my surprise, I soon found I was gasping for breath.

"Slow down," said Birch, "You're not acclimatised to the altitude yet." He explained that as Limuru was well over 8,000 feet, the air had much less oxygen than I was used to. I don't remember if I arrived first; I was more concerned that I got a ride back.

Noreen had several horses running in the upcoming Race Day. They went to the track a few days early to get used to different stables and train on the same track as they would race on. Ma and I went with Noreen to watch the horses prepare, and mingled with trainers and jockeys from all over the country and listened to their talk. It was an exciting new world of competition, which had an air of intrigue. Ma spent some time trying to learn about likely winners, from talking with trainers and jockeys in the stables, off the record, but when the day came it did not result in any dramatic returns from the bookies. Race days were one of the most important social events in Nairobi and it seemed to me that almost the whole city was there, though carefully segregated by colour. Ma decided to dress for the occasion, in a tailored white dress, white gloves, and a white pill-box hat with a cluster of grapes hanging down one side. Her photo appeared in the East African Standard the next day, with the caption "…obviously a newcomer." Most locals dressed much more casually, though most of the women did wear dresses.

W.A.A.F. was to race. Noreen had promised to bet five pounds on her for me, as I had been thrown off a few days before. We had been out for a ride when she suddenly shied and jumped sideways. I fell off and was dragged for a while, as one of my feet stuck in the stirrup. At eleven, my feet were too large for the small jockey-size stirrups that were fitted to the light racing saddle. Fortunately I was only bruised and shaken up. W.A.A.F. won easily. I went to meet her at the exit to the track and, full of self-importance, led her into the winners circle to the applause of onlookers. When I went to collect my winnings from the bookie, I received four pounds, fifteen shillings. I thought I had been cheated, but was afraid to ask why. Where was the five pounds Noreen had bet? After much thought it finally dawned on me that Noreen had bet on credit; I had just received the winnings, which were so low because W.A.A.F. was the hot favourite.

I slipped easily into the routine at the farm and enjoyed every day. I loved the drives around the country, seeing the grass-thatched mud huts of rural Africans, surrounded by banana trees, with children, often clothed in little more than rags, looking after cattle and goats that comprised the family's wealth. Children often stood beside the dirt roads waving to us as we drove past, leaving them engulfed in a cloud of red dust. Neither I nor they (I expect) understood the concept of social justice then.

Noreen and Terrance, her brother, had not been on speaking terms for some time, but we arranged to visit him at his farm, which was far out in the bush, for one night. It was much more of an 'African' farm than Noreen's. The house was more primitive, thatched with the same mud wall construction used by Africans, and surrounded by bush. Heads of trophy animals decorated the living room walls and skins covered the floor. Along with ranching, there was plenty of hunting for game, though I didn't get the chance to shoot. We had plans to meet again in Malindi, an Arab town on the coast that was also a budding seaside resort, but communications were fouled up so we didn't meet him again. He blamed both Noreen and Ma. I don't know who was at fault, but the result was I never saw him again.

But Ma and I spent a wonderful week in Malindi during which she treated me more as a companion than a child. We stayed at Lawford's Hotel, whose rooms were individual huts, known as *rondavals,* set in the sand dunes. The communal area was a thatched building with a bar and a dining area in the back, and a semi-circular dance-floor protruding onto a beach that was pounded by surf. To the left, the beach (smoothed by the surf) extended for a few miles to the mouth of the Galana River. About a mile to the right was a rocky promontory that created a sheltered harbour in front of the Arab village, where *dhows,* Arab sailing vessels with lateen sails, were anchored, waiting for the next monsoon to take them to Arabia or India. The village was made up of simple, white buildings on narrow, dusty streets, its commerce focused on the local population rather than on the few European tourists in the two hotels along the beach. On the promontory was a monument to Vasco da Gama, who was the first European to visit the area in the late fifteenth century. Beyond that was a calm lagoon, with a white beach behind a coral reef. We sailed out to the reef in a dugout with two outriggers and a lateen sail to snorkel. I was enchanted by the beauty of the brightly coloured coral and exotic fish, but it did not deter me from shooting some of them with a spear-gun for sport.

All too soon it was time to return home. As I had been sick flying, Ma decided that I should return by sea, while she flew home as originally planned. I was booked on the SS *Ascanius,* an ancient Blue Funnel Line ship that had been chartered by the British Government for a troop ship, and was now on her last voyage before going to the scrap yard. Ma arranged for Betty, an attractive twenty-three-year-old passenger, to look after me. I was assigned to an eight-person cabin in the officer's quarters, which I shared with an elderly Roman Catholic priest, an army major in his forties, and five subalterns (junior officers) in their twenties. Betty was on the other side of the ship, in a similar cabin designated for the few female passengers.

Betty, who was one of the very few unattached women aboard, clearly didn't have much experience with children, and her interest in me was tempered by the large number of young officers who were attracted to her like bees to honey. Thus, I pretty much had the run of the ship, as long as I didn't upset anyone important. Betty's three main suitors—Ginger, who had red hair; Wooley, which was his surname but who happened to have a very hairy chest, arms, and back; and a third man whose name I forget, did pay attention to me, perhaps in the hope of winning Betty's approval. I revelled in their adult company.

Our first stop was Mogadishu in Somalia, where we picked up more troops. The harbour had not been repaired since it was bombed in the war, so the ship had to stand off in the open sea, where it rolled in the swells. Two barges, crammed so full that the soldiers had to stand up, were towed out to the ship, where they also wallowed in the swells for some time while a debate took place as to how best to board them. Eventually, the barges were brought along the lee side of the ship, and rope boarding nets were thrown over the side so that the soldiers, carrying a full pack and a rifle, could scramble aboard. Considering the troops had been waiting on the dock, in temperatures over ninety degrees, for almost eight hours, and that many of them had been sea sick on the barge, it was a miracle that no one fell overboard to be squashed between the hull of the ship and the barge.

The troops were housed in what had been cargo holds, both fore and aft of the central decks where the officers and civilian passengers lived. I sometimes went down to their area where I was welcomed, as the troops saw me as a small diversion from their monotonous life aboard, with few activities other than the morning parade and inspection. The decks were always crowded with soldiers playing cards, smoking, or talking. The holds were crammed with bunks three high, and other than the overhead opening to the deck there was little ventilation. The few times I did go below, the atmosphere was rank and humid.

I made friends with the Coxswain, whose job was to refurbish the life-boat supplies. I climbed up into the lifeboat in which he was working, where he told me stories about his life at sea as he checked the containers of water, biscuits, barley sugar, and Horlicks tablets. Any container that was rusted or damaged was thrown out and replaced. As a result, I had an endless supply of barley sugar and Horlicks tablets from damaged containers in my cabin, but soon became sick of guzzling them.

Our next port of call was Aden, where as soon as the ship anchored it was surrounded by 'bum boats'—small rowing craft—that offered goods such as leather work or local trinkets for sale. If a passenger was interested, the Arab vendor would heave a line up to the interested purchaser on the ship, who then pulled the goods up in a basket and either returned them or sent down the cash payment—after bargaining for the best price by shouting back and forth, much to the amusement of the many spectators. If a price was agreed upon, I don't remember any instances of cheating by either party. I was more intrigued by the boats that carried young boys, who dove for coins thrown by passengers. I threw several coins into the clear blue water to watch the lithe brown bodies diving for the undulating coins. They would return to the surface, almost always triumphant, with a wide grin and hold up the coin in their hand. I later found out that sharks were abundant in the area.

As we were in port for a couple of days, a small group of us were taken out to a beach club, for Europeans only, which had a thick shark net made out of rusty metal set out into the sea to protect swimmers. I swam out to the diving station at the far end of the shark net. I don't know now if they were real or imagined, but dark shadows seemed to be cruising along the outside of the netting. I was the only one swimming. What if there was a hole in the rusty netting? I looked towards the shore, which seemed much farther away than it had when I had swum out. It took a while to pluck up the courage to return and when I did, I swam faster than I'd ever swum before.

As we sailed through the Suez Canal, the ship was surrounded by a sea of shimmering yellow sand for as far as the eye could see. We must have stopped in Alexandria at the north end of the canal, but I have no memory of it.

Just before we arrived in Malta, Betty and I were summoned to the bridge. There was a message from the Admiral to say that a launch would come and pick us up to take us ashore for the day, a trip that Ma had arranged through friends. We dressed up, I in a jacket and tie, and Betty in a dress, hat, and white gloves. We stood at the rail, watching a smart, blue and white launch, with naval ratings dressed in immaculate whites—one standing on the bow and one on the stern, and both holding wooden poles with polished brass hooks on the end—swung neatly alongside the boarding ladder. Betty and I descended, much to the interest of the other passengers. A naval officer saluted before holding out his had to help us aboard. I felt like the Captain of Marines with his beau. I don't remember much of the tour of the town or who gave us an excellent tea, but I revelled in every one of the few minutes we spent sailing to and fro in that launch. I knew I wanted to be part of that when I grew up.

We stopped in Gibraltar, where I saw the monkeys that live on the top of the rock. Then, on her last leg home, the old Ascanius ploughed directly into a storm in the Bay of Biscay, which sent waves crashing over the ship. The foredeck was continually awash, so the poor troops were confined below, where the conditions must have been atrocious.

Ma, who had arrived home a week ahead of me, met me in Southampton.

"I've left Max so that we can go and live in Kenya," she told me. "Penelope and I will go out this summer, but I think it best that you finish prep school at Fernden and join us next year."

I had no forewarning of this momentous change in my life.

Chapter 7

Many years later, Ma told me what happened when she told Max she was leaving him. On her first night home from Kenya, she was sitting up in bed. As Max came out of the bathroom, she said, "Max, I've decided to leave you and go and live in Kenya."

After a moment's stunned silence, he shouted, "No, you're bloody not!" He grabbed the red roses that he had bought her off her dressing table, threw them into the waste paper basket, and stamped on them. His foot jammed. He tried to pull it out, but it remained wedged in. He hopped around the room desperately trying to dislodge the wastepaper basket from his foot. Ma dissolved into giggles.

As the intricacies of parental relationships had always been well hidden from me, and Max had had little impact on my life, I accepted this break-up as just another thing that adults did. Nobody told me it was wrong, nobody criticized Ma, at least not within my earshot. I knew that there was a stigma against divorce, but I had little if any awareness of what it meant at the time. Maybe the prospect of going to live in Kenya enabled me to focus on an exciting future.

I returned to school. Ma and Penelope went to Kenya.

There was nothing notable about that summer term at school until the end. I caught up with the school work that I had missed, I played cricket, but not as well as I hoped, and I ran in track races, but not as fast as I wanted. The big disappointment was that the swimming pool started to leak, was out of action for most of the term, and the swimming sports, in which I thought I might do well, were cancelled. Prize-giving, which was the last formal school activity before scout camp, was held in the classrooms adjacent to the chapel, with the screens between the four classrooms pulled back so as to make one long room that could accommodate the entire school of one hundred and forty boys plus staff. Rather than listen to the endless accolades for those who won awards in either academics or sports, I was sitting at the very back watching Quenten, a boy with sandy hair and multiple freckles, who was living up to his reputation by spreading ink from his fountain pen on his hands, face, and clothes while he doodled.

"And finally we come to the Cup for the Best All-round Swimmer," said the headmaster. He went on to comment on what a shame it was that the pool was closed and the swimming sports cancelled, "...but there is one boy whose ability in all aspects of swimming and diving is exceptional..."

I wonder who that can be, I thought.

"... and that boy is, of course, Brind-Sheridan."

I was stunned. With the swimming sports cancelled, I had assumed there would be no trophy and, while I had expected that I would have done well in swimming sports, it had never occurred to me that I would win the cup. I stood up, wished I had time to straighten my tie, pull up my socks, and brush my unruly hair. As I walked to the front of the room to receive my award, I felt as if I was in a dream, surrounded by clapping phantoms.

When scout camp was over, I spent the first part of the summer holidays with my grandmother, who had sold Staplehurst and was living in the Hindehead Hotel, not far from school and very close to the old Grover home where she had grown up. My mother's friend Babs' mother, Robyn, was also staying there, and so I was chaperoned by two ladies in their eighties. Robyn was tiny, talkative, and bossy, while granny was quiet, determined, and stubborn. They sparked off all the time. As Robyn had a car—Granny had never learnt to drive—she had an ace-in-the-hole and poor Granny had to acquiesce to some of her whims. In retrospect, it had the makings of a great sitcom, but at the time I found it both aggravating and tedious. My saving grace was my bicycle, which allowed me to explore the mainly rural area. My favourite place was on the old Portsmouth Road, which circled the Devil's Punch Bowl—a deep valley with heather growing on the steep slopes that led down to dense woods in the hollow. A stone marked the spot where an infamous highwayman, who had terrorized the area in the eighteenth century, was eventually hanged. Babs did rescue me for a brief respite and took me to London to see places like the Tower of London, but as she worked, she was only available on the weekends.

I went through a religious spell while I stayed with Granny. My spiritual questioning had begun a couple of years before, when I'd grappled with the concept of eternity. How could time never begin and never end? But if time began, what came before and how did it start? And if time ended, what happened after it finished? Ma was no help in explaining this unsolvable question and I sometimes ended up in tears of frustration. As I could find no satisfactory answer, I refused to say, "I believe in the life everlasting," when I repeated the creed, as we did in chapel at school. At Willow Green, I had slunk away to church a few times without telling Ma, who hadn't been to church for years. The vicar dropped round to see me once and I was covered with embarrassment, though Ma was very civil to him. When I stayed with Granny I decided that, if I read the bible every night, I would find some answers. I thought that if it was such a wise book I could just open it anywhere and it would reveal its wisdom. I stuck it out for about ten nights but in the end I was more bewildered than when I started. My reading had only confused me more and consequently my interest in religion waned.

Later in the summer, I stayed with Aunt Joan—who was now married, had two small daughters, and lived in Winchmore Hill, a suburb of London. Joan's marriage had caused consternation in the family. She married the local wood merchant who was considered lower class, and therefore beneath her. His motive was believed to be Joan's money. Ma was quite hostile to him by being overly polite, Granny tolerated him, though her disdain was often evident, but I enjoyed working in the garden with him. He had three daughters by a previous marriage, so he and I became male allies in a female enclave. I loved his ribald sense of humour.

Skating became my main recreation. I had learned to skate outside during an exceptional cold spell a couple of winters before. I took an hour-long bus ride to the Harringay Arena, where they had skating every afternoon. I loved speeding around the rink, and my only frustration was that I had figure skates when I desperately wanted hockey skates.

When I returned to school, I was appointed a Dormitory Captain (DC) which brought about a significant change in my attitude and behaviour. Now I had to set an example, rather than find ways to undermine the system. I think I was overly officious at first, but hopefully learned to be a better leader with time. The system emphasized leading by example, and suddenly some of the rules that had seemed nonsensical to me in the past took on a new meaning. A DC's role was similar to that of an NCO in the military—make sure the boys (troops) carried out the orders of the masters (officers). Often the DC would modify the rules, because they were impractical, but always had to strike a balance between two, often competing expectations. A DC could impose some restrictions on boys but not punishment. If a situation was becoming out of control, he reported it to the headmaster or Biffer, who were the only ones authorized to administer corporal punishment. Beatings were not frequent. I experienced my share and like many, but not all, of my contemporaries, believed that a beating was a reasonable punishment. I certainly felt no resentment at being beaten unless I was unfairly punished—but I would have felt the same regardless of the punishment. One of Fernden's strengths was clearly stated rules and expectations with fair administration. Another was respect. Although teasing and bullying happened covertly, the school message was clear: respect others regardless of their age or status. When you were appointed to a position of authority, it was your responsibility to earn the respect of those you supervised. The philosophy on the playing field was to cheer on your own team, but applaud good play by your opponents. If you won, be modest—complement, don't taunt the losers. If you lost, never sulk and always congratulate the winning team. Good sportsmanship sometimes seemed more important than winning. It is a philosophy that some of the more successful professional coaches deride as creating good losers, not winners. This may have been the case with me, for when I competed in sports as an adult, mainly racquet sports and sailing, I never developed the killer instinct to win at any cost. I also absorbed the school message so well that, in those days, I believed that everyone who played sports at any level, played fairly. Many years later, when I played water polo against an army team, I was bewildered when, rather than swim for the ball, my opponent tried to pull down my swimming trunks.

DCs had to read the lesson in chapel. I dreaded my turn coming as I didn't enjoy performing and knew from English classes that I didn't read aloud well. When my turn came, I read and reread the assigned verses in my own bible the day before. On the morning, I went into the chapel early so I could open the large bible on the lectern in front of the altar at the correct page and read through the lesson yet again. The last few verses required turning over the page. I was reading the end of my passage when the headmaster came in and I had to sit down. When the hymn ended I walked up to the lectern, knees shaking.

"The lesson is taken from the ninth chapter, verses one to eleven, of the Gospel according to Saint Mark," I said, without looking at the bible, while I gripped the lectern so hard that my fingers ached. I paused to give the boys time to find the place in their own bibles so they could follow the reading. When the rustling of pages stopped, I started to read. But the words weren't right. Boys started to look at each other or at me. My voice tapered off. I had forgotten to turn the page back when I was rehearsing and had read from chapter ten, which just happened to start in the same place on the page as chapter nine started on the previous one.

In the dining room, the DCs sat at a long head table, parallel to the other tables, on a platform about eighteen inches high. Being physically higher meant that, when I sat with my back to the wall, I looked across the table and down onto eleven tables of boisterous boys. It gave me a sense of superiority, but it also meant my behaviour was visible to the rest of the school. The set up—typical of English schools—was designed to reinforce status and responsibility. At the head table we rotated our seating. The four boys adjacent to the headmaster had to speak French. I dreaded this as I was never very good at languages and didn't like to display my weakness. One lunch, shortly before Christmas, I came in late, as I had had to go to the matron's room for a reason that I no longer recall. As soon as I sat down, my companions started to laugh at me. Finally, after repeated questions, they told me I had lipstick on my cheek. Miss Prince, the pretty, twenty-one-year-old matron who had freckles on her turned-up nose, had hung mistletoe above the door of the matron's room. When I stood below it waiting to ask a question, she had walked up and given me a kiss on the cheek. I had never enjoyed being teased so much.

By Christmas time, Granny had moved to a residential hotel for wealthy, old people in Surrey. It was a beautiful, old, country-estate house set among rolling farmlands, but that winter it was shrouded in a pervasive, Scotch mist that created a dreary scene that matched my mood. Granny and I played cards together—she taught me how to play bridge—but I spent much time on my own. There was no companion close to my age, though I did play a few rounds of golf on a soggy, nine-hole, par 3 course with a young man who came to visit his mother, who was one of the residents. I explored the estate and the surrounding farm area, but the only thing of interest was an extensive pet cemetery that went back for over two centuries. There was no TV and I did not enjoy reading or working on the large puzzles, so I was bored for much of the time. The one big event while I stayed there was a fancy dress ball held on New Year's Eve, for which I made up my own pirate's costume out of an old pair of pyjamas. The photo of the event suggests I wasn't enthralled, as I had no friends and looked like a ragamuffin among the other costumes, many of which had been tailor made.

While I was staying with Granny, shortly after Christmas, I had an attack of severe pain in my right side. About three years earlier, I had experienced that pain for the first time. The pain gradually increased over a three-hour period, until I was in agony and vomiting. I threw up over the next hour or so, until there was nothing left in my stomach and the pain gradually subsided. A year passed before I had another attack. The frequency of the attacks gradually increased, though I didn't have one while I was in Kenya or Switzerland. Granny was desperately worried and contacted Babs. Between them they arranged for me to see a specialist on Harley Street— the street where most of the top medical specialists in England have their clinics—as the doctor I had seen previously did not know what was wrong. But that had to wait, as I was scheduled to go to Switzerland again with the same school group as before.

On my return I stayed with Joan, as my appointment with the specialist was a few days away. I took up skating again and became an ice-hockey fan. I took the bus by myself to cheer on the Harringay Harriers, most of whom were Canadians. Joan's home was a much more congenial atmosphere than Granny's hotel. I developed a great affection for Joan and John during that stay, but as individuals rather than as a couple. As John frequently came home late from work, I, Joan, the children, and one of John's grown-up daughters who lived with them, had usually eaten before he came in. After he changed out of his dirty work clothes and washed, John sat down to eat alone. Sometimes I sat with him and he'd tell me about his work day. He worked with people who were considered working or lower class, people who I had been taught were inferior and untrustworthy. But when John talked about them, they seemed like fun people to me. After supper, John usually went to the pub so Joan was left on her own. She spent most evenings in front of the gas fire, playing solitaire while listening to a radio drama, with a fag (as she referred to cigarettes) hanging out of the corner of her mouth, which inevitably dropped ash on her large bosom—she weighed over three hundred pounds. With me, she was jovial and friendly. I felt she loved me, though she never said so.

I went to stay with Babs in London, so that I could go and see the specialist. There appeared to be no decision after the first consultation. I was still staying with Babs when I had another attack.

"I want that damn doctor to see what's happening to you," she said, clearly distraught at my condition. We drove to his consulting room, while I groaned and held my side. We didn't have an appointment, but Babs forced him to see us. The specialist was sitting behind an antique desk in the corner of a large panelled room, with a Persian carpet on a polished wooden floor.

"I'm going to be sick," I said. He looked shocked, held out a waste-paper basket for me to throw up in.

"Don't be sick on the carpet," he said, with an anxious expression on his face

I don't remember what was said afterwards, but a few days later I was admitted to the Queensway private hospital in London, for a nephrectomy—the removal of a diseased kidney. The day before I was to have the operation, Babs sat down on my hospital bed to try and tell me that I didn't have to worry, as he was the best surgeon in England, and so on. Despite the disinterested approach of the specialist or perhaps because of it, I was not worried about the operation.

"I suppose it is just like having an appendix removed and they do that every day," I remember replying. Babs was stunned. From somewhere, probably Ma, I had developed an almost unshakeable (and unreasonable) faith in doctors and surgery, a trait that has stayed with me throughout my life. I was also very fortunate to have a grandmother who could afford to pay what I'm sure was an exorbitant fee, for the surgeon was a top specialist and the private hospital in Queensway is in one of the more expensive locations in London. The hospital was like a hotel with large individual rooms.

Ma had wanted to fly back to England, but Babs persuaded her not to, as she couldn't afford it. Babs took over the role of surrogate mother, which she filled with love and care. She had never married so I, and her other godson, whom I never met, were her surrogate children. She had been a constant in my life from the time I was an infant, although I only saw her intermittently. In the war, she had been in the army reaching the rank of colonel in the ATS, the army for women. Her most important role was being in charge of locating and preparing several thousand lorries to support the D-Day Operation. After the war, she worked as a buyer for Harrods, so my stays with her had been, through necessity, of short duration. Her focus was on educating me, and it was she who took me to historic sites and museums in London.

The operation was much more complex than an appendectomy, but it was successful and, with encouragement from Babs' daily visits, I recovered well and returned to school shortly after the start of the summer term.

I was walking with a cane when I arrived at school. Much to my surprise, I was given a rousing welcome as the headmaster had told the school that I had been through a very serious operation.

Results on the national Common Entrance exams, which all boys wrote in their final year, determined if a boy was accepted into the Public (private schools for the upper-middle and upper classes) School of his choice. Acceptance into the top schools was very competitive and boys lived on tenterhooks, waiting to learn if they were successful. Although I had taken the exam, I had no worries, as Ma had told me some time before that I had been accepted at the Prince of Wales School in Nairobi without them seeing my exam results—at the time it was the only boy's school for Europeans in East Africa. I felt relieved, but at the same time guilty that I did not have to go through the same anxiety as my friends. Mail was handed out during lunch. If a sixth-form boy blanched when he was handed a large brown envelope, everyone knew he had received his school's decision and every one was intrigued to see how he would react. Most boys opened their letters at once. Most were successful and broke out into wide smiles—cheering would have been severely frowned upon—but a few were disappointed and had to fight back tears and try to continue as if nothing had happened. All my friends were successful so I was not faced with supporting a friend who had received a public humiliation, and was consequently branded as a loser. Those who failed tended to receive only nominal sympathy and a few words of encouragement. They were expected to learn how to handle their disappointment on their own.

When I first returned to school, my physical activity was limited, but after a few weeks I was allowed some activity, which included swimming, but not diving. Four weeks before the Swimming Sports, the doctor told me that I could compete in swimming, but I was not to dive. I was out of practice, so I decided to train myself by swimming one hundred lengths over three days. I was surprised how easy it was to reach my goal. The speed competition was two races, a one-length sprint and a longer four-length race. Both races were started by diving from the edge of the pool. Biffer allowed me start both races standing in the water rather than diving. I won them both, though some complained that starting in the water gave me an advantage. Swimmers were also rated on five styles of swimming. I won the crawl, trudgen, and sidestroke and was second in breast stroke and backstroke. I think I was fortunate not being able to enter the diving competition, as I had grown a lot and was rather uncoordinated. I doubt that I could have beaten some of the other divers who were more coordinated than I. I won the cup again, though some thought I didn't deserve it as I hadn't been in the diving competition. I brushed off the criticism as poor sportsmanship and had more faith in the school's judgement. I felt more comfortable accepting the award this time than the previous year, but was still very proud.

Leaving Fernden was bitter sweet. I had spent over six years there, which had given me the base of a value system and a code of conduct that governed my life. The school's values and expectations were compatible with Ma's, as they should be when parents choose a private school, so there was little if any difference in expectations whether I was at home or school. It was difficult to leave behind the familiar routine, friends, staff, most of whom I respected, and more than half a life-time of memories. Now, I don't remember my friends, but I do remember some of the stars: Kipper Heal, who ran like the wind, kicking up his heels so high that few could tackle him in Rugby and who scored more tries than the rest of the team put together; Geoffrey Dunn, who disliked his red-brown hair and freckles, but who was a brilliant goal scorer in soccer; Hallam, who kept us riveted in anticipation as he weaved intricate ghost stories; Weldon who, when no one visited him on Sports Day, climbed to the tip of the tallest fir tree, from which he waved to the crowd, much to the admiration of the boys and horror of the adults. Swimming had been my triumph, but I had learned to live with my limitations. I had friends; I got along with most people; I had school spirit, and felt I belonged. But I and my friends were thirteen and moving on. I had a new life in Africa, but I fought back the tears when I left.

After the scout camp, I went to stay with granny. She had gone to live with Mrs Watson, her old house-keeper at Staplehurst, who now ran a boarding house in the seaside town of Southend. I didn't realize how frail and difficult Granny was becoming. She had been troublesome in the hotels, acting as if she owned them and telling staff what to do, so she had been asked to leave. I was unaware of it at the time, but she was desperately searching for a place to live other than a nursing home. Sadly, she had to move into a nursing home shortly after I left for Kenya. During the time I stayed, Mrs Watson looked after her and made sure that I did not tire her. We always had our meals together and played cards every day, but I was sent out of the house for most of the time. I knew no one so I had to entertain myself. My favourite occupation was going down to the pier that had a small permanent fun fair. All my attention was focused on driving the electrically powered race cars, with a steel guard rail surrounding the entire car, around a circular track about fifty yards long. Top speed was about ten miles per hour. It cost two shillings for about a two-minute drive. I was very fortunate that Granny gave me a generous allowance, probably about ten shillings a day, all of which I spent on driving. After a couple of drives I learnt that the orange car, which was a different make from the rest, was slightly faster. It became the only one I would drive. My goal was to pass every other car on the track. The more I drove, the more cars I passed, and the more I loved my few minutes behind the wheel. It instilled in me a love of driving that has stayed with me for all my life. For the rest of the time, I went swimming off the pebble beach or walked around watching for, but never finding, any friends.

Southend was a holiday resort primarily for working class people from London. The sea front that overlooked the beach was lined with deck chairs, rented for a shilling a day, in which older holiday makers spent their time, watching the sea and any action on the beach. The women tended to wear flowered frocks with a hat, but might roll down their stockings, and a few took off their shoes. The men wore suits, some of heavy worsted material, with a tie, but as the day warmed up, they took off their ties and detachable shirt collars and even their jackets, while those without a hat would tie a knot on the four corners of a handkerchief and put it on their heads. Their treats were Walls ice cream from a bicycle vendor, or fish and chips in newspaper, which was a standard in every seaside town. I thought they looked funny and felt rather superior. What I didn't realize then was that it was only after the war, when wages and working conditions improved significantly, that many of them were able to afford a holiday for the first time.

Dennis, the Watson's son, came down for a few days holiday. He had just completed his training for the Metropolitan police and had a few days leave before starting duty. I had seen him a few times at Staplehurst, where he helped his father with his chores. He had always been kind to me and I looked up to him, but he wasn't able to spend much time with me as his father made sure he earned his money. For the few days he was in Southend, he took me to the evening concert on the pier—I suspect that

Granny paid. They played light classical music that I didn't enjoy much, but I liked Dennis and felt very grown-up in his company. He explained things to me and told me stories about the police. The "Twelfth Street Rag" was a very popular tune at the time. After about the third piece of music, the piano player would hammer out a few bars of it. The conductor would make a derisive comment and continue on with the program. In each break the piano player persisted and the audience slowly lost its inhibitions and applauded louder and louder until the conductor asked, "Do you really want it?" Every evening the cry was the same: "Yes!" The orchestra, much to my delight, would let loose with a rousing version of the ragtime tune as the finale.

I was very sad to leave Granny, as we both feared it would be the last time we would see each other. She had been a steady rock in my life, never demonstrative but always a secure and safe haven where I knew I would be cared for and loved. She was also a very generous benefactor, which I didn't realize or fully appreciate then.

My last few days in England were spent with Babs in London. Early in the morning, in September 1949, she drove me to the airline office where I had another emotional farewell. Babs had been another rock in my life, but I was sure I would see her again. After checking in, passengers were put on a bus to Southampton, to board a Sunderland flying boat for the flight to Kenya. This trip took about twenty-four hours, with brief refueling stops at Malta and Khartoum on the Nile River, and finally landing on Lake Naivasha about fifty miles west of Nairobi. I sat with a family, two parents and a son a bit younger than me, in seats that faced each other with a table in between. The flight was uneventful until we started our final descent. Flying over the Kenya highlands in mid-afternoon is well known for excessive turbulence and the flying boat bounced around erratically as we descended. I was determined not to be sick and thought I had succeeded, but as the plane came to a stop, I threw up all over the table onto my companions' passports and papers. Everyone was very understanding, but I was mortified.

Chapter 8

Ma met me on the dock after I had cleared customs. In my excitement at seeing her, I quickly forgot the discomfort and embarrassment of throwing up so dramatically. We drove home along one of Kenya's few tarmac roads across the floor of the Great Rift Valley: through rolling grasslands dotted with flat-topped, thorn trees, where herds of wildebeest, zebra, and buck grazed peacefully; past Logonot, an extinct volcano, which rose from the plains with thorn scrub crawling up into the lava runs that had spilt from the jagged rim of its crater. We passed the little stone chapel, built by the Italian prisoners of war who constructed the road, and then started to climb the four-thousand-feet-high escarpment to the rim of the Rift Valley. The road then dropped a couple of thousand feet to the bustling city of Nairobi before climbing back up several hundred feet to Langata, the area where Ma lived. While the scenery was spectacular, I hardly noticed it, for I had so much I needed to say that words tumbled out of me like a river breaching a dam. I think I talked for the entire two hours of the drive. One of the few questions Ma asked was if I knew what I wanted to be when I grew up. I said I wanted to be a film star like Danny Kaye, because he could be funny or serious and sing. It was a nonsensical answer. I had no aspirations to be an actor and I still believed that my destiny was the Royal Marines. I must have been very hyper. Ma didn't comment.

About seven miles outside Nairobi, we turned down a dirt road, drove down a *donga*, a deep ravine where flash floods rampage after heavy rain, and along a hedge of giant succulent plants with sword-shaped leaves sprouting from a central base.

"Here's home," Ma said, and turned into a narrow dirt driveway. We bounced over rocks embedded in the black clay and stopped in the circular end of the driveway beside an oblong hut, about sixteen by sixty feet, with white siding and a tar-paper roof, set amidst the *vlei*, an Afrikaans word for flat grassland. A low Crown of Thorns hedge (dense bushes with sharp spikes and a small red flower) enclosed the circular end to the driveway, while the small, ornamental tree in the centre of the driveway was the only other thing that stuck above the tall grass. In front of the house, a rough lawn had been cut from the coarse local grass, bordered by a line of *cannas* with red flowers. At the back of the house, a small, vegetable garden was irrigated by waste water from the kitchen.

"*Jambo Bwana.*"

I was greeted by Kamau the houseboy, Maruri the cook, and Njugi the garden boy. These three 'boys' ranged in age from their thirties to their fifties.

"*Jambo*," I replied enthusiastically, but as I had retained no more Swahili words, I turned my attention to the dogs. Ma had brought two bull terriers with her from Willow Green, Dinah and her son William. Dinah had another litter in Kenya. Unfortunately, Dinah had attacked the child of a friend and had to be put down. Ma had kept one of the litter though, who was also named Dinah, and who became my dog. There was also a red setter whom Ma was looking after, but who stayed with us to become a permanent resident, and a cross between the red setter and a Labrador, called Ridiculous, or Dicky for short, who was Penelope's dog. They seemed keen to get to know me and I wondered if William remembered me from the games I'd played with him in England.

After saying something to the Africans in Swahili and telling me not to bother with my cases, Ma led me into a narrow passage. On my right was a small kitchen, no more than ten by eight feet, with a wood-burning stove, a sink that drained into the vegetable garden, and rough shelves for kitchen utensils. Next to the kitchen was a small pantry that was always kept locked—I soon learnt that Ma handed out needed stores each morning, always allowing a little extra for the boys to purloin. Beyond the kitchen was a roofed verandah that ran the length of the back of the house, adjacent to which was the hot water system: a forty-four gallon drum perched above a stone fireplace—a wood fire had to be lit under the drum to heat the water for the evening bath.

"This is where the boys do their work, like ironing," Ma explained, "and that's the loo at the end of the passage. It flushes." Flush toilets were a rarity in rural Kenya.

She opened a door to the left, which led into a small living room with a sofa and two chairs, covered with chintz, loose covers, with the oak, refectory dining table that had been in our house for as long as I could remember standing in the corner. A familiar copper bed-warming pan hung by the open fireplace, which had black smoke stains on the stones above the opening. I followed her across the red, polished-concrete floor to a door on the right.

"This is yours and Penelope's room. That's a bath in that box beside the basin. It was cheaper to put a bath in each bedroom than build a bathroom."

Ma had already told me that Penelope was away boarding at the convent school. My school started the next day, a Thursday, but Ma said that (as I had just arrived) I could go on Sunday night instead. Ma did not explain why she had arranged for me to spend the school holidays in England rather than in Kenya—perhaps as she worked she was concerned about leaving me on my own in a strange country.

Ma's room was at the other end of the living room, and was the same size as mine with another 'bath in a coffin.'

After looking around the house, I walked out onto the small veranda in the front, which faced west and so was filled with blazing afternoon sunlight. I looked out over the *vlei* that stretched beyond our property for some distance before it reached a dense forest, out of which rose the Ngong Hills some ten miles away. This was when Ma told me the ancient African myth about a giant falling and creating hills and valleys with his outstretched hands. Whenever I think of Kenya, that story and the image of the hills in the shape of a giant's hand print comes to my mind.

Kamau served us tea shortly thereafter and, as I wrote in the prologue, gave me the name Bwana Mrefu.

As I tucked into some chocolate cake, Ma continued with her story. "I bought this land very cheap, as people said it was impossible to build a house on this black clay." The house was in the middle of fifty acres, enclosed by the *sisal* hedge along the road and by a wire fence that Ma had built on the other three sides. She had designed the simple house herself and built it with a couple of Indian *fundis*. They did not dig out enough clay under the house so, when first rains came, the clay had swollen and caused cracks in the concrete floor that made it difficult to open some of the doors, but she was unperturbed. "I just got a *fundi* to shave a little off the bottom of the door." She shrugged and continued, "They said I would never be able to get a car up the driveway in the rains. Well, we filled it up with stones and I've never gotten stuck. All we need is a few more rocks and it will be fine." She must have had immense courage, and perhaps a little foolhardiness, to have done all this in a strange country on her own. Both Terrance and Noreen lived too far away to be of much practical help and I suspect she was too proud to ask. At the time I had no concept of the magnitude of her achievement, I just loved the wild frontier feeling of the property, particularly as the National Game Park, which was teaming with game, was just across the road.

We drove to the Prince of Wales School (PoW) at five o'clock the next day, so that Ma could tell the headmaster that I would not be coming to school until Sunday evening—we, like most people outside the city, didn't have a telephone or electric lights.

"I see why you are suggesting that," the headmaster said, as he sucked on his unlit pipe, "but I would strongly recommend that he come today, or if that is not possible, tomorrow morning. The new boys will be quick to make friends and, if your son doesn't come until Sunday, he will be an outsider."

The Head's wisdom or his authority or a combination of both convinced Ma. She quickly decided that I should come at eight o'clock the next morning—I could not stay immediately as I had no luggage with me.

The Head turned to me: "I assume you want to be called Brind-Sheridan, not Sheridan?"

I had never considered I had choice, but on the spur of the moment I replied, "Sheridan."

Ma looked astonished, but said nothing.

"We'll change all your records then," was his only comment. I also decided that I would introduce myself as Tony not Anthony. I had never liked my name and a new identity appealed to me.

I arrived shortly before eight o'clock the following morning. We parked in front of an imposing, two level, cream-coloured building with Grecian-style columns supporting a balcony along the front of the building, which had a tall clock tower in the centre. I was met by the headmaster, who handed me over to a prefect who was to take responsibility for me. My luggage was temporarily stowed and the prefect led me through the archway, which was under the clock tower, into the quadrangle—a grass rectangle, about thirty yards by eighty, that was surrounded by a covered walkway (with a shiny stone floor) on three sides. The roof was supported by the same Grecian-style of pillars. The fourth side was open, overlooking the countryside. I soon learnt that wooden classrooms were nestled on the slope below the horizon. The entire school population, of over five hundred boys, was standing two deep and grouped by houses around the quadrangle. I stood with the forty or so first-year boys who were allocated to Junior House, some of whom, like me, were new to the school that term. The prefect told me to stand at the end of the line, keep my mouth shut, and follow directions. I stood head and shoulders above every boy in the house, wearing a navy blue Aertex shirt, while the rest of the boys wore light blue, cotton shirts, which were part of the school uniform. I usually enjoyed being tall, but that morning, as I felt everyone was staring at me, I wanted to shrink into insignificance. We were not allowed to talk so I was spared answering questions. Soon I heard drums. The school bugle band marched into the quad and up to the flag pole, which stood in the middle of the open side of the quadrangle. The Union Jack was raised to the playing of a bugle call. The headmaster made some announcements and then we were dismissed to report to our classrooms. I have no other memory of that first morning, but I survived.

To get to Junior House from the classrooms, I walked through the passageway under the clock tower into the Quadrangle, past the gym, and along a road in a park-like setting for about two hundred yards. Having yet to make a friend, I felt as if I were walking a gauntlet surrounded by uncertainty, but I received nothing more than a few stares. Junior House, like the classrooms, was a series of wooden huts, built on stilts that were coated in some substance that kept ants from eating the wood. The House was composed of a dining room with kitchen attached, a prep room, and two dormitories—which housed about twenty boys in each. Lunch was bland, uninteresting food, not dissimilar to what I had at Fernden, so I ate it without complaint. I found that, true to the headmaster's words, new boys had already formed into cliques that were largely self-protective in nature. One boy seemed to be alone. Like me, he had just arrived from England. His style was very English and he had already been nicknamed Pongo, a derisive label for recent arrivals from the "Old Country". I think he had made a poor start the night before. He was not my type, nor do I suspect I was his, but we quickly formed a friendly alliance. The main advantage for me was that he was big—not as tall as me, but stronger, which would be a definite advantage in a potentially hostile environment

My experience at Fernden stood me in good stead. I adapted quickly to the environment that, though different, had many similarities. I knew how to follow directions and handle teasing, get along with a variety of boys, and never, ever rat out to a prefect or master. I made other friends, but Pongo and I remained a team for the whole of my first term. On a couple of occasions we stood back to back, fighting to defend our honour, and gradually earned respect.

Pongo became somewhat of a celebrity when boys learned that his father owned the Buick in which Lord Errol had been murdered in 1941—one of the most sensational murders in the British Empire. Errol had been having an affair with Lord Broughton's wife. Broughton was acquitted of his murder but, Ma told me later, he had confessed to a friend of hers who was a teenager at the time. He subsequently committed suicide. The bullet holes were visible in the foot well of the front passenger seat and everyone wanted to see them. I was one of the first.

One new routine for me was compulsory bed-rest for forty-five minutes after lunch. On that first day I had nothing to read, but soon I started reading comics; Kit Carson, the famous scout in the Wild West, was my favourite. As time passed, I began to read books and gradually learnt to love reading. Over time, I read all of the Horatio Hornblower series written by C.S.Forrester. Hornblower's exploits had far more influence in developing my values of service, duty, honesty, and loyalty (which were coincidentally reinforced by the school philosophy) than any other books or religious instruction.

Dormitory life was similar but tougher than Fernden. Boys came from a greater variety of backgrounds, from poor to rich, from isolated farms to city boys, as well as from twenty-six different nationalities. Some had traditional hostility towards the British. The largest group was the Afrikaners, whose culture still harboured resentment over how they had been treated by the British, particularly during and after the Boer War. There were also some boys from Germany and Italy, who only four years before, had been the hated enemy. This mixture of backgrounds with a variety of values made it easy to upset someone without realizing it. Though this did not cause major problems for me, it did complicate some relationships. But all boys were white. Though segregation was not legally sanctioned, it was accepted and enforced by custom.

We had two prefects in the dormitory, both of Greek origin. One was rather overweight and studious. He accused me of not washing in the morning, as I didn't wet my hair with water, and would not accept my explanation that I could wash my face without wetting my hair. After three days of being hassled, I took the lesser of evils and wet my hair. The other prefect was a rather immature show-off who, on one occasion, walked to the washroom in the morning with his sponge bag hanging on his erect penis. After initial surprise and curiosity, most of us just ignored him and thought him vulgar. But it was important to keep on the good side of prefects, as they held an inspection each morning to ensure our bed area and clothes were orderly and clean. This provided them a great opportunity to hassle boys they didn't like.

After the afternoon rest we had an hour of prep, followed by sports. During the term that started in September, we played soccer or cricket—I chose cricket because I was better at it, though I wished I could play soccer well. The next term we played field hockey and, for the third term, we played rugby during the first half of the term—while the ground was still soft from the rainy season—and track and field in the latter half, after the rains ended. I was very disappointed that there was no swimming pool. I worked hard at sports, as I still wanted to be a good athlete, but no matter how hard I tried, I never rose much above average. Cross country was a new experience for me. As I was no good at sprinting, I hoped that I would be a good long-distance runner, but it did not take me long to find out that I was even worse at long distance than sprinting. I soon dropped in with a small group who had a way of avoiding the rigours of the run. The course was out of the school grounds, across the railway line, and round a circuit through a coffee plantation. Some boys had figured out that if we ran fast enough to keep out of sight of the prefect who brought up the rear, we could duck into the coffee bushes, have a smoke, then join the rear pack of runners just after they rounded a bend on the other side of the coffee plantation before the prefect came in sight. That way we ran less than half the course. The ruse didn't always work, but when it did I got more satisfaction from beating the system than I ever did by running the whole course.

I played cricket during my first term with moderate success.

Fernden's teaching also stood me in good stead. My first term report indicated that, while I didn't work too hard in class, I received A on five of six exams and finished tenth out of 32 students.

Each form at PoW was graded into four levels, A, B, C, and D according to academic ability. I stayed in the A, or the top the level, for my first four years, though as I grew older I gradually slipped from the top third to the bottom third of the A class and some of my A grades became B's, C's, and an occasional D. Often my reports recorded comments such as:

"Quite good, he could make more effort."

"Rather disappointing. More effort needed."

"He must try to eradicate his careless attitude (I think carefree maybe a better word.)"

But I did have some positive comments and some A's as well.

To deal with lack of effort in class, the school had a system of monitoring class performance called "satis" cards. If a half term report showed a lack of effort, the housemaster called in the slacker for a dressing down and put him on satis for any or all of his courses. At the end of each week, the slacker had to present his satis card to each master who would rate the miscreant: very satis, satis, or non-satis. A non-satis rating led to loss of privileges, particularly being gated for the weekend, while removal from the program was earned after several satis or better ratings. The system worked for me. I was placed on satis about three times and it definitely improved my performance. I'm not sure why I did not do as well at schoolwork as I could. I certainly had a lazy streak, but I seldom saw any direct relationship between so much of what I did in the classroom and my expectations. Too often, schoolwork seemed like an unnecessary chore. This was particularly true of Latin. As a result of what I had learnt at Fernden I came top of the class for two years without having to study. But when we progressed beyond what I already knew, my marks dropped to D. I also had a tendency to resent authority and not working may have been a form of passive resistance.

Gym was part of our regular classes and, like Fernden, was run by an ex-army sergeant. In one of the first classes I attended, Mr Riddle, or Johnny as we called him, asked us who had boxed. Hoping to make a good impression, I put up my hand. As a result I was entered in the school boxing competition. Because I was so much taller than boys my own age, I ended up fighting against older boys. In my first bout, I fought against a boy of fifteen called Dennis Stevenson who, to put it mildly, beat the crap out of me. I never boxed again and was very careful about what I volunteered for after that. I met Dennis again some fifty years later. He told me that it was just as well that I lost to him, as he got the crap beaten out of him in the next round.

Bath time was after sports. There were four showers, but only enough hot water for about five or six showers before it ran cold. Prefects had priority in the showers so the remaining twenty boys shared four baths. There was only enough hot water to fill each bath once. Two boys got in the bath at the same time and those that followed were faced with increasingly dirty and cooler water. Your status in the house could be measured by your ability to get in a bath first. Pongo and I worked our way up the scale. After supper there was another hour of prep followed by an hour of free time before lights out at ten o'clock.

One of the social dividers in the school was between smokers and non-smokers. The former tended to be more rebellious, the latter more conforming, or as the smokers described them, "wet". Though I didn't enjoy smoking at first—it made me dizzy—I quickly joined the smokers as a way of thumbing my nose at authority and showing bravado. The punishment for those caught smoking was six whacks on the bum with a tacky (gym shoe), administered by the head prefect of the house. During my time at the PoW, I was caught smoking several times and beaten accordingly, but the excitement of getting away with breaking the rules with friends was well worth the occasional beating. The challenge for those who were beaten was to stand up after the beating, look the prefect in the eye, and shake his hand without showing any signs of pain.

Boys who lived near school were able to go home on Sundays after the church service, which finished at about ten o'clock, and return by six for supper at six-thirty. Once I was comfortable in my new environment, I started to hitchhike home on Sundays and Ma drove me back to school in the evening. Drivers were good about picking up boys in their PoW uniform, so it usually took between one and two hours to hitchhike home, a journey that took about thirty-five minutes to drive. I was able to invite friends who lived far from school home for the day. Our big treat was a decent lunch, which soon, if not during that first term, included a glass of beer. Ma believed that she should teach me and my friends how to drink responsibly, though many would consider her drinking excessive. She was often suffering from a hangover when I arrived home on Sunday mornings, but among her friends that was considered normal. After lunch, Ma would take us out to explore the local area that included the National Park. During the months before Christmas, it was common to see a pride of lion resting under a shade tree a few miles from the house. By the time the Christmas holidays arrived, I felt I was a Kenyan, even if some others still saw me as a *pongo*.

Ma had been putting money in a post office account for me, which had reached thirty pounds. She decided, without consulting me, that I should buy a horse. I didn't really want one, but as she had saved the money, I felt I had no alternative but to accept. Ma had selected an untrained pony named Gaiety who was a four-year-old, chestnut mare with a white blaze on her face and three white socks. She arranged for Colonel Sheppard, the show-jumping instructor at the local riding school, to train her. He was sceptical about Gaiety's abilities, but Ma's choice turned out to be fortuitous. Col. Sheppard found Gaiety to be very responsive with good potential for show jumping, and offered to buy her for fifty pounds. Ma refused.

I was very apprehensive as we drove over to the riding school for my first lesson, at the beginning of the Christmas holidays. I hadn't ridden for some time and had never jumped. At first Col. Sheppard taught me basic riding skills. The combination of the colonel's excellent teaching and Gaiety's natural ability quickly turned me into a confident, if not competent, horse-man. I soon progressed to jumping. The first round of jumps we took were low and, much to my surprise, I found myself keeping in tune with Gaiety's movement. The ride went smoothly. The colonel appeared pleased and pointed out another series of jumps. I thought the last one he pointed to was much bigger than the others, but figured that if he thought we could do it, we could. After completing the first three low jumps smoothly, I lined Gaiety up for the last jump. It was about twice as high as the previous ones. Rather than a simple bar, it was made of compacted brush with a white rail at the front and short, wooden wings on either side, to lead the horse into the jump. Gaiety looked at the jump, pricked up her ears, and sped up. I leant forward, grabbed hold of her mane, and let her have her head. Without a moment's hesitation, she took off. I rode with her, clinging onto her mane as well as the reins, so I wouldn't pull on her mouth. She cleared the jump easily. I sighed with relief as we trotted up to Col. Sheppard.

"I didn't mean you to take that big one, but you did it very well," he said. I was now a committed horseman. After that lesson, I rode Gaiety to our home where a stable awaited her. For the next three years, riding was to become my main leisure activity.

My first Christmas in Kenya was memorable for two events. On Christmas Eve, a friend of Ma's, Colonel Buller, invited me to go with him on a drive up to a farm near Ol Kalou, where he had some business. I jumped at the chance, as it would give me an opportunity to see a farm set in the wilds, as well as see a lot of game on the drive there. We drove down into the Rift Valley, past Lake Naivasha, where I had arrived three months before. On this drive I absorbed the wild beauty of the expansive, dry grassland, dotted with flat-topped, thorn trees, which was home to seemingly endless herds of buck, zebra, wildebeest, and giraffe. We turned off the main road into the hills, where we had lunch with a settler family who owned a farm that stretched as far as the eye could see. I don't remember what they farmed, but it was probably cattle and maize. As we left the farm in the early afternoon, the colonel pointed to Lake Nakuru, which was pink in colour and below us to the right.

"Those are millions of flamingo," he said. "How would you like to go and see them up close?"

I was not that enthusiastic, as I was not a great lover of birds, but as the colonel seemed keen, I agreed. We drove down to the lake and onto the sand, which was firm at the edge. As we drove towards the mass of birds, the ones closest to us took off. They flew in a great arc, the evening sun highlighting the pink on their wings, which flapped in slow, graceful movements, their black legs trailing behind. In his excitement, the colonel strayed too far from the firm sand at the edge of the lake and the car sunk up to its axles in soft mud. He carried a shovel and we took turns digging. Though there was no sign of habitation in the area, a small group of Africans, carrying *pangas*, suddenly appeared out of the bush. After some discussion in Swahili that I didn't understand, they agreed to help by digging with their *pangas,* and then pushing as the colonel tried to back the car out. It soon became evident that we needed a tow. One of the Africans went to ask the local Indian *duka wallah* (store keeper) if he would come and pull us out with his lorry. It was after dark when he appeared. The colonel negotiated a price with the lorry owner and the leader of the group of Africans, who took all his cash and cigarettes plus a case of beer that was in the back of the car. Some of the Africans cleared more sand from under the car, while others cut armfuls of brush to lay a track for the car to reverse onto. After three attempts, we were back on firm ground and finally free to head for home.

We were supposed to be home by seven, but it was about nine-thirty when we got back on the road. There was no phone within ten miles of the house so we couldn't call to let Ma know what had happened. We arrived home after midnight. I thought it had all been an exciting adventure, but Ma was beside herself with worry. I didn't see Colonel Buller again.

My first African Christmas with Ma and Penelope, was celebrated in the same manner as we did back in England—with a decorated fir tree, and a turkey lunch with traditional trimmings, held behind curtains drawn to block out the brilliant African sun so we could see the candles. I was not a great fan of Christmas, and aping an English tradition in Africa seemed out of context to me, but I was quite content to receive presents. Ma gave me a bolt action, single shot .22 rifle. A school mate, JJ, who lived about a half mile away, received a single shot 410 shotgun and a head lamp. We decided to spend Christmas evening hunting, hoping to put up a small buck, but prepared to shoot anything that was unfortunate enough to come into our sights. After an hour of tramping through the long grass with the dogs, who didn't put up any game, we returned to our respective homes. The next day we learned that a lioness with her three, almost full grown, cubs had been on an adjacent property, and killed three dogs.

Chapter 9

Coming home from school on Sundays for the day gave me a gradual rein-
troduction to living with Ma. One advantage of a boarding school was that
it set the standards so parents didn't have to be the main disciplinarians.
For the most part, Ma and I had a very easy relationship. Occasionally
she lowered the boom, if I pushed the limits too far, and when she did, I
did not push back. I felt she treated me like an adult most of the time and
our relationship was, from my perspective, more like brother and sister. In
some areas she was permissive. I was allowed to smoke, have a beer a day,
and escort her into bars that, in Kenya, seldom enforced the age limit. She
encouraged me to mix with her friends, but expected me to live up to her
idea of behaving like an adult. As long as I conformed to her expectations,
she supported me and I became comfortable with older people. She taught
me how to drive when I was fourteen, and let me drive on back roads when
she was in the car. She believed treating me this way was the best way to
teach me how to be a responsible adult, rather than being a lax parent. Her
values were a mix of upper-middle class, conservative British, and rebel.
She had strong opinions about public behaviour and dress, but let loose at
parties; she was generally polite and proper, but could be cutting and did
not suffer lightly those who did not conform to her values. She believed
in keeping a stiff upper lip rather than being demonstrative, but I always
felt loved.

We did not see my grandmother, although she lived only a few miles away. Ma told me she didn't want to see us—she never met Penelope—but gave me no explanation. I thought it was odd, but I was not very concerned as I had never gotten close to the old lady. Later I learnt that Max had written a letter to her, saying that Ma was an irresponsible and loose woman who was coming to Kenya to sponge off the family. We saw my aunt Noreen often and she became a significant part of my life. We didn't see my uncle Terrance again though, as he had moved to South Africa. Noreen and Terrance still weren't speaking to each other, but I never knew why.

Much to Ma's surprise, Granny in England decided to visit, about a year after I arrived. She flew out on the same flying-boat service that I had taken. It was unusual for eighty-two year olds, particularly as infirm and doddery as Granny was, to fly in those days. While Ma was very anxious for her welfare, I just assumed she would be fine as I knew she was a very determined old lady. As soon as the door of the plane opened we saw several attendants helping Granny, the first to disembark, down some steep steps onto the dock. With an attendant on each arm, she half strode and half stumbled down the dock, with an enormous smile on her face, waving her cane. After an emotional greeting, she collapsed in the car and fell asleep. I suspect that she was surprised at the small size and simplicity of Ma's house, but said nothing in my hearing. As Ma was working as an air-traffic controller—in those days it was strictly daylight flight rules—Granny spent most of her days sitting in a chair, reading, knitting, sleeping, and becoming frustrated because she couldn't communicate with the houseboy to get him to do what she wanted. She had an imperious attitude towards staff, whom she liked to boss around. Penelope and I spent a bit of time with her, but for most of the time we had other priorities. Her days must have been quite dreary as she was not very active and there was little more for her to do than look at the Ngong hills.

As she had looked at the hills so much, Ma decided to drive Granny around them on one of her days off. Granny, Penelope, Ma, and I, plus two bull terriers, set off after lunch in Ma's Morris Oxford, which was not exactly designed for rough, back roads. As we drove down into the valley behind the hills, and left civilization behind, the road became little more than a dusty track with frequent pot holes and dried washouts from the previous rainy season. The country turned to semi-desert, dry, scrub bushes and stunted flat-topped, thorn trees growing out of sandy soil. Though we bounced over the rough road, Granny seemed delighted with the giraffe we saw munching on the greenery off the top of the trees. We rounded a corner and dropped into a large pot-hole. The car bounced and landed with a horrendous crash on a rock in the middle of the road. The oil sump was holed. As we had seen no other cars, waiting for help was not an option. Ma decided to drive on. After driving a short distance the engine seized completely and we skidded to a halt in a cloud of dust. Our only choice was to walk out. Granny, Penelope and one dog stayed in the car, with seven-year-old Penelope in charge of my .22 rifle, which I had taught her how to use, although Ma decided it should not be loaded. Ma, William (the bull terrier), and I set off to walk the nine or ten miles to the nearest civilization. Due to the poor road conditions the trip had taken much longer than antici-pated and it was now nearing nightfall. As we walked into growing darkness we were bombarded by the symphony of the African night—some sounds were harmless, like the chirping of crickets or the creaking call of a hyrax [a small rodent], others were scary, like the lonesome howl of a hyena, which seemed much closer than it probably was. I became increasingly anxious. To add to our apprehension, we knew that lions hunted in the area. William was not happy and kept darting from side to side on his leash. After about two hours, the road began to climb steeply, beside tall, rock cliffs that rose high above us like a great, black wave. It was a home for baboons and their sworn enemies, leopards, both of whom loved eating dogs. Ma and I sang "Ten green bottles" at the top of our voices, laughed hysterically, and clapped our hands. William was not reassured by our display of bravado and continued to dart between us. After almost four hours of walking, we arrived at the District Commissioner's (DC) *Boma* (compound,) guarded by two African *askaris* who were amazed to see two *Mzungus* (white people) arrive on foot more than three hours after sundown. The DC was eating dinner when we were shown into his house. After listening to Ma's story, he said, "Have a drink while I finish my dinner; then we'll organize a rescue." A little while later, we set off in a lorry, with three police *askaris,* to rescue Granny, Penelope, and the dog. One *askari* remained with the car to protect it from vandals until it was towed in to have a new engine a couple of days later. Granny appeared to survive her ordeal remarkably well.

In my second term at the PoW, I was promoted to Intermediate house, designated for boys in their second year, and in my third term to my senior house, Clive, where my school report stated: "He has settled down well …." There were six Houses in the school. Clive and Scott were located in buildings that were attached to the main quadrangle, while Grigg, Hawke, Rhodes, and Nicholson were located about half a mile away in twin buildings at the far end of the spectacular, park-like school grounds. Inter-house competition, particularly in sports, was strongly fostered.

Clive had two dormitories, junior and senior, with about twenty-five boys in each, plus two prep rooms and a prefects' study. The dining room was shared with Scott house, where we sat at long tables with twelve boys aside and a prefect at each end. The junior boys sat in the middle and gradually progressed to one end or the other until they sat close or next to the prefect. They were then promoted to the next senior table where they started in the middle and had to work their way up again. The prefect controlled the distribution of food, thus the main advantage of sitting near him was better access to choice bits or preference for limited seconds. The food was not appealing and a popular way to spice it up was with a communal bottle of Worcestershire Sauce, which was paid by a system of fines, mainly for swearing, imposed by the prefect.

The house master and his family lived in an apartment under the senior dormitory, and the assistant house master had a smaller apartment adjacent to the junior dormitory. While there was a duty master in the dining room for all meals, masters only came to the dormitories and prep rooms occasionally, on unscheduled visits. Prefects were expected to keep order. One evening, after lights out, a boy was demonstrating how a fart could be turned into a blue flame with a cigarette lighter when the house master, Mr. Fyfe, suddenly appeared. He happened to teach chemistry, and instead of disciplining us, gave a brief lecture on how methane gas was created and what it could be used for. But he did confiscate the lighter. I never saw the

assistant housemaster visit a dormitory during the four years I was there—
rumour had it that he was too drunk to do so.

The school philosophy was based on the British Public School system.
The headmaster, the third since the school's origin in 1929, was Mr. Phillip
Fletcher, commonly known as Flakey. His own school record was impres-
sive, culminating as assistant head boy at a prestigious British public school.
After attending Cambridge and Princeton, where he was successful in both
academics and sport, he became a school master in England, working up
to assistant headmaster. In 1945, at age 42, he was selected by the Colonial
Office, from fifty applicants, to become the headmaster of the Prince of
Wales School, an appointment in which the Governor of Kenya took part.
My predominant memory of Flakey is of him sucking on his pipe—sleeves
rolled up to reveal muscular forearms covered in ginger hair, tie askew, shirt
collar points curled up, and trousers that looked as if he had slept in them—
watching every boy at the end of morning classes, when the whole school
had to walk through the entrance to the quadrangle on the way back to their
houses for lunch. He often made me feel guilty as I walked by him, usually
with good reason. I suspect that this was his way of sensing the mood of the
school and reminding us who was in control. He knew every boy by name,
and at least some of their history, and would often make remarks to either
compliment, warn, or censure a few boys each day. He was a strict discipli-
narian who believed in punishment, often beating boys himself, but he was
always ready to help a boy who needed it. His belief in honesty, respect, and
fair play permeated the school, and he was responsible for the positive environment that I experienced while I was there. He was a bachelor who was
so dedicated to the school that he had no outside interests that I was aware
of. These days a bachelor teacher so dedicated to the welfare of boys might
be suspected of being a pedophile, but at the time, as well as looking back
with the wisdom of hindsight, I can see no indication of any deviance, other
than him being a workaholic. His regular work hours were from 7:30 a.m.
to 11 p.m., five days a week, with slightly shorter hours on the weekend.

I checked the Old Cambrian's (old boys of the school) website to see
if my impression of Flakey was shared, and though he was not faultless, I

found many overwhelmingly positive comments. The following three comments reflect his style and philosophy.

On being beaten:

"The only staff name that could strike terror was 'Flakey' – especially when he was on your trail. When it all ended in his study, he had a big smile and said, 'I'm going to beat you. Heh, heh, heh!' It wasn't too bad and I always got a handshake and his usual saying of 'Well stood, Dyack'. That meant I didn't flinch or cry. Empire stuff!"

From one of his speeches that aptly describes how I felt at school:

"I wonder if we all realize what happiness and freedom can here be found? This was not always a happy school, and of course at this or at any other time there are unhappy individuals in it, but for some years now I believe it has been a school where the vast majority of boys have been happy for the greater part of their time. I should think something was wrong if all boys were always happy, for school is a training for life, and life is full of rough patches, through which one must live and help others to live. But I do think it tremendously important that there should be an atmosphere of happiness, confidence, trust, mutual liking and respect, and that boys should consciously cherish this and do their best to maintain and increase it. It has to be constantly worked for—and prayed for—by staff, by prefects, by boys of all ages and sizes; like all the precious things of life, it can easily be lost."

This incident occurred after I left, but reflects his attitude, which pervaded the school:

*"At morning assembly, 'Jake' Fletcher, the legendary
headmaster, then nearing retirement, clad in his black gown,
made a speech to the boys. He had received a complaint from
an African small-holder growing maize next to the school
boundary. Two boys had been smoking 'out of bounds' in
his field the previous day, and had damaged some of his
crop. 'Jake' requested that the culprits report to his office
that morning. He said that they would be beaten (six of
the best with a cane) for the offences of breaking out and
smoking, and that their parents would be required to pay
compensation for the damaged mealies. He said that he knew
the calibre of boys of the school, and expected the culprits to
report to him, despite the promised punishment.*

*Next day, he announced that he had been proud that the
boys had reported as expected, had taken their punishment
like men, and had acted honourably."*

One role Flakey reserved for himself was to give a lecture on sex to boys about to leave school. The tone was distinctly moral rather than practical, though he did suggest we could laugh when he referred to the significant role our balls played in life. One of my contemporaries reported on the Old Cambrian website that:

*"His advice to those who would be tempted by ladies of
doubtful character was to raise one's hat and say, 'No thank
you madam.'"*

The calibre of teaching was generally good. Liver sausage—his real name was Liversidge—was very much the retired army officer and had a no-nonsense approach to teaching that appealed to me. I learnt a lot from him. In one class, he saw that I was drawing pictures rather than paying attention. He threw the wooden chalkboard duster a good fifteen feet, hitting me on my knuckles and spoiling my drawing. Baldy Lamont was very different. Erratic and volatile, we never knew what to expect, but our favourite tactic was to get him to talk about his experiences in the First World War, rather than teach French, which he did in a very pedantic manner. His stories of surviving in the trenches taught me about taking responsibility for myself rather than relying on luck or others—particularly those in authority—to look after my interests. He was fired for publishing poetry that was deemed pornographic. We were sad to see him go, but even sadder that we could never find a copy of his poetry.

Mr Nel—he must have had a nickname but I don't remember it—had played Rugby for the Springboks, the South African national team. When he arrived at school, a few weeks after term had started in my fourth year, Clive's rugby team, in which I played wing forward, was at the bottom of the house league. He got us out of bed an hour early, much to our chagrin, to run around the field, gradually urging us on faster and faster as he ran beside us—there was no escape. After some physical exercises, he taught us tactics; the most successful was the 'wheel and break' from the scrum. Instead of the scrum pushing straight forward against the opposing team and heeling the ball back to the scrum-half, the ball was held by the second row forwards, and on command, the eight-man scrum wheeled to one side, broke free, and charged down the field together, dribbling the ball in front of them. The only defence was for an unfortunate defender to fall on the ball in front of sixteen pounding boots with cleats—not an appealing activity. As a result of this, and other coaching, Clive, with no players from the school's team, moved from last to first place in the inter-house competition and won the 'Cock of the Walk' trophy.

Also in my fourth year, the school hired a music master, Mr Lockhart. In his first class, he talked about the orchestra and its instruments. Although I loved singing the current hit tunes, and knew the words of a great many, I had no interest in playing an instrument in a classical orchestra. As he identified the role of each instrument, he asked who was interested in playing one and boys put up their hands. Suddenly, I realized that I was the only boy who hadn't shown an interest in an instrument, when Mr Lockhart said, "Let's see, what have we left? Ah yes, the trombone. Who would like to play the trombone?" I put up my hand. "Good," he responded, "that's the only instrument we have. You can start practising tonight." I was flummoxed. It was soon evident that I was not destined to become a musician, but the few weeks that I practised it provided a useful subterfuge. I went to the middle of the playing fields to practice my trombone, but also to have a smoke, which allowed me to exhale the telltale smoke through the instrument.

Some other masters were not good at keeping order and they became the victims of many schoolboy pranks, some funny, some cruel, some silly, but they all kept us amused, and though the stories became greatly embellished over time, they gave me a good feeling of being able to pull one over on authority.

For me, social life at school was more important than success at schoolwork, which, too often, I continued to find irrelevant. It also became more important than sports, as it quickly became clear that, in spite of all my efforts, I would never be a good athlete. So making friends and establishing status among my schoolmates was the most crucial aspect of my day to day life. By the time I reached Clive House, I had largely shaken off the *pongo* label, though it arose on a few occasions when a boy tried to insult me. I was a committed smoker and established a common bond with others by planning and sharing a risky experience together. The bond was increased when we were caught, as we had to wait together for the inevitable beating.

Status was gained by creatively breaking rules, such as going out of bounds after dark. To become a fully recognized member of the group I belonged to, we had to sneak onto the grounds of the girls' convent school, which was across the valley, and make contact with a girl. To meet this requirement, Titch, Martin, and I slipped out of school one Saturday evening, crossed the main road and scrambled through the woods to the Ki-apple hedge, a thick, thorn bush that had small, green, apple-like fruit, which surrounded the convent. We found a hole through the hedge and saw that the girls were watching a film. A couple of girls were sitting on a windowsill, high above us. One of us made a comment to them, to which a girl replied, "You better go; the nuns know you're here." We heard someone coming, so we beat a hasty retreat, diving through the hole in the hedge. Titch, who as his nickname suggests, was very small, was at the rear. He jumped through the hole after Martin and I, but his belt caught on some barbed-wire that we hadn't seen before. As he swung for a moment before his belt broke lose, an arrow shot by a Wakamba (one of the tribes whose traditional weapon was a bow and arrow) night watchman whizzed into the bushes overhead. At the time we thought it was a great joke, but it could have had very painful and dangerous consequences. Though the conversation with the one girl was extremely limited, we had reached or goal—I suspect details of our contact was dramatically embellished when we got back to the dormitory. But one of our group went too far. Sven was Norwegian. When he arrived at school, at age fourteen, he spoke no English. There were no special classes, only some tutoring, to teach him the language. Though he learnt English quickly, he didn't do well at schoolwork, and though big and tough, I don't think he ever felt at ease at school. He disappeared one Saturday night without telling any of us. The next morning he was lying on his bed fully clothed. An old school boy had found him downtown, dead drunk, and brought him back to school and left him on his bed. Sven was expelled.

During school holidays, I spent most of my time riding Gaiety. Part of my riding time was spent training and competing in show-jumping, the rest was spent exploring the plains, which were populated by wild animals. I took riding lessons both at school and during the holidays, so my skills were continually improving. Gaiety's jumping ability flourished and it seemed all I had to do was point her at a jump. When I was fifteen, we entered the show-jumping competition at the Nakuru Show, the biggest agriculture show in the country. The arena was about the size of a North American football field, surrounded by a few rows of seats, which were sheltered by a thatched roof. I was called to the entrance area, as I was scheduled to jump first. I expected to go straight into the arena to start, but the steward held us back for what seemed like an eternity. I'm not sure who became agitated first, Gaiety or I, but we fed off each other's frustration. Gaiety was throwing her head up and down and prancing from side to side, while I directed my anger at her, rather than at the steward who refused to allow us leave the area to walk around calmly. When I was finally directed to start, Gaiety's neck was lathered in sweat and her canter felt awkward. Instead of calming her down by cantering around in a circle, I lined her up for the first jump. She seemed hesitant. I kicked her hard and urged her on. Just before the jump, her hind quarters went down, her forelegs straightened, and she skidded to a halt right in front of the jump. I ended up hanging around her neck with the noise of the crowd pulsating in my ears. I pushed myself back in the saddle, circled around, regained some level of composure and headed for the jump. I held her back in a tight canter until we were about thirty feet from the jump, eased the reins, and then gave Gaiety her head. She arched her neck and pricked up her ears. As I felt her get ready to spring, I leant forward, pressed my heels into her flank, rose in the saddle as she jumped, and followed her leap, landing without pulling her mouth. I lined her up for the next jump. We found our rhythm again and went on to complete a clear round, but the penalty for the refusal knocked us out of the top finishers. I was bitterly disappointed. I had won several previous competitions and was one of the favourites to win the biggest juvenile show-jumping prize in Kenya.

Later that year, I attended the Pony Club camp, held on a large farm near Nanuyki, with eighty-seven girls and eight other boys. We slept in tents, boys well separated from girls, ate in a marquee, and spent the days on different riding exercises. In the evenings there were campfire activities and then some free time. Though I was desperately shy with girls, I and a couple of other boys were invited to visit a girls' tent. I was attracted to Jenny, a redhead with freckles on her nose. I was so enamoured with her that I wasn't paying much attention to the riding activities. During the final event, which was the show-jumping competition, I went into the ring with no knowledge of how those who had gone before had done. When I came in after a clear round, I was greeted with enthusiastic yells from the members of my club. I had the best round so far. My lead held up and I won the cup. Unfortunately, Jenny lived many miles away on an up-country farm, but we swore eternal love and vowed to write to each other when we returned to our respective boarding schools the next week. I wrote to her, but never received a reply. Some years later, I met a girl who had been at school with Jenny. She told me that Jenny did write back to me, but her letter had been intercepted by the headmistress. Writing to boys was strictly forbidden and poor Jenny had her letter to me read out in front of the entire school.

While I loved show jumping, I loved my long rides over the plains even more. None of my school friends lived around Nairobi and, as Ma worked during the day and arranged for Penelope to spend the day with a family who had a girl her age, I spent much of my holidays on my own. Joseph, the *syce*, would saddle up Gaiety and, after breakfast, I'd call the dogs and we set off for the plains to the south. The first couple of miles were along paths, in between private properties, that led to the scrub bush at the edge of a shallow valley. There I followed a game trail down to a small stream, forded it, and rode up through the bush on the other side to the plains, which stretched as far as I could see in front of me, while on my right, the Ngong Hills, silhouetted against the sky, looked down over my shoulder. The plains, covered in brown grass cropped close by the large herds of buck, zebra, and wildebeest that roamed at will, provided a wonderful venue to gallop in any direction. When my heels touched Gaiety's flank, she'd stretch her neck, flatten her ears, and leap into a gallop. I stood in my stirrups so that I could move with the pounding rhythm of her gallop; the sound of her hooves drumming on the hard dirt was music to my ears. I yelled at the top of my voice as the wind tore at my face.

My favourite game was to chase a herd of wildebeest and try to cut out a young bull from the herd—a goal that I seldom achieved, as wildebeest, who to survive must escape a pack of lions, cannot only run fast but also weave and duck faster than a professional football player.

As I was alone, my fantasies were my companions. I was the lone cowboy, reliant only on myself, out to right the wrongs of the world: to seek out and kill the outlaw gunslinger who had shot the sheriff; to rescue the young and beautiful widow left alone on the wild prairie; to help the settlers set up a new town by the next river, which was marked by a row of flat-topped, thorn trees in the distance. My fantasies meant that I was never lonely on my solitary rides. They gave me confidence that I could look after myself, while the heroic deeds I dreamed of bolstered my self-esteem. As for the dogs, they were faithful companions who always followed me.

On one ride I was shocked out of my reverie when Gaiety started to prance nervously and snort through her nostrils. About twenty-five yards away, a leopard was lying in a tree, resting its chin on a branch while one front leg and one back leg dangled below the branch. I was in no danger on a horse, but I left hurriedly, as leopards love to eat dogs. When I was a safe distance away, I realized that Wopsy, a black Labrador was missing. My heart sank. I rode back towards the tree. The leopard had disappeared. I whistled and yelled for Wopsy, but there was no response. I was sure the leopard had killed him. The bush by the stream was thick and I was afraid to go into it, but I rode back and forth along edge of the bush yelling Wopsy's name, while the image of him crammed into the fork of a tree with blood dripping from his throat, which had been ripped open by steely leopard claws, floated around in my mind. I was about to give up when Wopsy, his coat covered in grass and leaves, suddenly appeared, wagging his tail but looking rather shamefaced. That day I took the dogs straight home, truly thankful that we all returned.

I didn't always ride alone. Sometimes I rode with Penelope, but she was not strong enough to control her pony, and we only went for short rides together on a few occasions. If I brought Titch, Neil, or Rusty home from school on a Sunday (one at a time) we would often go riding on the plains—Martin and Mac, the other friends whom I brought home, didn't ride. But I did have one ride during one of my holidays with a beautiful girl named Joy, who was visiting some friends with her parents. She had big, brown eyes, short, curly, brown hair, a smile that made my knees weak, and a figure that made me gulp. She was fifteen, one year older than me. I didn't have the nerve to ask her myself, but our parents arranged for me to take her for a ride. I couldn't believe my luck, but at the same time I wasn't sure how to behave. We set off through the forest towards the Ngong hills, with me in the lead and playing the male guide looking out for his beautiful companion. We came to a grassy glade in the middle of the forest. "Let's canter," I said over my shoulder. She nodded and I spurred Gaiety on, intent on showing off my horsemanship. Gaiety's front feet went into a hole, and she stumbled and fell. I flew over her head. As I struggled to regain consciousness, I felt warm breath on my face and soft lips nuzzling my cheeks. For one delicious moment I thought that Joy was cradling me in her arms, but when I opened my eyes, I was lying in the grass with Gaiety blowing in my face and rubbing her velvety nostrils across my cheek. Joy was sitting on her horse, looking stunned. Fortunately Gaiety was not injured. The fall broke my collar bone and I had an agonizing ride home.

My life at home was about to change. One day, a year or so after I arrived in Kenya, Ma told me she had decided to build an addition to the house—two rooms and a bathroom—which she could rent out. Looking back, it obviously wasn't only for financial reasons. The first tenants were Gus and Skeperhorn. Skep only stayed for a few weeks and it slowly dawned on me that Gus was more than a tenant. After a short while, Gus moved into Ma's room and I moved into his room in the addition, so that Penelope had her own room. They were not married; Ma's divorce had not come through, but their cohabiting seemed natural enough to me. At the time there was a common saying: 'Are you married or do you live in Kenya?' Gus had not been married before and was ten years younger than Ma. He acted more like an elder brother than a father to me, and I enjoyed his company, particularly his wicked sense of humour and endless supply of off-colour jokes. He was the managing director of the Cooper Motor Corporation (CMC) that had the Land Rover Agency. Shortly after he moved in, he went on a business trip to Germany and was ecstatic when he returned. He had obtained the Volkswagen agency for East Africa. He showed me the brochures for what appeared to me to be a very peculiar car that came to be known as the Beetle. "You'll never sell any of those," I said, with all the wisdom of my fourteen years. Two years later, over half the new vehicles sold in East Africa were Volkswagens, due to their superior construction, dust-free interior, excellent suspension, and reliable air-cooled engines.

With Gus part of the family, we began a tradition of spending Christmas at Malindi, a small Arab village about eighty miles north of Mombasa. The four-hundred mile drive took us through Nairobi and onto the dusty, dirt road, the surface of which was corrugated by traffic so that cars shook and rattled as they weaved to avoid the many potholes. The route that dropped from 6000 feet to sea level, led across the almost treeless Athi Plains, past Donyasabuk, the giant beehive-like hill over which the giant had tripped in mythical times, past the turn-off to Machakos, the home of the Wakamba Tribe and location of an historic Kenyan tale that captured my imagination:

In the early part of the century, the Kikuyu, with spears, and the Wakamba, armed with bows and arrows, were about to go to at war. The two armies were massed on the plains ready for battle. Just before they clashed, the local District Commissioner, unarmed, took a table and some chairs and set them down in between the two armies. He invited the leaders of the two tribes to meet with him. All day long they sat in the blazing sun and negotiated. By nightfall, they agreed on a treaty and the armies went home.

The open plains gave way to the scrub bush of Tsavo, with an elevation of about 3000 feet, renowned for the abundance of game. We occasionally saw game along the road, including the odd elephant, but never a lion, which frustrated me. My imagination had been fired by the book the *Man Eaters of Tsavo*, the story of how the Indian indentured labourers, who had been imported to build the railway from Mombasa to Uganda at the turn of the century, were hunted and killed by lions. We usually spent the night at the Tsavo Hotel, where the rooms were individual *bandas*—made in the traditional African style of mud and wattle walls covered with plaster, with thatched roofs and wide verandas—set on the edge of the game park with a majestic view of Mount Kilimanjaro.

The coast was very different from home. Not only was it much hotter than the Nairobi area but it also had a strong Arab and Islamic heritage. For centuries it had been ruled by the Sultan of Zanzibar. *Dhows* with lateen sails traded with Arabia, Persia, and the Indian subcontinent, sailing east on the monsoon winds and returning six months later when the winds reversed. Narrow, dusty streets threaded through white, Arab-styled buildings, with minarets sprouting like sentinels on the horizon. Many, though not all, of the newer European buildings were built in a similar style, but more spread out with wider roads suitable for cars. The population was an eclectic mix. The Portuguese had arrived in the fifteenth century and assorted European and Asian traders had visited, and some settled in the area over the years. There was a major African presence—most noticed by a teenage boy in the form of bare-breasted women, wearing only a short skirt, which were made of strips of cotton, and beaded jewellery. But, for me, it was the Arabs in long, flowing, white gowns that gave the place its special sense of romance and mystery. They remained an enigma, for in all the time I spent there, I never met one other than in a store or passing on the street.

The road to Malindi was sandy, mainly through dense, thorn scrub but with the occasional palm trees, usually around a small village or farm. The road was cut by two creeks, one about a hundred yards wide and the other, some twenty miles farther on, about five hundred yards wide. The ferries were metal barges attached to a chain that spanned the creek. The ferry would take two or three vehicles, depending on size. When loaded—no one placed stops under the wheels—the captain began his work song. The crew responded with a chorus, then pulled the ferry across the creek by grabbing the chain at the front of the barge and heaving on it while walking to the stern in a line, and then returning to the front to repeat the exercise. The captain and crew sang for the entire trip, making up songs that included mentions of their current passengers. Their songs were partly in Swahili and partly in some obscure dialect so we couldn't understand. As the ferry approached the shore, the captain picked up a conch shell and blew out a melodic beat. The crew let go of the chain, clapped their hands and stamped their feet in time, turning the barge into a giant drum as it glided to the shore, grinding to a halt on the pebble beach. The display was magical and ended all too soon, but their performance earned them a good tip.

On our first visit to Malindi, we stayed at the Sinbad Hotel, a white building fronted with rounded arches and turrets that, to me, suggested an Arabian palace. From the hotel's arched entrance-way, six curved, wide steps led down to a bar and sitting area, which overlooked the dining area for about sixty people another six steps below. Beyond that, six more wide steps led down to a dance floor that overlooked a sandy beach, pounded by surf. The hotel was up the beach from Lawford's, where Ma and I had stayed on our first visit, but seemed much more exotic. Days were spent surfing on the beach in front of the hotel or driving to the blue and white lagoons to swim in the calm water behind the reef. Sometimes we hired an Arab dugout canoe, with two outriggers and a lateen sail, to explore the unspoiled coral reefs. I was still as fascinated with snorkeling as I was the first time, and spent many hours exploring the brilliant coral and shooting fish with my spear gun. Ma and Gus were great party-goers and evenings were spent in the bar and on the dance floor. During most of our stays there were few if any kids my own age, so I spent a lot of time with adults and drank far more John Collins than was good for me—by some modern definitions I would have been considered a teenage alcoholic. Christmas holidays at Malindi became the highlight of my year.

MY GRANDFATHER NORMAN SHERIDAN,
PROBABLY TAKEN DURING HIS TWENTIES.

MY GRANDMOTHER, WINIFREDE
[NEE KENDALL,] AGED ABOUT EIGHTEEN.

MY GRANDFATHER, PERCIVAL PICKFORD,
PROBABLY TAKEN DURING HIS FIFTIES.

MY GRANDMOTHER, HELEN PICKFORD,
PROBABLY TAKEN DURING HER LATE FORTIES.

MY FATHER, AGED TWENTY-TWO, IN FULL DRESS UNIFORM.

MY MOTHER, AGED 19.

NOVEMBER 9TH, 1935.

JAMES INSPECTS...

"SIT UP STRAIGHT AND GRIP WITH YOUR KNEES."

H.M.S. AJAX

MY FATHER'S MEMENTO OF A "FRIENDLY" MEETING BETWEEN
THE CREWS OF AJAX AND THE ADMIRAL GRAF SPEE IN 1938.

THE BAYVIEW TERRACE GANG ... ME, MICHAEL AND
PETER MITCHELL AND ANTHONY SEAGRAVE.

PENELOPE'S CHRISTENING, SUMMER 1943

HOW MY MOTHER LEARNT THAT HER HUSBAND WAS
DEAD, TWELVE DAYS AFTER HE WAS KILLED.

LEADING W.A.A.F. INTO THE WINNERS CIRCLE.

GAIETY JUMPING HIGH ENOUGH FOR MY FEET TO CLEAR THE BAR.

RACING THE FLYING ELSON AT TITCH'S FARM.

PENELOPE, AGED THREE, JUST BEFORE SHE WENT TO KENYA.

THE LAST PICTURE OF MA, PENELOPE AND ME,
TAKEN ELEVEN MONTHS BEFORE SHE DIED.

THE SMOKERS: MAC, MARTIN, ALAN, TITCH,
ME AND DES IN OUR HIDEAWAY.

MA AND ME, DURING MY BRIEF RETURN TO KENYA IN 1955/56.

DAWN STAR [IN THE FOREGROUND] AND
SEAWARD IN LAS PALMAS HARBOUR.

ENGLISH HARBOUR WITH SEAWARD
MOORED STERN-TO ON THE RIGHT.

Chapter 10

Eight days before the end of the term, in December 1951, the house master called me in to say that Penelope was ill. I thought it strange that he would tell me, as there was nothing I could do. Her boarding school was over a hundred miles away, and anyway, she would soon get better. I didn't think much more about it. As I was leaving the dining room after lunch the next day, the house master said the headmaster wanted to see me at his house, as he had some news about my sister. That meant something was terribly wrong, as he usually saw boys in his study. As I walked along the road to his house, with the mid-day sun burning my shoulders through my shirt, it suddenly occurred to me that if she had died, there would be more room in the car going down to the coast for our Christmas holiday. I stopped dead in my tracks, appalled at my thoughts. Shame rolled over me. I trembled. I shook my head, and then hurried on. When I arrived at Flakey's house, I stood on the doorstep for a while, not wanting to go in. Finally I rang the bell. Flakey showed me into his living room and pointed to the sofa. I sat down. Flakey took a seat opposite me.

"I have some bad news," he said, looking directly at me. "Your sister died yesterday." He handed me a freshly ironed handkerchief

He told me that Ma didn't know yet, as she and Gus were on holiday on the remote island of Pemba, north of Zanzibar, and couldn't be contacted. The manager of Cooper Motors in Dar es Salaam, the nearest place on the mainland, had gone out on a boat to locate them.

I gritted my teeth, determined not to cry and use the handkerchief.

I left Flakey's house in a daze, walked past my dormitory, where boys were resting on their beds, and headed for an old, corrugated iron shed on the edge of the school's property, in which discarded furniture was stored and where we sometimes went to smoke. I lit a cigarette, stood for a moment, then knelt down at an old desk. I clasped my hands together, my cigarette hanging from the corner of my mouth, looked up, and spoke through gritted teeth.

"God, if you exist, it's clear you don't give a damn about me or my family, so I don't give a damn about you." I have not prayed since.

The dam behind my eyes finally burst. Tears streamed down my cheeks and sobs racked my body.

Some indeterminate time later, I went back into the school routine. At first I didn't tell anyone what had happened, but they'd been told. An uneasy tension filled the air. I didn't know what to do or say, and neither did the other boys. Later that day, I did talk to some of my friends, but none of us knew how to handle such raw emotion, so after a few sympathetic but uncomfortable words, the subject was dropped and we tried to carry on as usual.

Two days later I was called to Flakey's house again. Ma and Gus had flown back from Zanzibar in a small plane. The Nairobi West Airport was flooded, so they landed on the road south of Nairobi and caught a lift to the school. It was an uneasy meeting. Gus paced around the room and said little. Ma and I sat on the sofa. We both cried a bit, but I had cried myself out. My overall sensation was one of utter futility and hopelessness. When we got up to leave, Flakey, who had waited in the hall, asked if I wanted to go home.

"I think it's better if I stay at school and finish the term," I replied. I had learned to cope with death by carrying on with life as if nothing had happened, leaving grief to solitary moments.

Penelope died at boarding school shortly before her ninth birthday. At age seven she had gone to the convent. One Sunday she came home and said she wanted to become a "caflic". When Ma asked her why, she replied that "caflics" were given cakes after mass but the "prodidents" didn't get any.

The next term Ma sent her to board at the Beehive School near Nanuyki, about one hundred miles from Nairobi. There were only about twenty-four children at the school. Her school reports said she did well and she was apparently happy there. One day she cut her foot while playing in the fields and came down with tetanus, also known as lock jaw. I remember hearing a story about a misdiagnosis that resulted in delayed treatment, and the doctor leaving the country, but I don't know the details and it is too late to find out about them now. I was told that, as the airport at Nanuyki was flooded, the police took an iron lung, which might have saved her life, by Land Rover from Nairobi, but they didn't arrive in time. She died far from home, and from what I learned later, her death would probably have been agonizing. The last time we had been together, the evening before she left for school, we went riding. Some unimportant thing had annoyed me and I lost my temper with her. Was that how she remembered me?

I did not attend her funeral, and did not see her grave until my family and I went to visit Ma in Kenya almost twenty years later.

Now, as I look back more than sixty years, I'm saddened at how little I remember of that sparkly little blonde girl, with bright blue eyes, who could twist Ma and me around her little finger. I look at the photo of Penelope, Ma, and me on the beach, the last one of the three of us, taken in December 1950, and wonder what she could have become and how she might have impacted my life. All I'm left with are a few anecdotes, some of which I have related in this memoir.

Penelope's death left me with a gaping emotional hole. For many years after Penelope died, as if desperately trying to replace her, I used to revel in playing big brother to the young daughters of some of Ma's friends. As for Ma, I don't recall her talking about Penelope's death or how it affected her. Perhaps she thought that it was so obvious that losing a child was an unimaginable sorrow that it was not necessary to talk about it. Babs told me that when she saw Ma, after she'd first met my wife, she often referred to Steph as Penelope.

Chapter 11

But life had to go on. Soon after I returned home for the school holidays, Ma and I drove to Malindi in her Ford van, with the two of us in the front, and Maruri, the cook, crammed into the back along with our luggage and the household gear we would need for the house we'd rented during the holiday. Gus followed a few days later in his Land Rover. The van was a small, utility model that bounced over four hundred miles of corrugations and potholes in the dirt road, sucking dust through poorly fitting doors, as the engine struggled to keep the speed over fifty mph. As I wriggled to get comfortable, with my long legs pressed up against the dash, I was too often reminded of the callous thought that had flashed into my mind as I walked over to Flakey's house, for with three of us, it would have been very cramped.

Ma and Gus had rented a house in Malindi rather than stay at the Sinbad for our annual holiday. The house was simple, made of mud and wattle, with a thatched roof. It had two bedrooms, with a dining area in between, and a long veranda in front for the living area, which overlooked the harbour where *dhows* and local fishing boats bobbed at anchor. A shower was in a separate building, the toilet was a thunderbox out back, and a kitchen was adjacent to the servants' quarters behind the main house. Furnishings were rough, simple, and locally made, and gave the house a rustic look that appealed to my sense of adventure. A short walk to the south, over Vasco de Gama Point, a path led to a lagoon behind the reef, with crystal clear waters that were great for swimming and snorkeling. A slightly longer walk to the north, along the beach and past the village of small, square, white houses and narrow, twisting streets, led to the surf beach, on which the Sinbad and three other small hotels were situated

Our social life revolved around the bar in the Sinbad hotel. The big event was New Year's Eve, when a parade was organized for midnight. Ma volunteered me to be the Old Year in 1951. I wore a long beard made out of sisal, a full-length, white *kanzu,* and had to carry a guest's baby with 1952 written on a white sash across her chest. The baby, along with her anxious parents and I, was ready at midnight, but the rest of the cast were absent. The clocks in the hotel were set back while the organizers went to look for the other participants. Corralling the inebriated cast was like herding sheep without a pen to keep them in, and it was well past midnight when they were finally assembled. I was handed the baby. She took one look at me and howled. I'm not sure who was the most apprehensive, her mother or I, but the parade went on. Instead of a slow graceful walk down the three sets of steps in the hotel, with the rest of the cast following, I strode out in the lead, holding the screaming baby at arm's length, desperate to return her to her mother. I suspect my embarrassing performance caused more mirth than a slow graceful walk would have done. Unfortunately, it did not disqualify me from being coerced into the parade the following year.

To welcome 1953, Gus drove his Land Rover down the three sets of steps through the length of the hotel, with a large cardboard replica of a cake on the back. Inside the cake was a six foot six, skinny, sixteen-year-old boy—me—wearing a diaper, with 1953 painted on his chest. When Gus hooted his horn, I was to jump out and yell "Happy New Year!" Once again, the clocks had to be put back and it was after one in the morning by the time the entire cast, or at least those that could still stand, were ready. I climbed into the cake, desperate to finally get this embarrassment over with. The Land Rover bounced down the steps with me bouncing around inside the cake. The horn sounded. I sprung out of the cake and disappeared into the gap between two ceiling beams. Nobody had thought to measure the height of the beams. If Gus had stopped a few inches further back or forward I would have smashed my head into a beam when I jumped.

I have never been a showman by nature, and I certainly did not relish my role at the centre of these parades, but I made little if any effort to get out of them. A clear incentive for me to expose myself in such an embarrassing way was that I was being treated as an adult, and I probably believed that to be accepted I had to participate. Now I wonder what some of the adults thought. I was also drinking and, though not drunk, I had consumed enough to lower my inhibitions. Finally, what Ma wanted, Ma usually got. I was always leery of going against her wishes. But I did learn an important lesson: how to shrug off embarrassment, laugh at myself, and return to the party.

Soon after New Year, 1953, Clark Gable, Grace Kelly, and Ava Gardner, the stars of the movie, *Mogambo,* which had been shot on location in Kenya, came to stay in the hotel for a few days before returning to Hollywood. Clark Gable was polite but kept to himself. Grace Kelly was aloof and distant, while Ava Gardner, who was the most beautiful woman I had ever seen, was friendly with all. After a couple of days, they were joined by Ava's then husband, Frank Sinatra, who was arrogant and disdainful towards other guests, who responded by ignoring him. One evening I was singing in the bar—singsongs were quite common—when Ava came in. She was wearing a skirt and sweater, inside out, and was quite tipsy. She asked me to sing to her. I was happy to oblige, as I was proud of my singing and, as I had had a few drinks myself, my inhibitions had been squashed. As I sang, I was mesmerized by her incredibly beautiful, green eyes, flecked with hazel. She bought me a bottle of Champagne and asked Ma if she could take me to Hollywood, to which Ma replied that they'd talk about it in the morning. Then she suggested we go skinny-dipping. To go skinny-dipping with any girl, let alone a film star, was beyond my wildest dreams. She told me to meet her at her room. With considerable trepidation, I rushed off to change into a swimsuit and grab a towel. But when I arrived at her room, she was having a flaming row with Frank. I stood outside her door and listened for a while, before reluctantly accepting that skinny-dipping with an exotic film star would remain beyond my wildest dreams—so, fortunately, would the invitation to go to Hollywood, where I would have been a dismal flop!

We spent the next two Christmas holidays at Malindi, but I managed to avoid participating in any more parades.

One year Mac, my friend from school, was also holidaying at Malindi. He hadn't snorkeled before, so I offered to take him out on the reef. We walked out to the tip of Vasco de Gama Point, where we could walk straight onto the reef. The water was knee deep, and walking on the uneven coral was hard going, so rather than struggle to where I had planned to snorkel, we donned our snorkeling gear and swam parallel to the reef, away from Vasco de Gama Point. Fish of all shapes, sizes, and colours swam around us as we swam along the reef, made of exotic and colourful growths, and which formed the edge of the lagoon. After a couple of hours gazing at this mesmerizing underwater world, we rested on the reef. As it was a shorter distance to swim across the lagoon to the shore and walk home along the beach, than to swim and walk back along the reef, I suggested to Mac that we swim to the beach, and he agreed. We were halfway across the lagoon, in about fifteen feet of water, when Mac, who was swimming behind me, called out that he couldn't go on any farther. I swam back to him and got him to float on his back. I held his head in my hands, so his face was just out of the water, told him to spread out his arms as I swam backwards, pulling him as I had been taught in life-saving class at Fernden. It didn't work well. Mac started to panic, and I was getting desperate when my foot hit something. I looked down and saw a giant coral mushroom about five feet below us. We were able to stand up. After resting for a while, Mac was able to swim the rest of the way to the beach.

The following year, on an outing from school, Mac and I were climbing up a cliff when my foothold gave way, leaving me hanging onto a shrub with one hand, fifty feet or so above a rocky stream. I panicked and was immobilized. Mac, who was above me, came back and talked away my panic so that he could guide me up to the top of the cliff.

Twice I went to stay with school friends in Kampala, with Neil in 1952 and Rusty in1953. Both times I travelled by train, a journey of some thirty hours, at the end of term, along with about thirty boys from school. As there was no supervision, the journeys were riotous. The train was a roller coaster ride. It started in Nairobi at an elevation of 5500 feet, climbed to about 8000 feet, dropped to about 4000 feet, and then climbed up to 8000 feet again before dropping to 3500 feet at Kampala, some four hundred miles later. Soon after leaving Nairobi, the tracks, which were alleged to be the steepest in the commonwealth, climbed past the PoW school. In 1950, some boys (I was not involved) scrounged a lot of oil and smeared it on the tracks. The train came, the engine's wheels spun, and the train had to go back so that both the tracks and the wheels could be cleaned before it could get up the hill. At one point on our journey, far into the Interior, the train was going so slowly up a steep grade that we jumped out of the carriage and ran up the hill ahead of the train, to jump back on board when our carriage caught us up—a dangerous game, as our carriage was near the rear of the train and, as the front part was already heading downhill, the train had sped up. On my second trip, Rusty and I paid the African engine driver ten shillings to let us ride on the engine plate between Naivasha and Nakuru. The flaming oil fire that drove the massive steam engine gave a warm, orange glow to the two black and two white faces, as we thundered through a dark, moonless night that accentuated the brightness of the mass of stars above us. I leant out of the cab and let a rush of warm air pull against my upper body and felt exhilarated.

Kampala was smaller than Nairobi, as Uganda, unlike Kenya, was a protectorate rather than a colony and there were no settlers, only Europeans who worked for the government or businesses. Both visits were fun but very different. With Neil, activities were organized by his mother. We had swimming parties in Lake Victoria, visited Murchison Falls, where the waters from Lake Victoria roared and pounded through a rocky gorge in a churning white mass to create the great Nile River, which ran north for many hundreds of miles through barren desert to the Mediterranean Sea. We toured a sugar plantation, where African workers, dripping sweat in the thirty-degree heat, shovelled about fifty pounds of sugar into bags and sewed them up. Four men lifted the bag by its corners, so another worker could walk underneath it with his back bent. The sack would then be lowered onto him, so that he could carry it to a railway car. They all sang to keep their production line running in time. I often wondered how much sweat was a part of the sugar that we all used. Now I wonder how long a worker could survive in those appalling conditions. We played sports, and did Scottish dancing, but the highlight for me was a party at Neil's home. We played Postman's Knock, a game designed to pair off a boy and a girl and send them out of the circle. I was paired with Pat, a girl with long, curly, blonde hair and blue eyes. We went outside, and walked across the lawn to look down on lights of the city, which ended at the waters of the lake that shimmered in the moonlight.

"What do we do now?" I asked.

"I don't know," she replied.

Gingerly, I put my arms around her waist. She moved closer and looked up at me expectantly. I swallowed and bent down towards her upturned face. My first kiss was cumbersome, but finally I had done it! I didn't see Pat again, as I left for home the next day, but I dreamt about her for many nights.

While my first visit had been well structured, Rusty's parents made no attempt to supervise us. We were both filled with the exuberant confidence of sixteen year olds and spent much time exploring on our bikes, both in the city, including the African areas where few Europeans visited, and the surrounding country, which was mainly small African farms and villages. While Kenya was facing an emergency, fighting the Mau Mau, the Uganda Africans appeared friendly, and if there was ever any danger, we were blissfully unaware of it. One day we visited a quarry and asked the African workers to show us how to use a jackhammer. I leant on the handles as I had been shown, and squeezed the hand lever that opened the forced air, so that the hammer pounded up and down, jangling my entire body while I was engulfed in dust and the clattering sound of steel reverberating against rock. I was bewitched by the brute force that drove the bit into the rock. After drilling a couple of holes, I returned the drill to its legitimate operator. Like the African workers, we wore no ear protection, and as we rode away my ears rang so loudly that it was hard to hear. The ringing gradually subsided to a level that, though always present, I subconsciously learned to block out most of the time. I have had a ringing in my ears ever since.

When I turned sixteen, in 1952, I became eligible for a driving license. The lure of a car, which would increase my mobility and provide better opportunities to chase after girls, trumped my love of riding. I sold Gaiety for one hundred pounds, seventy more than I had paid for her, and became the proud owner of a 1934 Austin Seven Tourer. Ma christened it the Flying Elson, an Elson being a metal chemical toilet. I felt surprisingly little sadness at saying farewell to the pony, who had been such a large part of my life. I sold Gaiety to a girl who was not only a far better rider than I but was also committed to competitive show jumping. They went on to become one of the best show-jumping combinations in Kenya. A few years later, Ma told me, they were selected for the national team. Gaiety was travelling on a train to a competition when she was spooked by something, reared up, and broke her leg. Sadly, she had to be put down.

Ma had a very permissive attitude about driving regulations. She had allowed me to drive when I was fourteen. I learnt quickly, I think, because of all the time I had spent racing around the track on the pier at Southend. I had no license when I bought the Austin, and when I went down to apply for one, I was told that the waiting list for a driving test was six months. I'm not sure whether I told Ma or not, but I drove anyway. My girlfriend at the time was an eighteen-year-old police woman (because of the Emergency, many eighteen year olds were in the security forces) who, after going out with me in the Elson a couple of times, said she couldn't go out with me again until I had a license. I told her my predicament, so she arranged for me to have a test—the police did driving tests then—in a couple of days. The test was very short, down the road, around a roundabout, and back to the police station. I thought that I had failed, as I nearly ran us under a lorry as the brakes were so poor, but after answering a couple of questions, the officer gave me my license.

The Elson was a very basic two-seater. I started the engine with a built-in crank handle. She could just reach a top speed of forty-plus miles an hour on the level, after about thirty seconds of pressing the accelerator hard to the floor. Her climbing ability was limited. On the road home from Nairobi there was a long hill that climbed about seven hundred feet, with a level patch about two thirds of the way up. The Elson just made it to the level patch before she boiled over. I'd stop, have a couple of cigarettes while she cooled down, before adding some water so she could make it to the top. The Elson also had limited leg room, so I took off the door on the driver's side so that my right knee stuck out the side, as it wouldn't fit under the steering wheel. Despite her limitations, I loved her dearly. She gave me freedom and a certain status, as very few boys my age had their own cars. When I was at home, I could go into town when I wanted to. When I was at school, I kept the Elson in the garden of some friends of Ma's, who lived close to the school, so I could go downtown, sometimes with approval, and sometimes by sneaking out. Above all, I just loved driving.

Ma and Gus married in 1953, after living together for a couple of years. I did not go to the Registry Office ceremony, but Rusty and I acted as barmen at the reception held at a local pub. Water had to be boiled before it was safe to drink, and the pub stored drinking water in gin bottles in the fridge. Serving drinks to a large group of Kenyans was a hectic business, and in the rush, gin was mistaken for water. Late in the evening, I was reported to, not only have served guests gin in their Scotch or brandy, but drinking a mixture of Scotch and gin myself. I was extremely drunk. It was lucky the Elson didn't go very fast, as I drove her home that night—only a quarter of a mile up the road—fighting to keep her on the road, which was, thankfully, deserted. The next morning, with Rusty, I left for Kampala on the train with the worst hangover of my young life. I can still remember the clackity-clack of the wheels on the rail lines reverberating in my head.

After a couple of years, shortly before I was to leave for England, I sold the Elson to Titch Leonoit, a school friend. He and his elder brother were mechanically inclined and they "hotted-up" the Elson. To show me what he had done, Titch invited me down to his parent's farm for a weekend. We set up a race track and spent the afternoon timing each other racing the Elson around a dusty field. On his fourth run, Titch beat my time. Determined to beat him on my fourth run, I went into a corner too fast, slid into a ditch, and rolled over in a cloud of dust. I was thrown clear and suffered no more than a few bruises, while there was only body damage to the Elson. We spent the rest of the afternoon and the next morning straightening out the Elson's body work, and by the time I left to go home, she was running again with slightly rumpled fenders.

Chapter 12

One day in 1952, Flakey called me into his office to tell me that, as I only had one kidney I would not be accepted into the Royal Marines. I was stunned. I had never questioned my assumption that I would follow in my father's footsteps, even though I was far removed from the pomp and circumstance that reinforced the appeal of a military career. I was also conditioned to accept a headmaster's opinion as gospel, as I had not been taught how to question or check information or look for alternatives. Rusty, who was not only my best friend at the time but also someone I looked up to, was going to be a mining engineer. He knew about the profession and was planning to attend the Cambourne School of Mines in Cornwall. Without much critical thought, and probably because any goal was preferable to none, I decided to join him. At the time, I thought there was something romantic about mining, perhaps from movies about the Gold Rush or because Rusty was the only boy in the school who was considering mining as a career. After completing fourth form and School Certificate (the British National School Exams), students were streamed according to their vocational interests. The choice was Arts, Biology, or Engineering. With my new-found goal, I was destined for Fifth Form Engineering, to study math, physics, chemistry, English, and French.

I don't think Ma was impressed with my choice of profession. Her image of mining was probably more that of the blackened faces of English coal miners, but she didn't criticize my choice. Instead, she arranged for me to work in a mine one school holiday, so I could see what it was really like. When Peter, another school friend who had also decided on becoming a mining engineer, heard that I was going spend my holiday working in a mine, he asked if he could join me.

The mine was operated by the African Land Development Corporation, a crown agency, whose mandate was to redevelop Kenya's dormant mining industry. The two of us flew to the mine, which was close to Lake Victoria in a twin-engined bi-plane which held ten passengers. We landed on a grass landing strip, close to an eclectic group of buildings that were dominated by a tall, wooden tower, which held the pulley systems that raised and lowered the underground mine elevators. The mine was surrounded by flat, dry grassland that was dotted with bushes about ten or twelve feet high. The vast expanse of Lake Victoria shimmered on the horizon. To me it looked like a Wild West movie set, which meant that it was filled with the potential for adventure. We were shown to the single men's quarters where Peter and I shared a room. We ate in the mess hall, which was also the 'club' or social centre for the European staff. Most of the miners were married and lived in company houses. The working mine produced copper, zinc, and lead, but there were also several small gold mines in the area that had closed. Our work experience, which in reality was little more than observation, was divided into three parts: a week underground; a week in the mill, the assay office, and the steam boiler room; and the third week prospecting. Peter and I were put on separate schedules, so we did not work together.

On my first morning, I was issued a hard hat and a lamp and assigned to Bill, a European miner, who took me underground. Stepping into the wire cage with a group of miners, all white, since the Africans had gone down earlier, was a thrilling moment. As we descended into the dark, the miners teased me good-naturedly, and their laughing faces, partially lit by our hand-held lamps, made me feel like I was already part of the team. The elevator stopped at a tunnel, called a drive, whose dark, wet walls were only lit by the lights we carried. I followed Bill, who stepped around or over snake-like hoses—some hissing air, others leaking water—that led us towards the noise of drilling.

"Keep your head down," Bill warned. "This mine was opened many years ago by Welsh miners who were all under five feet six, so that's the height of the drive."

It was not long before I bumped my head on the uneven roof, and the top of my shiny new helmet was soon scarred, which made me feel like I was an old hand rather than a neophyte. Bill took me into a huge cavern of dark rock glistening with dripping water, in which African miners, standing on wooden platforms, drilled overhead. Each drill was fed by two hoses, one for compressed air to power the drill, the other to feed water into the place where the drill bit twisted and pounded into the rock, both to cool the drill bit and to control the dust. Water from the drills cascaded around us, forming a series of puddles and streams, through which we trudged. Bill checked the construction of the platforms to make sure they were secure, and monitored the placement and angle of the drilling. Though he often made derogatory comments about the Africans to me in English—such as: "You can't trust these dumb monkeys to do anything right."—he seemed to have a good working relationship with his men, as they shouted to each other in Swahili, often with much laughter. The pounding of the drills ricocheted around the enclosed walls, so the noise was horrendous. Once again we did not wear ear protection, which undoubtedly increased the ringing in my ears. Away from the drilling, Bill checked on those who were shovelling rocks, loosened by previous explosions, into small rail cars, which they then pushed by hand to an elevator, where they tipped their load into buckets to be sent up to the mill. The signal for the end of the shift heralded an eerie silence. Most of the African miners went up above, while the African blasters packed the holes they had drilled with dynamite and attached the fuses, under close supervision of Bill and the other white miners. The last of the Africans were sent up above. Bill, with me in tow, checked the fuses before lighting them. When he could see the sparks on the fuses speeding towards the deep holes that contained the charges, he ambled nonchalantly to the elevator, with me trying to be just as nonchalant trotting behind. Going up the elevator into bright sunshine was like a second awakening for the day. The communal showers led to good-natured bantering and the occasional water fight.

Looking back, the mine was a dank, dreary, dirty, and ear-busting place, but at the time I was intrigued by exploring this strange new world. After the initial day, my only problem was boredom. As a European, I was not expected to labour; that was left to the Africans. The white miners supervised, but as I didn't know anything about mining, I couldn't take on that role, except by acting as a gopher to relay instructions. Some of the time I shovelled rocks along with the Africans, just for something to do. When my five and a half working days underground (we worked a half day on Saturday) ended, I was still enthralled with the drama of underground work, though I expect my fascination would have dwindled fast if I had stayed down much longer. But what stories I would have to tell when I returned to school, to both boys and staff, about the wonders of the great underground caverns connected by a myriad of drives, which had been built long before I was born!

The next week was pretty dull, as all I could do was watch the machinery at work or the assayer testing ore, but the third week was the highlight. Along with another white miner, Gerald, I went off in a Land Rover to locate and take samples from abandoned gold mines. The mines in the area had been operated in the early twenties, when the ore had to be raised by hand. Apparently lifting ore by man power alone limited the depth of the mine to eighty feet. The company wanted to find out if any of the old mines had untapped gold seams below eighty feet. Gerald had a map of dubious accuracy, so we had to drive carefully through the bush—as open shafts had been left without any sign or protection around them. We drove slowly through the bush, looking for holes in the ground. When we found the first hole, we marked it with a pole and placed a metal beam across the opening with a chain-ladder attached. Gerald suggested I go down. My desire not to appear chicken overcame the fear I had of descending into the unknown. With a prospector's hammer in a bag, and a lantern, I gingerly climbed onto the beam and down the ladder into increasing blackness with no sign of a bottom. I yelled up a description of what I saw to Gerald who took notes. He yelled back, telling me when and how to take samples. As I hammered out my first sample, I heard a great flapping noise and saw a mass of dark shapes hurtling towards me. I froze with fear. At the last minute, they rose above my head and disappeared into the other end of the cavern. "Something's flying around," I yelled, when I had relaxed a bit.

I heard a laugh. "Just bats."

I was not enamoured with bats, as they were usually depicted in literature as evil, but I couldn't chicken out now. I gritted my teeth and collected my samples, placing each in a separate bag. The bats ignored me. When I finally reached the bottom of the mine, it was covered with about six feet of bat shit. I stayed on the chain-ladder and only took samples from rock that was within reach. I went down about a dozen different mines during that week.

When I returned home, my enthusiasm for a career in mining had not dwindled. Ma seemed to accept my enthusiasm, but with hindsight, I wonder if she didn't talk to Flakey, as soon after I returned to school the next term, I was again summoned into his office for a chat. His message was one I had heard before. No mining company would hire me with only one kidney. My only reasonable option was a desk job. I was not enthused. Desk jobs were for people who couldn't do a "proper" job. I suspect this new development contributed to my relatively poor performance in fifth form engineering, but at least my school report indicated that I performed well as a prefect—a role that was far more meaningful to me.

When I left for the school holidays in December 1953, I was expecting to return to school the next term. Rusty had earned enough credits to be accepted at Cambourne and was leaving school. I was very envious, as for the past year we had regular gripe sessions about how boring and dull school was, and fantasized about how great it would be to be free and earning money. Our fantasies were wildly unrealistic, especially those that involved women—a subject about which we knew far less than we were prepared to admit, even to ourselves. When Rusty and I walked out of the school grounds together, I talked about how lucky he was and how I was going to have to suffer through more school, when I realized that he was unusually quiet. I looked at him and saw tears in his eyes. Rusty was not a boy to show emotion. I fell silent and it slowly dawned on me that perhaps school wasn't so bad after all.

During the school holidays, Gus, Ma, and I talked more seriously about what I would do with my life. As I didn't want an office job, I said impulsively that I'd become a big game hunter, because no one would bother about my lack of a kidney. This was soon shot down as totally unrealistic—my interest in big game hunting was based on fantasy rather than fact. I didn't have a real interest in wildlife or nature. Ma wanted me to go to university, so I would have a professional career, even though she was not enamoured with intellectuals. I didn't want to leave Kenya, as I believed then that the sun rose and set on that part of Africa. Gus said that, if I had to work in an office, I should become a chartered accountant, and suggested that I talk to the financial officer in his company. I don't know if Gus did any research, but I did surprisingly little. I don't remember studying any books or brochures about accountancy. I had an interview with Gus' accountant. While I was not overly enthused, I figured that maybe accountancy was the least of all evils. Gus arranged a job for me in an accountant's office and I started working there rather than return to school.

The firm did mainly audit work. My job was to sort through piles of invoices and receipts, check that they had been entered correctly into the books, then check the addition. I was very quickly bored stiff, though it took me a while longer to admit that I was a fish out of water to myself, and longer still to admit it to Ma and Gus. My career as a budding accountant lasted for three months. At home with nothing to do, and no income—the accountants pay had been measly but at least was something—Gus came to the rescue again. It was impossible for Cooper Motors to get new cars on the train from Mombasa to Nairobi, so they drove convoys of brand new cars up from the coast to Nairobi. I was paid ten pounds, plus expenses, to supervise a convoy of eight African drivers to bring new cars to Nairobi. It was a three day job—down to Mombasa on the overnight train, organize the convoy with the Mombasa rep, then drive three hundred and thirty miles, at thirty miles an hour (in those days, new car engines were 'run-in' at 30 mph for the first 500 miles) with an overnight stop. The head African driver, a man in his fifties called Wilson, was really the leader, as he had done the drive many times, but Africa being what it was, a European, even if he was only a wet-behind-the-ears seventeen year old, was put in charge.

Wilson led the convoy; I brought up the rear, engulfed in clouds of dust. I led two convoys, fortunately without any problems. I also drove a new Land Rover up to Nairobi, following Gus and Ma in Gus's car, after a holiday at the coast. As I could only drive at thirty mph, I was well behind them. It was well after sunset when I approached Tsavo, where we were to stay the night. There had been no other traffic, and feeling tired, I rested my chin on my knuckles on the top of the steering wheel. I was staring absent-mindedly at the narrow dirt road and bush that were illuminated by the edge of head-light's beam, when the road suddenly seemed to move sideways. I slammed on the brakes and skidded to a stop, with clouds of dust overtaking me. A few yards ahead of me an enormous bull elephant was crossing the road. He stopped, and as he turned to look at me, his ears moved forward and he raised trunk above his giant tusks, as if preparing to strike. I didn't know much about elephants, but someone had told me that flapping their ears forward meant hostility. That new Land Rover went in reverse faster than it was supposed to. When I turned to look, after nearly running off the road backwards, the elephant had disappeared.

During the time I drove cars up from Mombasa, I was once again without a career goal, but I was not worried. There were girls and parties and, despite the very real danger posed by Mau Mau, life was a ball. Ma and Gus were more concerned about my future than I was, and I seemed quite happy to leave it up to them to come up with ideas. I finally accepted that a university education was important, which meant moving to what Ma referred to as a "civilized" part of the world. What career was still a mystery. Again, I didn't do any real research into university education, and what career it might lead to. I still wanted to work outside, rather in an office, so from somewhere, I suspect it was Gus again, surveying was suggested. I was sent to apply for a job as a surveyor, laying out an irrigation canal in the bush, about sixty miles from Nairobi, and even though I had no skills, I was accepted, no doubt facilitated by Gus or Ma's connections.

The survey camp was next to a small village on a dusty side road, set in rolling plains and surrounded by scrub bushes growing in sandy, red soil—the area was semi-desert. The focus of the village was a *duka* (a general store with a petrol pump), which was engulfed in red dust each time a vehicle passed, so that the once-white building was stained brick red and the limited range of goods for sale in the barren interior was covered in red dust. Behind the *duka*, to the south, was the District Officer's *boma* (compound), which consisted of a house and offices for the European District Officer, who was responsible for all government programs in the area, including acting as the magistrate. His African staff lived in the native part of the village farther to the east, which was a collection of windowless *rondavals*, round huts made of mud and wattle, with thatched roofs through which smoke permeated as they had no chimney. Such was the separation of the races that I never went to the African part of the village. South of the *boma* was a small police station, encircled with barbed wire, with tents for the two white officers, an armoury made of concrete blocks, and a row of corrugated iron huts for the fourteen *askaris*. The village was in Wakamba tribal territory but close to the border with the Kikuyu. The relative large police detachment was tasked with preventing Kikuyu Mau Mau from infiltrating and co-opting the Wakamba into joining their uprising. The survey camp was next to the police station, the focal point of which was the mess hut, a rectangular building, about 24x12 feet, made of corrugated metal, with a packed dirt floor that held a table with four upright chairs, a cupboard for all the eating utensils, a book case with a few old paperbacks, some out-of-date magazines, and a wind-up gramophone. Adjacent to it was an open kitchen, with an iron wood stove, a cupboard, and a rickety table, under a tin shed roof. There was no electricity, refrigeration, or telephone, while water was carried from a well in buckets made from old four-gallon kerosene cans. Each of the three surveyors had a tin hut, about ten feet square and set on a packed-dirt floor, that contained a camp bed, a folding chair, a drafting table, and a small floor mat. My clothes were kept in a suitcase stored under the bed. I was assigned to the southern-most hut, which overlooked untamed bush with low mountains on the western horizon.

I was driven out to the camp by Michael, the supervisor, who worked in Nairobi. He introduced me to Andrew, the senior surveyor, a surly 'older' man of twenty-seven who, after acknowledging my presence, gave no evidence of a welcome. Michael and Andrew discussed some business; then Michael left, saying that Andrew would explain my responsibilities. Andrew told me that he had already laid out the approximate route for the canal, which had already been cleared. My job was to take sights with a level, where he had surveyed, and from those sights, draw a topographical map. My map was to be taken into the office in Nairobi at the end of each week, where someone in a back room drew the precise position for the canal, and indicated how deep it should be. Andrew then laid out the exact location of the dig, with the depth marked on it. Paul, the third surveyor, worked with the crew who were digging the canal, to check that the track, gradient, and depth were correct.

The next morning, Andrew introduced me to Moses, an African of about forty, who was the boss of the three rodmen who were to work for me. He drove me and my crew out to where I was to work. He showed me where the survey pegs he had planted were, how to set up a level, where to place the rodmen and how to take a sight. After three or four hours instruction, we returned to camp, and he showed me how to transcribe the sightings we had taken onto paper and draw a map. After one day's training, he told me I was on my own and not to bother him, as he was not paid to supervise me. "If you have a problem, ask Moses, or check with the boss in Nairobi," he said. But we had no phone or radio. As he was about to leave me, Andrew turned and added, "My boy will look after you tonight, but you'll have to get one of your own tomorrow. My boy will find someone for you." One man could have easily have looked after the three of us, but there was so little employment in the area that the local community, with encouragement from the DC, expected us to have one servant each. The next morning, I hired my 'boy', Kibaki, who was probably twice my age, from the local village. I paid him the going rate of forty shillings a month—I was paid four hundred.

Paul, only a couple of years older than me, was friendly. "Just ignore Andrew," he advised me, "and he won't bother you. He likes to keep to himself."

I felt strangely confident the next morning, as I prepared for my first day on the job. As I was about to set off, Andrew said, "You have to pick up a work crew from the prison camp. Moses will show you where to go."

"What do I do with them?" I asked.

"You just take them out there and take them back at the end of the day. They clear the bush ahead of you, but they're not your responsibility."

So that's why I had been assigned a three-ton lorry as transport.

I drove to the camp for suspected Mau Mau detainees, composed of rows of wooden huts surrounded by barbed wire, which looked like a prisoner of war camp from a movie. I was greeted by a friendly, middle-aged warder from central Europe. Waiting for me was a crew of ten men carrying *pangas*, the ubiquitous machete that was used for all kinds of cutting and digging, but was also the primary weapon of the Mau Mau, who used them to hack up their victims. They were guarded by two *askaris* carrying Lee Enfield .303 rifles.

"This lot won't give you any trouble; they're our best wogs," the warder said. "Just drop 'em off. They know what to do. Sign this, will you? Just confirms that you've taken ten out so we have a record of where they are." As I signed the paper he added. "Do you play crib?" When I said that I did, he invited me to come and have a game the next evening after supper. He was the first reformed alcoholic I had met. During my weekly visit, he always drank Coke, but had three or four bottles of beer waiting for me.

Taking sights with the level was not a complicated procedure, though my accuracy was likely compromised by my tendency to be impatient. Moses guided me to the appropriate spot to set up the level, and helped me check that it was properly balanced. I was wise enough to accept his guidance. I directed the rodmen where to stand for a sight, sometimes Moses suggested they should move and again I followed his advice. This situation was not dissimilar to a brand new subaltern in the British Army, just out of training, being coached by an older and wiser sergeant. When I came back into camp after my first day, Andrew ignored me, but later Paul asked if I was okay. "Everything went fine," I told him confidently, but I was not proud of my map. I was a lousy draughtsman and my product looked distinctly amateurish.

For his forty shillings a month, Kibaki woke me with a glass of orange juice and poured some hot water into a canvas wash basin. I shaved every morning, although I didn't need to. Andrew's boy did the cooking, while the other two served at table. After I left for work with a packed lunch,

Kibaki made my bed, cleaned the hut, and laid out a clean shirt, shorts, and socks for when I returned from work. When I came back in the evening, he filled a square canvas bath—set on the ground in front of my hut—with water that had been heated over an open fire in the kitchen, and took away the clothes I had worn that day to wash and iron. After serving supper and washing up, his day was done.

The evening bath became my favourite part of the day. I lay with my head resting on a rock, smoking a cigarette, with most of my torso immersed in the hot water while my feet rested on another rock. I watched the sun go down behind the hills and listened to the slowly increasing symphony of the African night: distant howls of hyenas accompanied by a cacophony from hundreds of different and unseen animals and insects. After supper, Andrew usually went back to his hut, while Paul and I listened to music on the wind-up gramophone, played cards, or read.

We were supposed to work five and a half days a week, but always finished our work by Friday, so we could go into town that evening. After I finished my survey work one Thursday afternoon, I went to collect the work crew who were clearing the bush around a bluff, ahead of where I had been working. I found them lying under a tree in the shade, including the two *askaris* with their rifles propped up against a tree, chatting and laughing together. As they had done little or no clearing, I would be delayed starting work the next morning, which might mean I wouldn't finish in time to leave for Nairobi that evening. As I lived for the weekends, I was furious. I bawled out the *askaris* for not making the crew work, and ordered them to clear fifty yards of bush before I took them back to the camp. The men looked at me sullenly, then turned to look at the *askaris*, who—though they appeared to resent me as much as the men they supervised—reluctantly motioned for them to get back to work. I stood and watched them slash down the bush with their *pangas* for about twenty minutes, before deciding it was tactful to reduce my expectations. When I got back to the camp, the administration was in a panic. As I was over thirty minutes late, they were afraid there had been a massive escape. I was told in no uncertain terms never to keep a crew out late again. More important to me, though, was that I *did* get to Nairobi the next evening.

Weekends were tight. We didn't arrive in Nairobi until nearly nine o'clock on Friday evening and had to leave at six on Sunday. There was always a party on Saturday night, but most Sundays, over a late breakfast (as Ma and Gus had usually been to a party as well), we talked about my future. University seemed inevitable, but I was not enthusiastic. I dreamed of a more adventurous life, such as being a bush pilot or working on a ranch, typical subjects of boys' adventure stories. But I kept these fantasies to myself. I don't think Gus or Ma knew much about university education either, just that it was seen as the road to a good future. But, having traveled extensively, they did know about living in different countries, and how that was an education in itself. I certainly needed to get a wider perspective on the world, though I didn't realize it at the time. One advantage of this plan, to me, was that it was a positive step without having to make a commitment to a particular career, a goal that was still beyond me. It also meant I would go to England, which was very important to Ma. She was a typical colonial, in that she considered England to be home, and the place where I would learn how to behave like a civilized adult rather than a raw colonial. She was a great sales person, extolling the wonders of English country life, fox hunting, shooting, debutante balls, and making the right connections.

Her stories brought back memories of a weekend when I stayed with the Dugdales (Peter Wise's stepfather), in Warwickshire, when I was twelve. They had been invited to a shoot on the estate of an earl, and Peter and I went along as beaters, putting up pheasant, by marching through dripping-wet kale that was over six feet tall, so that they could be shot in flight. After the shoot, we went to the palatial mansion where I was given a glass of sherry to warm myself at an indoor picnic in the baronial hall. Through my twelve-year-old eyes, watching the adults laugh and joke as they became inebriated appeared very grand and enviable. As a result of Ma's coaching, I began to see England as an exciting and rather magical place, in which I could have a good time. What Ma never talked about, and what I never seriously questioned, was why then she had left England for a better life in Kenya.

As I was approaching eighteen, I would become eligible for call-up for National Service in the Kenya Regiment. Though the regiment wasn't the

Royal Marines, it was a reputable part of the British military. Looking back, I would have thought I would have pushed to join the regiment, not only as it was the right thing to do—serving my country—but a chance to get close to my early dream of serving in the military along with many of my friends from school. But I did not. I was resigned to being continually rejected because of my lack of one kidney.

I was now committed to go to university in England. I would study to prepare for some undefined career under the umbrella of engineering. I would go to the best university—Cambridge. The only problem was that I had left school before completing my A levels, and had failed O level Latin, the requirements for entrance to Cambridge. But there was a solution. I was to attend Davies, Laing, and Dick [DLD], a crammer in London, where I could take the courses I needed for university entrance. Gaining admittance to the crammer was no problem; they needed students. My passage to England was booked aboard the Durban Castle from Mombasa to Southampton, in September 1954.

My six months surveying in the African bush had given me a lot of confidence. Though I lacked any training as a surveyor, and had never learnt to draw a professional-looking map, they must have been accurate enough, as ten or so years later Ma sent me a newspaper cutting about the successful opening of the canal. But I was not sad to leave. Life was an adventure and that meant moving on. I was to return to my country of origin to learn how to become a gentleman. I was sure my new English friends would be impressed with my African experiences.

Chapter 13

It seems strange to have written so much about Africa with so little about native Africans. But in those days, I had absorbed the racist values that were prevalent amongst my family and friends, and consistent with the majority of European settlers. Africans outnumbered Europeans by about 100 to 1, but in my life, they were more like fleeting shadows in the background rather than real people. We employed a cook, a houseboy, a kitchen *toto* (teenager), a *shamba* boy to look after the garden (although those referred to as boys were grown men), and a *syce* to look after the horses. They were trained to be servants and be servile. The total staff costs were probably no more than fifteen percent of our disposable income, though this figure is a guess. I was awakened each morning by the houseboy—wearing a long, white *Kanzu*, and an embroidered Arab cap—who, after knocking on my bedroom door, placed a glass of freshly squeezed orange juice beside my bed. I was served breakfast by the same houseboy, who glided in the background on his bare feet and whose removal of a dirty plate or serving of a new dish did not change or interrupt the flow of conversation at the table. My room was cleaned, my bed made, and my shoes polished. If I was going riding, a brief comment to the houseboy meant that the *syce* would have my horse groomed and saddled by the time I arrived at the stables. If I forgot something, a brief order and the *syce* would run back to the house to fetch it for me. It seemed natural, even at the age of thirteen, to assume the role of '*bwana*'—which meant I was the boss. My Swahili was only good enough to give orders, not to carry on a meaningful conversation.

At school we had to make our own beds, clean our shoes, lay the tables, and clear away the dirty dishes, but Africans cooked the food, cleaned the buildings, and looked after the grounds, all under the direction of Europeans. The only African whom I knew by name at school was the "boy"—in his forties—who cleaned our dormitory and took our dirty clothes to the *dhobi* (laundry) and returned them washed and ironed.

In the part of town frequented by Europeans, Africans did menial jobs. They served in hotels and restaurants, cleaned the streets, and ran errands. If they were not actively employed, they were regarded with suspicion and often moved on by the police. If not outfitted in a uniform, most were dressed in fairly ragged cloths and often walked barefoot. A few held clerical level jobs and dressed like Europeans. If whites were walking along the sidewalk, they expected Africans to move aside and mostly they did.

There were African police, called *askaris*, but their main job was to control other Africans, under the direction of white officers. If a European was in trouble with the law (minor infractions were usually overlooked if you were white), a white officer was expected to deal with it. Africans lived in separate areas of town. Some established areas had small stone houses, usually no more than two rooms, with basic services such as communal running water and a rudimentary sewer system, but there were growing shanty towns, where houses were built of whatever material could be scrounged and municipal infrastructure was nonexistent. Whites avoided these areas as they were considered unpleasant and potentially dangerous, particularly at night. But when the Mau Mau became active, even the police became leery of entering the shanty towns, except *en masse*. In the country, Africans were restricted to Reserves, so settlers could farm most of the land—the economy of Kenya was based on agriculture. Europeans believed that, as colonizers bringing 'civilization' to the Africans and improving the country (which they did but largely for their own benefit), they had a right to the land. The Reserves, most of which were on fertile ground, were becoming increasingly crowded as the population, but not the land base, increased. But that problem tended to be minimized by the *bwanas*, as Africans were needed to work on farms, in towns, or wherever industry grew up.

There was also a large Indian community, composed of a mixture of Hindus, Moslems, Sikhs, Goans and Arabs, numbering about ten to every European. In the settler social hierarchy, they were below whites, but above blacks—though they were often regarded with more suspicion by whites, perhaps because of their relative wealth. Originally brought to the colony as indentured labour to build the railway from Mombasa to Uganda, at the beginning of the twentieth century, Asians grew into a prosperous, entrepreneurial middle class. Despite their skills and wealth, whites generally considered them people who couldn't be trusted, or attain the "standards" of the white community. Asians couldn't own land in areas designated for whites, which included most of the best farming areas. They lived in a part of towns designated for Asians. As I have already pointed out, one of the ironies of the times was that, due to fluctuating farm prices and poor farming skills of some white land owners, some whites were deeply in debt to the local Indian *duka wallah* (store keeper) who supplied most of their needs.

There were three public toilets, one for each race.

Through my immature eyes, most Africans and Asians appeared to tacitly accept the separation of the races, but for anybody who bothered to look and listen, the rumblings of discontent were growing like a runaway freight train.

Most Europeans treated their staff with consideration, though within the prevailing hierarchical and racial context. Ma treated her staff like children, but was basically fair and considerate. I never sensed any overt hostility from any who worked for us—though I was conditioned not to look for it. To me, they appeared content, thus reinforcing my conviction that all was well. I tried to treat our staff, and other Africans with whom I came in contact, respectfully, though they may not have interpreted it that way. I didn't yell and swear at them, and never hit one. I would laugh and joke with some of them, especially Joseph, the *syce*, who was not much older than I and who appeared very appreciative that I had taught him how to ride, but it was always clear in my mind that they were servants, who were expected to do what I wanted.

On the farms, which often had a labour force of over a hundred, some farmers set up schools and held regular medical clinics for their workers and their families, providing better services than they would have received back on their Reserve. But there were abusive and violent employers. How wide spread that abuse was is a matter of debate, and opinions often reflect the biases of the critic as much as reality. But no matter how well-meaning a European employer was, time has exposed how oppressive racism can be.

When I arrived in Kenya in 1949, there was ample evidence, for those who looked, of discontent among both Africans and Asians, but many (if not most) European settlers, and certainly those we associated with, tended to live in a state of denial and assume that their privileged lifestyle would continue. A few dared to challenge this attitude, but they were dismissed by most as "socialist trouble makers" who didn't understand that Africans needed to be kept in their place.

However, there were some incidents that made me begin to question the prevailing culture in which I was brought up. Ma had a large crop of tomatoes that grew from seeds, in the waste water from the kitchen that irrigated the vegetable garden. One morning, I took a large bag of tomatoes to an African vendor in the market, who gave us wholesale price. As I left the vendor, I saw a young African stealing some produce. I ran after him, grabbed him around the neck, and pulled his arm behind his back into a half nelson. Full of pride, I started to march him off to the police station when an elderly white man stepped in my way, raised his cane in the air, and demanded to know what I was doing. I explained what had happened, expecting to be congratulated. Instead he berated me. "How dare you treat an African like that. Don't you realize this country belongs to them. Whites will soon be leaving." I was flabbergasted and attempted to defend my actions. But I was soon surrounded by a hostile crowd of Africans, yelling abuse at me—most in Swahili, some in English—with the elderly white man demanding that I release my captive. For a short while I resisted, believing that I was in the right, but soon I decided that discretion was the better part of valour. I released the thief and slunk off, humiliated.

When I told Ma, she responded by dismissing my critic as a misguided old fool who didn't understand the country, but I thought a lot about what had happened to me. What had I done wrong? Why did so many people support a thief? Why should Europeans leave the country? After all, we were running the place properly, weren't we? Though I had, at times, sensed that Kenya society was unfair, this was the first time I remember trying to understand why. But my unanswered questioned slipped to the back of my mind. My life was too comfortable and far too seldom did any adults, friends or teachers, encourage me to think about those questions.

My school held a special church service on November 11th, Remembrance Day, to commemorate those killed in the two world wars. It was a very emotional day for me, and I always cried during the "Naval Hymn" when we sang *"For those in peril on the sea..."* and when the bugler played the "Last Post". But I did wonder why, if Europeans were so superior, our white school with its own bugle band had to bring in a black, African bugler from the army to play the "Last Post" in honour of the victims of European wars. Others voiced their criticisms too, but the matter was usually dismissed with some irrational justification rather than being seriously questioned.

Another school activity that required our racist heads to hide in the sand was the Triangular Sports. Once a year we competed in a track and field meet with the Alliance High School for Black Africans and the Government Indian High School for Asians. At the meets while I was at school, the Alliance School won (because they are much older than us, we rationalized, and anyway they're born at this altitude and run everywhere), we came second, and the Asians came third. But it was an uncomfortable day. How come we were well and truly trounced by these "inferior beings"? Once again, we tended to avoid the question.

In October 1952, Kikuyu Chief Warahiu was murdered. He had spoken out against the use of the violent tactics used by the secret society, known as Mau Mau, who were dedicated to evicting the settlers from Kenya. The press interpreted his speech as being pro-government, rather than anti-violence. Later that month, a State of Emergency was declared and the British Army was called in. Two weeks later, a white farmer was killed. Then two more. In January 1953, the Ruck family—father, mother, and six-year-old child—were all brutally hacked to death with *pangas* by a Mau Mau gang. The picture of the mutilated body of the child, lying among the toys in his bedroom, was on the front page of the papers. The settler community was inflamed. Not only was an innocent child brutally murdered, but his parents were known to treat their staff exceptionally well. They had established a school and provided medical services not only to their employees but also to anyone who needed it. Though police intelligence had known about the goals and violent tactics of the Mau Mau since the early forties, their potential threat had not received much credence amongst the majority of settlers until the Ruck murders. After this horrific event, the settlers extracted their collective heads out of the sand and, motivated by fear, demanded a swift and forceful reaction.

The government responded with a well-orchestrated propaganda campaign that emphasized that the Mau Mau was a small criminal element, with little support among the majority of Kikuyu who were loyal to the government. The British Army arrived. On a visit to Nairobi, I saw several lorries holding two rows of Lancashire Fusiliers, wearing impeccable uniforms that included bright yellow feather hackles rising out of the cap badge on their berets, and holding rifles with fixed bayonets that flashed in the sunlight as they were driven around the city. I don't know what impact they had on the Africans, but it filled me with confidence. In my mind, which flashed back to the Commando camp at Wrexham, I believed the British Army was not only invincible but acted honourably. I felt in safe hands. So while the settler fear was justified, I thought that not only right but also might was on our side and that these violent criminals would soon be brought to justice. Reports of arrests and trials reassured me. In my state of gullibility and naivety, Mau Mau was more of an inconvenience than a real threat.

As the Emergency progressed, my movements were gradually curtailed. Breaking bounds at school became increasingly difficult, as African police—with orders to shoot on sight at night—guarded the grounds. In my last two terms, the houses were surrounded by barbed-wire fences, but I was a prefect by then and had been co-opted into enforcing the rules rather than breaking them. As masters had to patrol the grounds at night, I and other senior boys were assigned to sleep in a master's house, when he was out on patrol duty, to protect his wife and children. I would have been little if any help, as I slept like a log, had no weapon, and my intuition was the only defensive plan. At home during the holidays, Ma decided that the Elson was not reliable enough, so she leant me her Volkswagen if I went out at night—which to me was a real plus. I did carry a .32 Walther automatic pistol and slept with it under my pillow, but to me it seemed more like a sign of my growing maturity than a symbol of fear. I did point it out of fear once. One morning I was deep asleep after a late night out when Kamau, our houseboy, knocked on the door, but I didn't wake up, so he pushed the door open to bring in my orange juice. The noise of the door grating across the floor aroused me. When I awoke, I was sitting bolt upright in bed and pointing the gun at Kamau, who turned grey. He was very careful about coming into my room after that.

A few weeks later, Kamau woke me at about ten in the morning after another late night out, to say a *bwana* wanted to see me. I struggled out of bed and put on a dressing gown. When I went outside, I found that the house was surrounded by British and African soldiers.

"I'm frightfully sorry to wake you," said a British Army officer, not much older than I, "but I have to take your chaps off to be checked." It was Operation Anvil, in which just about every African in the Nairobi area was taken to a screening camp. The routine practice was to parade the detainees in front of hooded figures, allegedly reformed Mau Mau, who had agreed to help the government by pointing out those who had taken the Mau Mau oath that bound them to kill white settlers. Those that appeared apprehensive were held in detention camps without trial.

"When will they be back?" I asked. I had no doubt that they would all return.

"Can't say, I'm afraid, but if they're OK, shouldn't be too long."

Kamau, Maruri, the cook, Mbuti, the kitchen *toto*, Njugi the garden boy, who were all Kikuyu, and Joseph, the *syce* who was a Wakamba, were loaded into a lorry at gun point and disappeared down the driveway.

That morning I had bread and marmalade for breakfast.

By late afternoon all had returned except Kamau. He had been the last I would have suspected to be held, though Gus and Ma did not share my opinion. To me, Kamau was the epitome of a good houseboy; efficient, courteous, and well dressed, but as he was only a shadow in the background, he was also somewhat of an enigma. A few days later, an *askari* came for Kamau's belongings, but did not know what had happened to him. I never saw him again. Mbuti, who was then a teenager, was trained to be the new houseboy. He worked for Ma until she left Kenya in 1977. Many Africans who had worked for settlers were spurned as turncoats by their people after *Uhuru*, which was when Kenya gained independence. Mbuti had trouble finding a job after Ma left, so she sent him money every year from Canada.

In a few cases, house servants who had worked for families for many years, and appeared loyal, did become involved in killing their employers. One story that was reported on a website told of a settler who tried to prevent the police from detaining his servant, with whom he had grown up. The servant was reported as saying, "It's better that they take me, *bwana*, because I will have to do something terrible if I stay." But though there was real danger, particularly for those living on isolated farms in the traditional Kikuyu lands, only thirty-two Europeans were killed by the Mau Mau, while they slaughtered over 1800 of their own people, whom they considered loyal to the government.

What I did not know about then was the brutality inflicted by the security forces. I had heard about a few incidents. The father of one of the boys at school, who was a captain in the army, was cashiered for wiring a pair of hands, cut off a dead Mau Mau, onto the front of his Land Rover. But that was an exception, I thought. Mr Nel, the master who had led us to victory in Rugby, had left school to join the Kenya Regiment. He came back to school to give an impassioned speech about the duty and obligation of Europeans in the security forces to treat the Mau Mau captives with dignity and respect. I was confused by what he said, as I thought that's what British soldiers did, but some of my schoolmates thought that Nel, an Afrikaaner, had gone soft in the head. "The damn wogs deserve whatever they get," they said.

A school friend, who had left school and joined the police, told me how he drove around the shanty towns with a group of Somali *askaris* in the back. When they thumped on the roof, he'd stop, they'd jumped out to chase suspects, but never returned with any. "They knew how to settle things," he told me. At the time, I thought that was pretty smart. When I left Kenya, I started to hear more stories about brutalities committed by the security forces, but I did not want to believe them. They were undermining the pride I had in my own upbringing, and what I had believed in. Many years later, I read several well-researched books and browsed the internet. I was appalled at what the government of Kenya had done. The book that was the most damning, and the hardest for me to read, was *Histories of the Hanged* by David Anderson. He documented how 1090 Africans were hanged, more than were executed during the fight for independence in Algeria and Malaya combined, after trials that lacked accepted legal safeguards. There were reports of vigilante groups, both white and black, being allowed to take the law into their own hands. Revenge killings were common. The detention camps were grossly overcrowded, with unsanitary conditions leading to outbreaks of typhoid and TB. But worse still, there were incidents of torture and murder in the camps. The book is beside me as I write this. On the cover is a photo of an African behind a barbed-wire fence, his face distorted with despair and his eyes burning with hatred. I have to force myself to look at it.

Once, an African stared at me with intense hatred. One afternoon, shortly before I turned eighteen, I went to visit Martin, a school friend who had joined the Kenya Police. He'd just finished his training and, at eighteen with the rank of Assistant Inspector (the starting rank for Europeans), he had been posted as second in command of a small police station, with about fifteen *askaris*, not far from Nairobi on the edge of a Kikuyu Reserve. He was in charge of the station for the weekend. Martin's father had been the Chief of Police in Uganda, and police work had always been Martin's career of choice. Most of the others who joined the police right out of school did so either because they wanted to fight the Mau Mau or because of demand—the police would hire almost anyone. After a cup of coffee— Martin wouldn't drink while on duty—and shooting the breeze, Martin said, "I have to fire off some practice rounds before the end of the week. How would you like to fire a Sten gun?" I jumped at the chance. Martin took a Sten, and two magazines of ammunition, from the armoury and we walked up a hill to a deserted gravel pit, which he used as a shooting range. A row of tin cans sat on a ridge.

"I'll fire off the first clip then you can shoot the second," he said.

The magazine, which was about eighteen inches long and held thirty-six bullets, clicked onto the gun at right angles to the barrel. Holding the Sten by the horizontal magazine, Martin pulled the butt into his stomach, pointed the gun towards the row of tin cans and, with his other hand, squeezed the trigger in front of the pistol grip. The first spurts of dust were about five feet in front of one of the cans. With his finger squeezing the trigger, Martin raised the barrel slowly so the line of dust spurts moved up to the first can, which flew in the air in a crazy spiral. As the loud "rat-a-tat" continued without a pause, several other cans danced in the air until, after only a few seconds, there was a click to signify that the magazine was empty.

Then it was my turn. I followed the brief instructions from Martin and copied his moves. I pointed the barrel towards the cans and squeezed the trigger. I felt a pounding in my stomach as I guided the bullets towards the cans, which began their deathly dance. All too soon it was over. I have not fired an automatic gun since, but to this day I can still feel the incredible and frightening sense of power it gave me.

Martin suggested I stay for supper and come with him on a night patrol. He had to check out a village that was suspected of housing members of the Mau Mau. I readily agreed. We set off at about nine o'clock, with Martin in the lead and me close behind, both armed with Sten guns, followed by six *askaris* armed with Lee Enfield rifles. As we approached the village, we saw several figures running towards the maize fields.

"Do we shoot?" I whispered.

"No," came Martin's authoritative response.

When we arrived in the village, the *askaris* surrounded one side, holding heir rifles at the ready.

"Stand back," Martin said, as he kicked open the door of one of the huts. When there was no response, he entered cautiously, his Sten levelled. After a moment, he beckoned me to follow.

"Search those bags," he ordered, pointing to a stack of sacks that appeared to contain *posho* (corn meal).

There were two women squatting by an open fire. They were both dressed in cotton dresses that were shabby and stained grey from smoke, with head scarves, and shawls over their shoulders. They were barefoot. The older woman bowed her head and looked away, but the younger one, probably about fifteen, looked up at me as I stood over her—my Sten gun, though not deliberately pointed *at* her, was pointing in her direction. She stared at me for only a moment, but in that brief space of time, her dark brown eyes conveyed such hate and contempt that it drained me of my confidence. My search of the sacks was so hurried that they could have contained a stash of arms and I wouldn't have found them. I don't remember anything about the remainder of the evening, other than feeling strangely uncomfortable. I can still see those eyes, which told me what was like to be a victim in a police state.

I knew no Asians on a personal level. Most of my contact with them was in shops, as they dominated the retail business. As they wanted the business, they treated their European customers with more deference than many of them deserved. I know my behaviour towards them was often disrespectful, particular in Shanker Dass, a record shop, where I and others would go to listen to new records in the soundproof rooms—with no intention to buy any. While that type of behaviour might be typical for teenagers, there was an underlying attitude of contempt for their race. Though I was guilty as well, there were some whose behaviour towards Asians was so abusive it embarrassed me.

One of the few places where there was no segregation between whites and Asians was at the movies. All the shows began with the National Anthem. We had been taught to stand to attention out of respect for the King, and did so whenever the anthem was played. Sometimes Asian kids refused to stand up, which immediately resulted in angry demands from white kids—yelling at them to stand up, with threats to evict them if they didn't. In my experience, they usually did and were not willing to fight, but this may have been because they were outnumbered by white kids.

One evening, after going to a movie, I went to the Queens Hotel for a beer with Pat, a friend of mine. Four young Asian men, also drinking beer, were sitting at another table not far from us. We paid no attention to them. After we had been there for about twenty minutes, Randy and four other men who had been at school with us, came over to our table. Randy had been the best Rugby player at school, a couple of years before, and was very tough. He nodded towards the Asian men. "They don't belong in here, do they? We're going to order them to leave."

The message was clear; we were expected to join in the eviction. The Asians presence hadn't bothered me, but I didn't have the courage to tell that to Randy. Instead, Pat and I followed Randy to the Asians' table. Randy was curt and to the point. The Asians tried to argue, but quickly realized it was useless. They left, muttering about returning. We went back to our tables.

Shortly after, two of those who had participated in the eviction got up to leave, and walked around the corner to the main entrance. Suddenly, one of them came back and yelled, "They're trying to come back in!" Randy sprung to his feet and beckoned to Pat and me to follow him—we did. Five of us ran to the door, to join the two who were already there. The manager, an Asian, was trying to talk his compatriots out of returning, in hopes of avoiding violence. Randy was more direct. "You are not welcome here," he told them in a manner that clearly indicated there was no room for negotiation. The Asians backed down. Seven white men stood shoulder to shoulder across the hotel entrance.

The Asians yelled at us from the pavement. We did not move and remained silent. Soon more Asian men came to join them, until a large crowd had gathered in front of the hotel. They shouted abuse and threatened us. We were soon outnumbered by more than five or six to one, but they made no attempt to enter. After some time, I have no idea how long, the police arrived. The one white officer stood in the no-man's land between us, while his *askaris* formed a line to hold back the Asians. The white officer suggested that it was time to go home, but Randy said that we weren't moving. Then the manager, perhaps on advice of the police, said the hotel was closed for the night. The white officer then told the Asians that, as the hotel was closed, they couldn't go in tonight, and so they might as well go home. After a while, they gradually dispersed, and the threat of a riot vanished. The only comment from the officer to us was that we should be more careful or we might get hurt. The press, fortunately, were not there.

The seven of us separated and went our respective ways. I don't remember seeing any of them again, except for Pat.

I look back on that evening with mixed emotions. It was a racist act that now I abhor. But what upsets me most was my failure to tell Randy that I had no problem drinking in the same room as the four Asian men, and to leave them alone. I went along with the crowd rather than stand alone and risk being isolated for my beliefs and receiving a possible beating. On the other hand, I learnt that when a small group appears confident and does not back down, they can successfully stand against powerful odds.

Not all Europeans were racist. During the Emergency, a small courageous minority fought for the rule of law and respect for all, including the Attorney General, but at the time their voices were largely drowned out by cries of indignation from the majority of the settler community, who at the time of the Mau Mau, were motivated by fear, both for their personal safety and the loss of their way of life. While I thought white Kenyans were good people, General Erskine, the commander of the British forces during the Emergency, said, "Kenya … is a sunny place for shady people … I dislike them all, with a few exceptions." (www.psywar.org). The white settlers days were numbered. The Colonial Office in London was losing patience with their demands, as colonialism was no longer in vogue, and Kenya, which was not economically self-sufficient, was a growing drain on the British treasury.

Chapter 14

The voyage to England was a two week party. I sat at a dining table with eleven other young singles and soon made shipboard friends, though I did not find a shipboard romance. I laughed and drank a lot, went to bed in the early hours of the morning, and got up late.

Our first port of call was the small town of Port Sudan, in the Red Sea. We only had a couple of hours ashore, in the blinding afternoon sun with the temperature well over a hundred degrees, Fahrenheit. The ancient Arab town, with narrow dusty streets between old mud houses, was deserted as the locals took a mid-day nap. Some friends and I were walking aimlessly around the deserted streets when we turned a corner and saw two fellow passengers, a young Swiss couple, walking ahead of us with their arms tightly around each other, so that her long blonde hair was almost hidden under his shoulder. She was wearing a loose blouse and very short, white shorts, which were the fashion then. As they walked down the street, they seemed to create a draft that dragged male heads out of doors and windows behind them, which only closed again once they were out of sight.

In Genoa, I was ripped off by a con man, who said he would give me the best exchange rate and instead gave me some bank notes that were not even Italian and proved worthless. Later, when I had met up with some friends, we ordered fish and chips. I enjoyed them, though they were different from anything I had tasted before. One man nudged the girl beside him and asked, "How do you like octopus?" Her eyes opened wide, followed by her mouth as she spat out a half-chewed mass of food onto the street, followed by the rest of her meal. A couple of others pushed their meal aside, but in a less dramatic manner. In Marseille, I explored the city on my own until my feet hurt so much that I dropped into a cinema, to see *Roman Holiday* for the second time,—I had a crush on Audrey Hepburn, the star of the film.

I enjoyed my shipboard companions, but not enough to keep in contact with any of them.

England was a new reality. As I was not yet twenty-one, the age of majority in England, Ma once again appointed Babs to be my legal guardian. She worked as a buyer for a large department store and lived in the centre of London, close to where I was to stay. I wanted to be totally independent, but I found her a receptive and understanding sounding-board on more than a few occasions—when I reluctantly admitted that I didn't know everything.

On the recommendation of the principal of Davies, Laing and Dick (DLD), who it appeared hadn't been asked for such advice before, I was booked in to stay at the Holland Park Hotel, a residential establishment that was close to the crammer. It was a large, Victorian house with wide, curved steps leading up to a terrace that was supported by Grecian-style pillars, and had large bay windows on each side of the front door. But the house was like some fading, dowager duchess, living on memories of grander times, for the garden was neglected, the terrace tiles cracked, the white paint blistered, and peeling in places and stained various shades of grey by the soot that pervaded the London atmosphere. The hotel was run by two old ladies and, to my surprise and disappointment, the twelve other long term residents were also elderly ladies. My arrival caused quite a stir, but not one that thrilled me—I had expected it to be home for others like me. But I had a room of my own on the fourth floor, with breakfast and supper served in the dining room on the main floor, at a rent that left me some spending money. I had an allowance of thirty pounds a month from my grandfather's legacy, which had been left to my father but, as he had been killed, had been split between Penelope and me. My room was fairly large, furnished with an armchair, table, upright chair, and an iron bedstead over a well-worn carpet, all of which had seen better days. Heat was from a gas fireplace that was activated by inserting coins into a metre box. A wash basin stood in one corner. The communal toilet and bathroom, containing a six foot pedestal tub for the four rooms on the floor, was adjacent to my room. But though the room was dreary, I was free, independent, and ready to explore a new world about which I knew very little.

My first venture was to Piccadilly Circus, a traffic circle that is one of the focal points of London's glamourous West End. I managed to figure out how to get there on the underground, a relatively simple procedure, and came up the escalator onto the street, where I stood mesmerized at the sight of more people and traffic than I had ever seen in one place before. I watched masses of pale-faced people, wrapped up in scarves and coats, staring intently forward as they jostled for space on the crowded pavements, all seeming to be earnestly striding to somewhere. Red double-decker buses vied for room with, what seemed to me, an endless supply of black London taxis, as they circled the statue of Eros at the centre of the traffic circle, which was fed by five main roads. Neon signs on the buildings that surrounded the circle flashed exotically coloured ads that contrasted with the prevailing greyness of the rest of the surroundings. I leant against a wall to watch. No one seemed to notice me nor spoke to me, and I didn't try to speak to anyone. I was content to watch and absorb this strange new environment. After an hour or so, I walked up a street until I found a pub and ordered a pint of bitter. I sat in the corner and watched a crowd of boisterous chatterers engulfed in clouds of blue cigarette smoke, which undulated just below the low ceiling, while I drank my pint and absorbed the slightly sour odour of beer that pervaded the room. It was a milieu that was soon to become a major part of my social life.

Piccadilly Circus was also the venue for my first New Year's Eve in London. Rusty came up to London from Cornwall, where he was studying at the Cambourne School of Mines. We went to the Windmill Theatre, the first topless show that either of us had seen, and about which we tried to be blasé, had a late dinner at a Chinese restaurant, and then joined the immense crowd that had come to celebrate New Year's in the West End. The statue of Eros had been boarded up and was ringed by bobbies (policemen). All the streets, which were closed to traffic, were a solid mass of people singing and dancing, the most common dance being the Cockney favourite, "Knees up Mother Brown." Rusty and I decided to sing and dance "The Zulu Warrior", a song from school. We were soon joined by others, who turned out to be from Rhodesia and South Africa. Before long we had a large audience of cheering admirers. Bottles were passed around, social differences ignored, and eternal friendships sworn. A sailor swapped my fancy paper hat for his uniform cap, which one of his mates later begged me to return. When the bells rang out at midnight, I kissed every girl in sight. Rusty and I picked up a couple of girls—there's a terrible photo of us—both wearing fancy silk waistcoats—with the two girls at about three o'clock in the morning, just before they left to go home. We stayed on until about four-thirty, when we were faced with walking seven miles home as there was no public transport. It was not until we were almost home that we saw the first vacant taxi. Though it was only a short distance, we took the expensive ride as our feet were killing us.

DLD was in two adjoining, elegant, four-storey, row houses on a quiet, treed street, a short walk from where I stayed. The houses, like the hotel, had been built in the Victorian era for those who could employ a batch of servants to maintain them, but most had subsequently been subdivided into up-scale apartments. The interior of DLD was functional, with small rooms, bare of any decoration, for students and teachers. About half the students were English, with the remainder from around the world. Among the more exotic students was a remarkably handsome Indian prince, who was far more intent on splurging his fortune than studying. One story of his antics that circulated among the students was that he had ridden a white stallion into the dining room of a posh London Hotel for a dare—a story that was far too colourful to question. Another student was a cousin of King Hussein of Jordan, who at age twenty-two, claimed to be a brigadier in the Jordanian Army. Bob, from Jersey, drove to school in a brand new, red Jaguar XK 120, the hottest sports cars at the time and the envy of every boy. Iain's grandfather was the head of a Scottish Clan. Arwas, who was a mixture of Hungarian, French, and Egyptian, dressed like a nineteenth-century dandy, and had a weekly allowance that was about the same as my monthly allowance, though he lived with his parents. Many years later, I learnt that DLD was often referred to as "the school for dumb rich kids."

My first day at DLD found me sitting at a desk in a study room, waiting to go to my first tutorial. There were about twelve other students, none of whom seemed to have much to do. The boy sitting next to me was about my age, with light olive-coloured skin, black hair, and green eyes. He asked me, in an upper-class English accent (in England your accent immediately identified your social standing), where I was from. He seemed genuinely interested when I told him I was from Kenya.

"Aren't there a lot of Asians there?" he asked. "What are they like?"

Without giving it any forethought, I launched into a diatribe on my prejudiced and uncomplimentary views on Asians. My seatmate listened, nodding occasionally, allowing me to finish without comment. After a moment's silence, I asked, "Where are you from?"

"Bombay."

I had assumed that he was of Latin origin. I started to apologize, but he cut me short, saying it was important to be honest with each other. To my surprise he spoke to me conversationally, with no hint of anger or hurt in his voice. He told me his name (something like 'Natasha Khourodi', but I don't think this is the correct spelling as I can't find a name like it on Parsee websites when I tried to locate him), but said that everyone called him Pogo. He said he was a Parsee, a small ethnic group in India who originally came from Persia, but were sometimes referred to as the 'Jews of Asia', as they focused on business and, as a result, often suffered discrimination from other Indians. Then he went on to explain that he didn't like the English because of their arrogance and contemptuous attitude towards all other races.

His calm and reasonable response impressed me and we soon became friends, a friendship that was to become one of the most significant of my young life.

Pogo and I were assigned to the same math tutor—Finn Bjelke, a Norwegian who had a degree in economics from the University of Florida. Finn, who was about 28, was new to the math he was to teach (he must have bluffed his way into the job or else they were desperate for teachers) and, before our sessions, he often went to another math tutor for help. Perhaps having just learnt the system himself helped make him a great teacher. He was filled with boundless enthusiasm and his math sessions often digressed to political, social, or religious discussions. As a newcomer to London, he had few contacts outside of DLD and soon I, along with some other students, including Pogo, became involved with him socially. He became somewhat of a mentor to me and, as another outsider, he put England and the English into a very different perspective from my mother's. While Ma saw it as the cradle of gentility and good taste, Finn saw it as mired by outdated traditions, with an oppressive class structure. For him, the US was at the cutting edge. For the first time I began to look at America with a more positive and inquisitive attitude. Finn helped me realize that the world was far more complex and contradictory than I had thought, and I began to question many of the beliefs that I had taken for granted. I became a frequent visitor to his apartment, where I often spent time playing with his three-year-old daughter, Anine—maybe to make up for the little sister I had lost. Beryl, his English wife, was friendly but cool to me and, I think, other students, as Finn spent so much time with us. Looking back, he appeared to want to be young and free again, rather than assume the responsibilities of a teacher, husband, and father.

At DLD I studied math, Latin, and English, the courses I needed to get into Cambridge—the exams were set for the following summer. I had two or three sessions a day with a tutor. Our math session with Finn lasted about an hour, as it was for a group of four or five. My other sessions were much shorter, as they were either individual or with a smaller group. The rest of the day was spent studying in a classroom.

More important to me, DLD provided a source of new friends and a good social life. I quickly learnt that pubs were great meeting places. My "local" was the Windsor Castle, which was in walking distance from DLD but far from the real castle. A frequent evening's entertainment was a pub crawl with a group of friends, usually all male. We drove to different pubs, sometimes finishing up at the Prospect of Whitby, far out on the river in the East End. If there was more than one car, a race usually ensued. It amazes me now that none of us were involved in an accident, especially as (foolishly) we didn't considered drinking an impediment to driving.

I was introduced to jazz clubs—I instantly took to Dixie Land jazz—where Toffs (upper-class public schoolboys), Teddy boys (working-class boys who greased back their hair into a duck tail and wore Edwardian-style clothes), and just about any other category appeared to mix comfortably, as they tapped their toes or bounced in time to the music. When we could afford it, we went to some of the many nightclubs in the city. One evening, four of us were driving around when we stopped at a traffic light next to a car with four girls in it. After driving alongside them, and yelling through the window for several traffic lights, they finally agreed to follow us to a nightclub. We went down steps into a low cellar, which was lit by candles that were stuck in straw-coated Chianti bottles, where a small jazz band was playing slow music. I asked the girl who appealed to me the most to dance before anyone else could grab her. I felt we were getting on well, gliding around the floor, but my friends and others were pointing in my direction and smirking. I finally asked them what the hell was up, and they pointed to the large tricolour flag that was draped under the ceiling. It was so low that as I moved around the dance floor, my head brushed against the flag, leaving a trail of where I had been and depositing a mass of dust in my hair. But I kept dancing, as I was getting on well with the girl and I didn't have enough money to buy another drink. It's strange that I didn't see her again—I have no recollection of why—as I have such a fond memory of the short time we spent together.

I spent most of my Sundays visiting Granny, now eighty-six, who lived in a nursing home on the outskirts of London. I took her to church, mainly because that is what she wanted but also because it cut down conversation time, which I found hard work. After church, we had lunch in her room at the nursing home, played cards, and went through family photographs, mainly of large wedding groups. She often confused time, place, and people, particularly identifying Ma as her younger sister, May. At first, I tried to correct her, but soon decided it was better to let her enjoy her reminiscences, even if they were not always accurate. Many years later, Ma told me that some of the relatives thought I visited Granny only because I was after the main chance. But I wanted to visit her because I truly loved her, and wanted to give her some of my time in return for all the love and care she had given to me. But though I never consciously went for financial gain, I certainly did benefit. Granny increased my monthly allowance by ten pounds a month, which significantly improved my discretionary spending and quality of life, and later helped out with other gifts.

Sometimes when I visited, during my first winter in England, she was bedridden and it was thought that she would not last long, but as the spring approached she perked up, and decided it was time for a family get-together. Aunt Joan was instructed to arrange a luncheon at a nearby restaurant. When I arrived, Aunt Joan beckoned me to the boot of her car. "Here, you'll need this," she said, as she handed me a stiff gin and tonic. No alcohol was to be served at lunch. Granny presided at the head of the table, with Aunt Joan on one side and me on the other, for about twenty-five other relatives. Before we started to eat, she pointed out who everyone was, sometimes requiring a gentle reminder for names and relationships from Aunt Joan. Then she sat back with a contented look on her face to survey the family. I didn't know many of them, as I had never been a keen family person. Ma's frequently stated attitude, which I had unconsciously absorbed, was: 'God gave me my relations, thank God I can choose my friends.' I didn't enjoy the party or make any new contacts. Other than Granny, the only family members I was involved with were Joan, whom I visited occasionally, and two cousins, Michael and Ian, with whom I was already in contact.

I did not see much of Michael, as he was away from home but Ian, who was about twenty-five, and his wife, Jane, invited me to visit often. At one of their parties, a guest asked how I was enjoying London. I replied that I was enjoying it very much, except that I wasn't getting any exercise. He suggested that I play Rugby for his club. He was an employee of Shell, which had a large residence, called Lensbury, in south London, for single, male employees. Though I was tall, six feet six, I was far too skinny to be a strong rugby forward, and too slow a runner to be a three-quarter, but undaunted, I accepted and arranged to play the following Saturday. Fortunately, I was placed in the third team, where expectations were not too high, and though I was far from a star, I played well enough to be invited to become an unofficial member of the club, and I played most Saturdays from then on. I enjoyed the comradeship that began after the game in the large communal bath, in which the entire team sat waist-deep in tepid water, which was soon thick with mud, singing vulgar songs and making lewd jokes. Those who did not have a date for the evening went on to a pub, drinking and singing more rugby songs. The team travelled by coach for away matches. For one game, which was far out of town, one of the team brought along his fiancée. On the return trip, he sat up front, leading the sing-along while she sat alone in the rear of the bus. Risking a beating from an irate boyfriend who was much tougher than me, I went back to chat with her. When the coach pulled into a pub, her fiancé yelled, "Just in case they don't like coach groups, you two go in first. When you've been served, you can order beer for the rest of us." The girl and I went in, ordered a gin and tonic for her and a pint of bitter for me. When I had paid for them, I asked for fourteen more pints of beer as the rest of the team marched in. I often wondered if that romance ever flourished, for I spent the rest of the journey cuddled up in the back of the bus with a delightful girl.

Travelling around London on the tube and in buses was cheap and easy, but service stopped around eleven at night. My first regular girlfriend, Clare, whom I dated for about five months, lived in Hampstead, about a twenty-minute tube ride and a short walk away. On occasion, I left her house too late. After sprinting to the tube station, I found the station gates closed, as the last train had left the station. I spent the next two hours walking home. I began to dream of having my own transportation. A car was out of the question, but a motorbike? Iain, one of my friends at DLD, rode a 500cc Norton, and I began to talk to him about bikes. The more we talked, the more I wanted one. I must have talked to Granny about it, as she gave me enough money to buy a second-hand bike—perhaps she was impressed that it would reduce my travel time to see her from about an hour and forty-five minutes to less than an hour. With Iain's help, I bought a 350cc Royal Enfield.

I found riding a motorbike truly exhilarating. At first I was nervous and cautious, but all too soon, I was weaving through traffic at speed. I loved the feel of the wind rushing past me as I sped along roads, passing cars and buses. In London, motorbikes did not stay in a line of traffic; they went between two lanes of cars or up the centre of the road—always when stopped for a light, and often when traffic was moving. One day I was riding home from work when it started to rain. As I didn't have any wet weather gear with me, I rode fast for home. Two long lines of traffic were waiting for the lights to change at the T-junction close to where I lived. I weaved my way up to the front, where two red, London double-decker buses were waiting, side by side, at the front of the two lanes. There was just enough room for me to squeeze my handlebars between them, and I arrived at the stop line just as the lights turned green. Needing to get clear of the buses in case one or both drivers had not seen me, I accelerated hard to get in front of them before turning left. The road was slick from fresh rain. As I leant into the corner, the back wheel slid out from under me. In a flash I was flat on my back in the middle of the road, looking up at two smirking bus drivers, both tapping their fingers on their steering wheels. My humiliation didn't last long though, for I was soon back to my wild riding style.

Omaya, a young Egyptian girl, had come to live at the hotel. She was very reserved and I was shy, so our contact was limited to little more than polite greetings. One evening as I was parking my bike in the back garden, Omaya emerged from the shadows and, with eyes lowered, pleaded in an anxious voice, "Please, would you take me for a ride?" I immediately agreed. She climbed on the rear of the double seat and I told her to hang on tight, pulling her arms around my waist. I took off fast and headed for the back streets, where traffic was rare and I could roar around corners with the bike heeled far over, to encourage her to keep on holding tight. She said nothing while I drove around the empty, darkened streets. When we got back to the hotel, a half hour or so later, she said politely, "Thank you very much," but her eyes sparkled with excitement.

"Your hair is really tangled," I said. "Would you like me to brush it out?"

She hesitated, said, "Yes, thank you," and followed me to my room. I took as long as I could brushing her long, thick, black hair, while I absorbed her strange exotic scent.

"I think that's okay now," I said. She immediately stood up, thanked me politely, and left. I took her for several more rides, usually late in the evening. As soon as I had brushed the tangles out of her hair, she'd thank me politely again and went back to her room.

On nights when I had nothing to do, I sometimes stopped by Hyde Park Corner, where anybody could set up a soap box to speak on any subject. Many speakers were crackpots, predicting the end of the world or, at least, floods and pestilence, but some were interesting and thoughtful. One evening, my friend Peter and I stopped to listen to an African ranting on about the evils of colonialism. His arguments were not well developed, and after he contradicted himself a couple of times, I challenged him. We began to argue. I scored a few points. A crowd, including many Africans, gathered. Soon I was being heckled. The original speaker had stepped down off his soap box and, as I was taller than anyone else in the crowd, it appeared that I was the one on the soap box, even though I was wearing my crash helmet. Peter kept tugging on my arm and pleading for me to leave, but I didn't want to back out of an argument. Soon some of my points were exposed as embarrassing and some of the crowd jeered. Peter whispered that he was leaving. I continued to argue. Eventually, realizing that I was losing, I conceded a few points and became conciliatory. I ended up shaking hands with some of the Africans in the crowd.

As I walked away from the crowd to find Peter, an older man dressed in a dark business suit approached me and said that he agreed with what I said and admired me for standing up for the Empire. "Would you like to come for a drink?" he asked, pointing to his Rolls Royce parked by the curb. I was about to accept, for both Peter and myself, when I sensed he had an ulterior motive and quickly left to find Peter.

Peter kept telling me how crazy I was to get involved, but I was thinking about some of the things that had been said. Perhaps colonialism was not as benevolent as I thought. Perhaps Africans were intelligent and competent people. I was not persuaded, but questions were racing around my head.

Out of the blue, in the spring of 1955, I received an invitation to Peter Wise's twenty-first birthday party in Warwickshire, about a two-hour ride from London, which included being billeted with nearby friends of the Dugdales—Peter's mother and step-father. I hadn't seen Peter for about six years, but through correspondence between our mothers, who were old friends from before the war, I knew he had graduated from the Royal Naval College, Dartmouth, with some award and was now an officer in the Royal Navy. Though Ma appeared genuinely fond of Lenore, Peter's mother, she often made jibes about her being a social climber. Lenore, who was originally from South Africa, was now a part of the 'county' set (the upper-middle class that lived in the country). They had a moderately large country house and were part of the set that chased foxes on horse-back (or at least watched others do it), shot game birds reared by a game keeper and put-up by beaters, had large house parties, and sent their children to Public Schools so that they would have the right accent and connections. Of course they had more money than most, but it was not proper to talk about it. This was the England that Ma admired and that she hoped would mould me into a gentleman.

But I had come under Finn's influence. Not only had he undermined the sanctity of the English class system but also, when I needed some new clothes, he persuaded me to go to an American-style tailor. Consequently, I had a single-breasted, two-button, blue blazer and gabardine trousers, rather than a double-breasted blazer and cavalry twill trousers, which were then ubiquitous for young men of the county set.

I arrived at the Dugdale's house on the afternoon of the party. After a brief welcome from Peter, who was busy preparing for the evening, he suggested I go out in the garden and meet some of the other guests. None of them appeared interested in meeting me and I was too shy to approach them. I was standing alone on the lawn, overlooking the rolling fields in front of the property, behind two young men, both wearing Vyella checked shirts with cravats, cavalry twill trousers with suede shoes—almost like a uniform for their class—when I overheard one ask his companion a question, in a contemptuous tone: "I say, who's that chap wearing gabardine trousers who arrived on a motorcycle?"

"Someone Peter knows from the colonies, I believe." After glancing around at me, they wandered off.

At that moment, though I wasn't sure what I wanted to be, I knew it was not an "English gentleman."

I don't remember much about the party, at which I drank Champagne cocktails and danced with a few young "English ladies", but I didn't meet anyone who changed my mind. Sadly, I haven't seen Peter since.

When I got back to London, I discovered that Clare had unceremoniously dumped me. What made it more humiliating was the drippy guy who had taken my place. But, I rationalized, it seemed he had bought her affections by promising to take her sailing on his father's thirty-five-foot yacht and, if that was the case, good riddance. I sulked for a while until, one afternoon, Finn told me that if I stopped moping he would introduce me to a beautiful girl who had just arrived from Norway. Berit had magnetic blue eyes, a radiant smile, short, curly, golden hair, and a willowy figure—all fine attributes in and of themselves, but it was the way they came together that counted. She was even more beautiful than Ava. She was also twenty-three, four years older than me, a fact which made me more insecure than did her beauty. But over the next couple of weeks we went out several times and got on well, though I was always a bit self-conscious with her, as I knew she had been out with older and more sophisticated men. One Thursday evening, while we were dancing at a small club I belonged to, I asked her spontaneously if she would like to come on a bike tour of Wales with me the next weekend. To my delight, and surprise, she said that she'd love to. But my ecstasy was tempered with trepidation. I had never taken a girl away over night; I didn't have much money; I had done no pre-planning for the trip, and my bike had just had an engine repair and needed to be run-in at slow speed before I could open her up on the highway. After I dropped Berit home, I decided to drive around to put a few more miles on the engine. Lost in the confusion of my excitement and anxiety, I was not paying attention to riding. I didn't see a stop sign, but I heard the screech of brakes and saw a Riley 2.5 litre sliding towards me. The point of contact was my left ankle. As I sailed through the air, I saw the sign for the Essoldo Cinema upside down and said, "Christ, Sheridan, this is your bloody lot."

Chapter 15

A police car brought Babs to St. Stephen's Hospital to sign a consent-to-operate form. A chunk of bone had broken off the bottom of my tibia, which had to be screwed back on, and my fibula was severed—relatively minor damage considering the circumstances. I came too shortly before dawn, still under the influence of the anaesthetic, to find my left leg in plaster and my right leg in a splint. I knew nothing was wrong with my right leg and, I was told later, woke up the entire ward of twenty-three other patients by yelling at the night nurse to "come and take this bloody thing off my leg!"—something I wouldn't have done if I hadn't still been under the influence of the anaesthetic. The night nurse was a bossy little Scotsman who was not popular in the ward, so my ordering him to take off my splint so authoritatively won the approval of my rudely awakened, new ward-mates. Later, when I asked the doctor why they had put a splint on my right leg, he said that under the anaesthetic my right ankle appeared to be dislocated. He asked if I had ever had a very severe case of influenza and, when I told him that I remembered being in bed for two weeks at age twelve, he said that it had very probably been a mild case of Polio, which had affected my ankle joints. He estimated that up to thirty percent of English children had had Polio but didn't know it

Lying flat on my back with minimal mobility was prescribed, but the hospital bed was too short for me. After much discussion between the nursing staff and maintenance personnel, a piece of plywood was placed under an extra mattress, so that the bed was extended by six inches. The main focus of the morning was doctors' rounds, which were scheduled for nine o'clock each day. The sister in charge of the ward, a solid woman in her fifties, with iron grey hair to match her stern disposition, ran the doctors' rounds much like a military parade. Both the ward and the patients were scrubbed clean. Hair was combed, pyjama tops straightened and buttoned to the top, all beds made to the same standard with not a wrinkle on the counterpanes, and pillows smoothed—even around those who could hardly move. The ward was a sparkling array of good order until my bed, the six-inch extension of which stuck out like a sore thumb. Sister never forgave me for disrupting the good order of her domain, and I was met with a steely scowl from her each time she stopped by my bed.

Visiting hours were strictly limited to one hour a day. I had asked Babs to contact Finn, so that he could tell Berit what had happened, but much to my disappointment, she didn't come on my first or second day in hospital. On the third day Clare appeared, soon followed by Omaya. As soon as I had a girl sitting on each side of my bed, Berit appeared at the entrance to the ward, dressed in a white dress with black streaks that had been designed specifically for her by a Danish artist. While both Clare and Omaya had been noticed when they came in, Berit caused a distinct lull in conversation. I introduced the three girls. I had been at ease with Clare and Omaya, but when Berit joined us, I was tongue-tied and could not create a harmonious atmosphere. It was not a successful encounter and none of them came to visit me again.

After a couple days, I only suffered minor discomfort from my broken leg so my main problem became boredom. While I got on well enough with the patients around me, I had little in common with most of them. Old Mr Holmes in the next bed had had both legs amputated. We joked for a while but soon ran out of conversation. I had been given a Lilliput magazine that had a three-foot pin-up photo of Ava Gardner in a black slip. When I showed it to Mr Holmes, he chuckled and, pointing to her breasts, said, "I'd like to snuggle m' nose between them two." I pinned the photo up beside his bed, but the nurses soon confiscated it before Sister could see it and discipline them. For a while a man about my age—a window cleaner who had fallen off a ladder—was in the next bed. He was illiterate and, other than making a few lewd comments, offered little conversation. I offered to teach him to read, but he turned me down. He was replaced by another window cleaner who had fallen off a ladder, who told me how much money he had made, while doing his National Service in the army, by selling driver's licenses to fellow soldiers without giving them a test.

A South African about my age, called Denis, was at the far end of the ward. He'd also had a motorcycle accident, but his was far worse than mine. He was hit by a taxi, dragged underneath it, and had very nearly died. When I came in, he had already been in hospital for about three months. We got to know each other by shouting across six or seven beds. We asked if one of our beds could be moved so we would be next to each other, but Sister refused on the grounds that medical needs—whatever they were—required that our beds stay put. Fortunately, Denis was on the mend and after a few days was able to hobble down to my bed on crutches. We became close friends.

For me, the greatest attraction was the nurses. Nearly all of them were from Ireland or France, as in those countries they had to pay for four years of on-the-job training (nurses were not trained in universities then) while in England they were provided with a residence and a small allowance— although not enough to attract many English girls, who had more lucrative alternatives. The staff nurses, who had completed their training, were both over twenty-five—old women to me but good targets for teasing. Their uniform, which Sister expected to be immaculate, was a starched, white cap, a starched, white apron over a blue dress with starched, white collars and cuffs, black stockings, and black, lace-up shoes with a medium-high heel. Somehow, I managed to acquire a water pistol. One morning, as two of the staff nurses came on duty, one definitely hung over, I squirted the front of their aprons, which left them hanging limply (instead of smoothly arched over their breasts). Everyone laughed, but it was not a trick I repeated. Later that day when Sister was out, they both snuck up on me while I was dozing, squirted me with water from two large hypodermic syringes, and then left me in a soaking wet bed. But there were younger nurses and soon I was smitten by Madeleine, a French girl. For nurses to be personally involved with patients was strictly taboo. Our budding romance, though obvious to everyone, had to be conducted furtively. We daren't steal a kiss, as the whole ward might have burst in cheers. Denis also teamed up with one of the few English nurses.

After eight weeks, I began walking around the ward on crutches and a few days later, when I had demonstrated I could manage, the doctor approved an afternoon pass—doctor's orders were believed to have the force of law. I put on my best suit, as I had a date with Madeleine, but found I had grown an inch while in hospital. Once again my trousers were too short, but I soon forgot that as the afternoon with Madeleine was all that I had hoped for. I also found out that, during rush hour, London taxis gave priority to potential passengers waving crutches.

A couple of days later, the doctor cut off my cast to reveal a spindly leg that was coated in dry, flaky skin. He said I would have arthritis when I was forty—a time that seemed so far in the distance that I didn't give it a second thought. He also told me I would be discharged when I could walk up and down the ward without showing pain. I started walking immediately and after four days of practice, I told Sister I was ready. At doctors' rounds the next morning, with staff and patients watching, I completed the walk with a false smile on my face to mask a grimace of pain. A nod from the doctor to Sister indicated that I was free. Aunt Noreen happened to be visiting England from Kenya and took me to stay in a hotel in the New Forest to get some fresh air, good food, and to build me up—a pint of Guinness with lunch and a glass of Burgundy with dinner, a recipe that was strange for someone who thought Ma had encouraged me to drink too much. I didn't complain and greatly appreciated both her company and kindness.

While I was in hospital, I had arranged to stay in a furnished flat with Peter and another boy from school, Alan. They shared one bedroom, while I had a small single room. The living room was heated by the ubiquitous gas fire fed by a coin metre, as was the geyser that provided hot water for the bath. We often ran out of money and so in the winter the house was frequently very cold. As I piled on more jerseys, and sometimes even wore gloves, I swore that when I was rich, I'd have my house so warm all winter that I would only wear a shirt while at home. Our house keeping was abysmal. Dust was rampant and at one stage we had about fifty empty, unwashed milk bottles standing on the kitchen floor. We finally returned them to the milkman when we could no longer walk around them to get to the table.

I had not written my exams, as they were scheduled while I was in hospital, so I returned to DLD. My life continued much as before. When DLD wasn't in session, I worked. Jobs were very easy to come by. Other students knew who hired temporary help, and passed on telephone numbers. It usually required only one phone call to start work the next day. The easiest place to get employed, and where I worked the most, was at Watney's Brewery. Each time, my job was in the warehouse that received the empty beer bottles. Lorries backed up to an unloading dock, for men to unload the wooden crates full of empties, and put them onto a mechanical lift, which sent them up to a chute with rollers that went into the bottling plant, where they were washed before being refilled. If too many cases came up and jammed the line, I took them off and stacked them. If not enough came up from the loading dock, I put cases back on to keep the bottling plant running. I probably worked no more than an hour of my eight hour shift, so I read a book a day. One day I forgot to take a book to work. Out of boredom I decided to drink. Policy was that employees were entitled to two free pints of draft beer a day, but the regular employees had created their own "pub". The wooden beer cases were stacked ten high in the warehouse. If you knew which two cases to pull aside at ground level, it exposed a tunnel that led to an open area in the centre of the pile, just large enough for four men to play cards. Four of the cases that made up the wall of the pub pulled out to expose a selection of bottled beer. For most of the shift, a rotation of regular employees played cards. Temps were not invited to play, but were welcomed to come in, have a beer, and watch the game. I usually had a couple a day, but without a book, I consumed a large number of "nips" (a seven ounce bottle of ale with 7% alcohol). I got drunk. Deciding that I would continue drinking at home, I put two bottles in the front pocket of my jeans and two in the back. I had been told that stealing beer meant dismissal. Regardless, I staggered past the security guards at the gate with the tops of all four bottles sticking out of my pockets and clearly visible, waved good night, and left unchecked.

It is no wonder that, a few years later, Britain was in a financial crisis due to inefficiency and poor productivity.

Soon after I came out of hospital, I had to go to court as a result of the accident. I was acquitted of dangerous driving, but convicted of driving without due care (which I was), fined, and had my license suspended for six months—back to the tube and buses, including the long Sunday ride to see Granny.

I went back to Kenya for Christmas. In many ways it was the same. The bright sunshine and warm weather lifted my spirits and it was good to see old friends and visit old places, particularly the white, sandy beaches and clear, turquoise waters on the coast. But I was beginning to see the country through eyes that had been opened a bit wider. Though I was primarily concerned with having a good time, which I did, I had time to think. During the previous year I had questioned as to whether I had a future in Africa. It was during this visit that I decided that my skin was the wrong colour. If I was a black African, I reasoned, I would have little tolerance for the way the *mzungus* (white people) had treated me, so why should I, a white African, expect them to treat me with respect? I now knew why I didn't want to live in Kenya, or any other part of Africa, but I didn't know where I wanted to live instead.

On my return to London, I went back to DLD and to the flat with Peter and Alan, which became an informal meeting place for boys from Kenya, some of whom crashed in the living room. Most of the time, gatherings were young guys having a good time, but there was one notable session. John had not been a friend at school, as he was three years older than me and had been the head prefect in Clive House. He had probably beaten me, as I don't think a term went by in which I wasn't beaten for some infraction, but I certainly didn't hold that against him. He joined the Kenya Police directly from school at the usual starting rank for Europeans of Assistant Inspector. Though he was not good at school work, John was a strong character and a fair athlete. A group of us were sitting around our living room, shooting the breeze, when John started talking about his experiences in the police. He had been in charge of a Police Station in Naivasha, a small town in the Rift Valley, in the heart of a European farming country. There was a lot of Mau Mau activity in the area and, as a result of a series of operations, the police cells in Naivasha had become grossly overcrowded with Mau Mau suspects. John told us he called his superior officer to ask for the prisoners to be removed. He was told there was nowhere for them to go and, if the cells became too overcrowded, perhaps he should arrange for a mass break out. This was interpreted to mean opening the cell doors and telling the prisoners to run while a Bren gun (the standard British Army machine gun) was set up to shoot the fleeing prisoners in the back. While I have a clear memory of the beginning of the story, my memory refuses to tell me the end and so I do not know what John did.

In those days I still didn't believe that the security forces could be guilty of committing such an atrocity, though I have learned since that atrocities were not only too common in Kenya, but also in all wars, particularly insurgencies. I have not been able to find any record of an incident such as John described at Naivasha, but there is now plenty of evidence that too many unforgivable atrocities occurred during the Emergency in Kenya. That afternoon, I was part of a small group of ordinary decent young men who chose not to react in horror to a story about a senior police officer encouraging a subordinate to commit mass murder. At the risk of appearing as if I am excusing myself, I have learnt that people, particularly the young, are prone to go along with the crowd rather than stand against what they perceive to be the group values. All the young men who heard John's story that day had grown up in a culture in which Africans were considered inferior at best, and less than human at worse. They had also been subjected to sophisticated propaganda and well-publicized stories about the atrocities committed by the Mau Mau. Unfortunately, I have found that this type of denial is not uncommon, so I have told my story to many to illustrate how easy it is for ordinary decent people to turn a blind eye rather that stand out against the perceived values of friends. It was a long time before I understood the emotion and disgust that was behind Mr Nel's impassioned plea to the boys at the Prince of Wales, that the security forces had a moral duty to respect the human rights of the Mau Mau. I'm also thankful that I did not join the Kenya Regiment, as I fear that I might have become involved in something that I would not want to remember.

As Peter had failed his exams, he had to leave the flat to work. Alan suggested that I move into the double room with him, so that his sister, who had just gone through a divorce, could have my single room. I thought that having a woman in the house would relieve me of housekeeping duties and promptly agreed. Pat was thirty-one, a pleasant but not particularly attractive woman. She fitted in easily, helped upgrade our living conditions, but made sure that Alan and I contributed to improving the standard of cleanliness. One evening, when Alan was away, Pat came into my room as soon as I had gotten into bed. She sat on the bed and talked for a while and then, to my astonishment, started to seduce me. I had never considered having anything but a platonic relationship with her, but after some initial hesitation, was a willing student. From then on we led a double life. For most of the time we related to each other as if nothing had changed, but when Alan was away we became lovers. Alan sensed his sister was having a relationship with someone and often asked me if I knew anything. I never told him.

On one of my visits to Granny, I mentioned that my six-month license suspension was soon up.

"You're not going to ride that dangerous motorbike again, are you?" she asked.

It had not occurred to me not to. If you fall off a horse, you got back in the saddle. Why would a motorbike be any different?

On my next visit, Granny told me that, if I promised never to ride a motorbike again, she'd give me enough money to buy a car. I promised and haven't ridden a bike since, though all my life I've looked at bikes with envy and imagined the adrenaline rush of weaving through traffic, leaning into the corners, or racing down a country road with the roar of the engine in my ears and the wind in my face. Granny gave me two hundred pounds. With the sale of my repaired motorbike, I was able to buy a used Citreon 15, a French car with a long, narrow bonnet (hood), framed by flared front mud guards with large, chrome headlights mounted on them. It had a unique, racy style that had always appealed to me. I would have preferred a sports car, but as Granny had paid for the car, I bought one that she could ride in. So my visits to her now included sedate drives around the countryside, with Granny not only giving instructions, but telling me how to drive.

Over the winter, my career plans modified and I was considering attending Bristol University, which had a program in quantity surveying—a more office-oriented type of engineering. I knew very little about this obscure and minor engineering discipline, but it appeared that my lack of a kidney would not be an impediment. It also had the advantage that I would not need Latin, which had become an anathema to me, to enter Bristol. It was still a requirement for Cambridge,

About the same time, I became close friends with Kerry, a Canadian student at DLD. His father, Harry, who was the Trade Commissioner at British Columbia House, was an enthusiastic advocate for the bright future of that province. Kerry, who had attended Westminster School in London, was going back to BC to attend university. Both Kerry and Harry encouraged me to join him. I did not require much persuading to sign on to another adventure, which provided me with a possible home other than Africa or England. An added appeal was that it postponed the need to commit to a career. I still had not learnt how to research careers properly, and despite my new interest in quantity surveying, I still didn't really know what I wanted to do with my life. Nor did I research the impact that my lack of a kidney would have on my career choice. I had been told it was a problem and just accepted that. As it turned out, it has never prevented me from doing anything I wanted to do, except for joining the marines, though it may be the cause of my relatively low energy level. Harry painted such a rosy picture of the opportunities in BC that I was confident something good would turn up, as it always had so far in my life. Once I committed to go, Kerry and I, with strong guidance from Harry, decided that after we had written our exams, we would sail to New York in the autumn, aboard the Queen Elizabeth—one of the last great ocean liners—then travel overland to British Columbia so we could see the country. We would then have almost a year to get settled before entering UBC the following September.

Ma supported my decision without reservation, though it must have been difficult for her to accept that her last remaining child was moving so far away from Kenya. Babs and Aunt Joan were also supportive. One evening I was having a drink with Babs and her friend Sheila, when the latter stared at me in amazement and said, in a raucous voice that could be heard around the bar, "What on earth do you want to go to that Godforsaken country for? It took me four days to cross it by train and I couldn't get a drink from one end to the other!" But telling Granny was gut wrenching. She was eighty-seven and we both knew that, when I went, it would be our last goodbye. She did not try to dissuade me.

Kerry suggested I move in with him at his parent's home on West Eaton Place, which was the location for the TV series, *Upstairs, Downstairs*. What once had been a private house was now four spacious apartments. As it would cost me much less, I decided to leave the flat, and my affair with Pat, which (for both of us) had run its course. Soon after I arrived, Kerry's parents allowed us to have a party to celebrate our twentieth birthdays, which were a few weeks apart. All night we played Elvis Presley's new 45 record, with 'Heartbreak Hotel' on one side and 'Blue Suede Shoes' on the other. By the end of the party, the record was worn out.

Being accepted as an immigrant was little more than a formality. Canada needed workers and gave preference to immigrants from Britain. Having the capital, which gave me a small income from the money my grandfather had left to me, undoubtedly improved my acceptability.

In the summer before I was to leave, Finn asked me to be Godfather to his second daughter, Tiril, and travel to Norway for the christening as soon as exams were over. I was honoured and agreed without hesitation. He and I were to drive in my Citroen, while Beryl and the two children travelled separately.

We drove to Dover, took the evening ferry to Calais, and drove through the night to Paris, where Finn had arranged to meet another student from DLD. While I knew Maurice, he was not a friend and I knew nothing about him. We arrived in Paris at about nine in the morning, and stopped at a sidewalk café near the Arc de Triomphe in the centre of Paris. While Finn phoned Maurice, I sat in the sun and watched the bustling throng on the sidewalk, and the mass of traffic jockeying for position as it rushed along the wide boulevard. It seemed so much more spacious and flamboyant than London that I felt full of life, although I had not slept all night. We ordered ham sandwiches for breakfast—piles of ham falling out of half a baguette, which seemed very exotic compared to an English sandwich made from sliced ham neatly tucked between sliced bread. Maurice arrived shortly after and suggested we go to the apartment, overlooking the Bois de Burlogne—which I later learned was one of the most exclusive residential areas in Paris—for a shower before driving out to the villa for lunch with his family, where we were to stay for one night. The apartment had a large entrance hall, an enormous living room and about six bedrooms. All the furniture was covered by dust sheets as the family spent the summer months at the villa outside of town.

"If you don't mind," Maurice said, "it would be more convenient if you used the servants quarters." The servants had, what I considered, a very comfortable, three bedroom apartment attached to the main one.

The villa was a large, rambling, Spanish-style building with red tile roofs, behind a high wall and locked gates. I parked the car among several others, and we were greeted by two servants, who took Finn's and my baggage up to our respective rooms while we were shown onto the terrace, surrounding a swimming pool, which overlooked a large fertile valley. About two miles from the villa was a large cement factory. We were introduced to about twelve people, but after a few words of greeting in English, every one spoke French. Finn was fluent enough to join in the conversation, but my French was so limited that I was relegated to observing. A waiter handed me a tall, slim glass of ice, into which he poured some 12-year-old Scotch. As soon as I had taken a sip, my glass was topped up. After some time, we were summoned to the dining table, which had been set up under a shady tree. A waiter came around with what I thought was a cold buffet. I was ladling food onto my plate when I noticed that some of the guests were looking at me askance, and that those who had been served had only a delicate portion on their plates. Suddenly I realized that there were three wine glasses and an abundance of cutlery in front of me—what I thought was a meal was only hors d'oeuvres. I can only assume that my lack of sleep, coupled with the whisky and warm sunshine, had made me so blind to the obvious message of the table setting. I managed to stay awake and eat some of the several courses that followed. For me, the meal took an eternity, during which I struggled to appear attentive. After lunch, Maurice's father asked if we would like a tour of the cement factory. Finn agreed, but I excused myself, saying that I needed to rest. I was shown to my room where, to my embarrassment, I found that my suitcase had not only been unpacked, but that my grubby, old clothes, which I had stuffed in my case, had been washed, ironed, and laid out on the bed. After we left the next day, Finn told me that our host was one of the richest men in France, and that the cement factory in the valley below the villa was one of several that he owned.

We drove through Northern France, Belgium, Holland, and Germany to Copenhagen, where we stayed with some friends of Finn's. Unlike our French hosts, they spoke English all the time I was in their company. My endearing memory of Copenhagen was having breakfast in a sidewalk café at the bottom of a long hill. As I sipped coffee and ate cheese and cold meats on rye crackers, I revelled in watching girls on bicycles leaning over their handle bars as they sped down the hill. When riding a bicycle in England, girls sat on their skirts holding them demurely tight to their knees; in Denmark the girls sat with their skirts over the saddles, so that they flew up around their waists as they sped down the hill—an intoxicating sight.

We took the ferry across to Sweden. Soon after entering Norway, we picked up two very attractive sisters, about my age, hitch-hiking. Finn told them that he was American, so they didn't know he spoke Norwegian. After we dropped them off on the outskirts of Oslo, Finn told me that, talking amongst themselves, they hoped we would invite them to stay with us.

In Oslo, we stayed with Finn's younger brother, where we met Beryl and the children. His apartment was next to their grandmother, a feisty woman in her late eighties, who had just started to learn a new language to keep her mind active. Tiril's christening was the next day. I suddenly realized that, as her Godfather, I ought to give her a present. My experience with christening presents was limited to what had happened to Penelope and me, namely engraved silver mugs. It was too late for that. Early the next morning I awoke with a brainstorm. I got up and wrote Tiril a letter, in which I told her about myself and how I came to be her Godfather. I said that I would invest one hundred pounds for her, which she would have when she was twenty-one. Finn asked me to read the letter out to all who attended the christening. I eventually invested $500 for her, when I came to Canada, which grew over the years and which I sent to her when she turned twenty-one. My original letter to her was lost.

After few fun days in Oslo, we drove up to a village near Trondheim to stay with Finn's mother and stepfather. En route, the engine of the Citroen began to make a horrible clanging. I didn't know what the trouble was, but I knew that it was serious. We managed to make it to our destination, where Finn's stepfather arranged for us to be towed to a garage, where the mechanic diagnosed worn rod bearings—a major repair. As he was a friend of the family, he told us that would repair it at cost. Even so, this seriously depleted our funds.

The home was elegant in an austere style, which I later learnt was typically Scandinavian, and gleaming with cleanliness and order. Finn's mother prepared meals for eight with no apparent effort. On our first morning, the breakfast table was set with an assortment of cold meats, cheese, fruit, and preserves, including a chocolate spread that was new to me and immediately became my favourite. Formality and politeness were the rule, even for Anine, Finn's four-year-old daughter, who (on leaving the table) went to curtsy to her grandmother and say, "Tak fer matten," (thank you for my food) to which her grandmother replied, "Welbecommen." My offer to help clear up was promptly rejected and in no time the kitchen was spotless. After breakfast, Finn and I went for a walk.

"Now you can see why Norwegian men who marry English women always have problems," he commented ruefully, "while everything works very well when an Englishman marries a Norwegian girl." This may have been a justification for the screaming row that he and Beryl had within my hearing, the night before the christening in Oslo. I didn't respond, as I had concluded that, although he was my friend, Finn did not treat Beryl with respect.

When the car was repaired, we drove back to Oslo. Halfway there the engine began to knock again, but as we were driving through the uninhabited mountains, we had no alternative but to continue. We made it to Oslo, but the engine was shot. I had offers to buy the car (even with its broken engine) for more than I paid for it, but in those days it was not possible to exchange Norwegian krona outside the country except on the black market—a process I knew nothing about and did not want to get involved in.

We met Pogo, who had been travelling around Europe, in Oslo. After a couple of days I said goodbye to Finn, who returned to England, and Pogo and I went to stay at a student work camp in the mountains outside Oslo. We paid two kroner for our board, and they paid us two and a half kroner a day to work. There were about forty students, boys and girls, from several countries—the largest two contingents being a group of five communists from the Midlands in England, and five Germans who behaved as if they were in the military. We slept in a dormitory in a large log cabin, which was a ski lodge in the winter, and spent about six hours a day breaking and hauling rocks to make a road to the cabin. Though we worked fairly hard, there was lots of time for kibitzing. Pogo and I talked a lot about racism and how similar our attitudes were, though in opposite directions. One morning, Pogo was sitting on a rock, while I and some others were still working.

"Hey, you lazy good-for-nothing wog, get to work!" I yelled at him.

There was a stunned silence from those around us.

"Don't play the colonial master with me," he retorted. "Why should coloured people do all the work when you sit on your fat arse and pay them nothing?"

The Germans moved in between us, ready to prevent a fight. Pogo and I grinned at each other. One of the communists started to laugh, and then others joined in, much to the confusion of the Germans who did not understand our sense of humour. We continued to slang each other for the rest of our stay, trying to outdo each other—Pogo often getting the best of it as his points had more credibility. It was a great way for me, and I expect for Pogo, to work through our prejudices, and it helped me to accept people for who they were rather than for their race, though traces of my prejudices remained.

After ten days at the camp, where I fell in love with a Danish girl whom I wrote to for the next eighteen months, my poor, abused Citroen and I boarded a ship bound for the North of England. I left the car in Newcastle to be repaired, and returned to London.

Shortly after I returned, Kerry announced that his father had arranged for him to crew on a sailboat leaving Gibraltar to sail to Victoria, via the Panama Canal. I was green with envy.

"Persuade them that they need another crew-member," I pleaded. Two days after Kerry arrived in Gibraltar, I received a telegram inviting me to come. I ran and jumped around the flat, yelling in excitement. When I calmed down, I sent a telegram to Ma, as I worried that I might need her permission as I was still under twenty-one. She approved of me going. I went to a travel agent, where I learnt that there were no airline seats to Gibraltar available for months; my best hope was the train, but that required a Spanish visa. I spent a day at the Spanish Embassy, only to come away with a pile of forms to complete and no assurance that I would get a visa quickly. Disheartened, I went to a bar for a drink.

"You look pretty down," commented David Korda, who was the grandson of the famous film producer and a fellow student at DLD, but not a close friend. "What's up?"

I told him my story.

"I think I can fix that," David replied, and went to make a phone call.

He came back after a few minutes and gave me the name and address of a travel agent. "Go and see him tomorrow morning and he'll book you on a flight." By noon the next day, I had a flight to Gibraltar.

The next few days were hectic, but I was high on anticipation. I sold the Citroen to a dealer, brought some gear, but not proper wet weather gear as I did not know what that was, gave away stuff like records to friends, and threw away stuff that no one wanted. On the morning of my flight, my notice to report for National Service in the British forces arrived in the post. I threw it in the wastepaper basket.

Chapter 16

As I waited for my connecting flight from Madrid to Gibraltar, I paced out seventeen paces, approximately 52 feet, from a wall on a balcony that was about twenty feet wide. I looked back. *Jesus, that's small*, I thought, *and Dawn Star* (the yacht on which I was to crew) *is not even that big.* But once again the thrill of adventure and my sense of optimism convinced me that the skipper would know what he was doing and that I was in for a great time. My apprehension subsided a bit. Later that evening, from the entrance to the dockyard high above the water, I looked down on Dawn Star, the only boat moored to a long, low dock. In the background, a large Royal Navy warship was silhouetted against a starlit sky.

"There she is," said Kerry, who had met me at the airport. The tone of his voice indicted that he was keenly interested in my response.

"She's beautiful," I replied, trying to appear far more enthusiastic than I felt about the boat, which was to sail all the way to Canada but, from where I stood, appeared not much larger than a dinghy.

As we climbed down to the dock, Dawn Star grew in stature. As I walked along the dock towards her, I was impressed by her jaunty prow, set off by the graceful curves of her hull. I felt a little less apprehensive. She was a fifty-two-foot ketch—two-masts with the mainmast forward. To my untrained eye, her graceful lines suggested seaworthiness. I bounded aboard to meet the skipper and the remainder of the crew.

The skipper was Major Jukes. His home port was Victoria, where he had sailed a number of boats over the years before buying Dawn Star in Ireland, where she was built some time after the war. He and Sylvia, his girlfriend, and some other crew, who were never identified to me, had sailed her around northwestern Europe before the planned voyage home. I knew he was seventy-six, but I had not expected someone who appeared so old, frail, and grumpy. Looking back, a sensible person might have abandoned the venture right then, but I was not about to lose the chance of a lifetime, even if risky, and having made a commitment, I didn't want to back out, or perhaps did not want the embarrassment of doing so. I understood that Sylvia, aged thirty-six, was the major's girlfriend and had been sailing with him for some time. She was a small, slim woman with deep worry lines on her tanned face. I didn't take to her personally, but neither did I dislike her, though I was soon to learn that she was very fussy, which I found aggravating. I saw her as the mate of the ship, while I would be part of the crew—composed, at this point, of myself, Kerry, and Veronica, a vivacious if solid English girl of nineteen, who had come to the airport with Kerry to meet me and whom I felt would be a 'good sort' rather than a romantic connection. Sylvia said that two others were to join us for the first leg from Gibraltar to the Canary Islands: Chalky and Rodney, both of whom were airmen stationed in Gibraltar, and would stay in barracks until we set sail. Chalky turned out to be a fun-loving Cockney, while I have little recollection of Rodney. I only remember him by checking the photograph album. The surprise was two miniature Poodles, not my favourite breed. To me, dogs and sailing didn't seem to mix. Where would they exercise? Where would they poop? I was not enthralled.

All the crew had agreed to pay a share of the food. As soon as I handed over my contribution, Sylvia ordered the ship's provisions and soon several cases arrived at the dock. Our first job was to tear off the paper labels from the cans, and write the ingredients on them in indelible pen. The reason for doing this was that the damp would unglue the labels, so we would not know which label belonged to which tin, and even worse, soggy labels floating in the bilge might block the pumps. This simple precaution increased my confidence that the major and Sylvia knew what they were doing. We had a few other jobs, the most intriguing of which was making "baggy-wrinkles"—short pieces of rope that were plaited into fenders on the rigging, to reduce chaffing of the sails when running before the wind. Otherwise, Dawn Star seemed ready for sea and much of our time was spent hanging around looking for something constructive to do, while Sylvia and the major disappeared on undisclosed "business". Kerry, Veronica, and I explored the town, went up the massive rock that looms over the town like a colossus, and fed some of the monkeys who scampered around the rocks and who, legend predicts, will disappear when the British are about to leave. In the evenings, we frequented a nightclub, along with about a hundred British servicemen and a few well-worn Spanish whores. Most of the soldiers were from the Black Watch, the majority of whom were of Scots/Irish descent and recruited from the Gobbles of Glasgow, a notoriously rough part of the city. They all seemed short, about five foot six, and very broad across the shoulders, which gave them a swagger that made their kilts swirl as they walked. Each time I went into the club, one or two of them would approach me individually and, out of the blue, ask, "De ye wan' a scrap, Loft?" Fortunately, my replies must have been diplomatic enough for them to back off with a comment like: "Jus' thought you might be inter a bit'f fun. No hard feelings." The first two times we went into the club, I asked the band to play "Sorrento" and they complied. On the third and subsequent visits they struck up "Sorrento" without my asking, which gave me a great sense of importance. One day we met some young naval officers, who invited us to their submarine for the evening. Intriguing though the tour of the ship was, the idea of being a submariner, encased in a tube of thick steel with no horizon whether the ship was on the sea or below it, did not appeal to me. But we had a fun evening, drinking their booze, fleecing them of cash playing Blackjack—probably no more than a couple of pounds as we were not into heavy gambling—and learning the intricacies of a submarine toilet. If you flush while still seated, the suction could keep you stuck there for up to ten minutes!

Finally, the major said that we would have a shakedown sail the next day and that, provided all went well, we'd set sail for Las Palmas in the Canary Isles a couple of days later. Excitement built. Chalky said that due to the delay in our departure he would not be able to come, but the major considered a total crew of six appropriate. As we motored out of the harbour, the sun shone from a deep blue sky, with cumulus clouds on the horizon, and a fair breeze of about twelve knots blowing in from the west. After a thorough briefing by the major, we hoisted the mainsail, followed in order by the staysail, jib [the two sails forward of the mast], and mizzen [the sail on the aft mast]. As the sails filled, Dawn Star heeled. Kerry looked startled. "Is she tipping over?" he asked. He hadn't been on a sailboat before. I didn't know much about sailing, but at least I knew that sailboats heeled. Veronica had crewed in fourteen-foot dinghies, while Rodney had never sailed before either. All we crew could do was follow orders, which the skipper gave clearly while Sylvia was at the wheel.

Our course gave us a "soldier's sail"—so named by sailors as it was the easiest point of sail—a reach (wind on the beam) across the strait towards Morocco and a reach back. Dawn Star charged through the seas, throwing a curtain of white spray from her bow each time she crashed through a wave. Not only did my confidence in Dawn Star grow immensely, I was exhilarated. On the way back to Gibraltar, I went down to the fore cabin and wrote a letter to Ma, in which I told her what a wonderful boat Dawn Star was, how well she sailed, and best of all, how I didn't feel the slightest bit sick, even though I was below and it was quite rough. The next day our bonded stores, mainly booze, arrived and were stowed aboard. We were committed to leave within twenty-four hours or return the stores unopened.

Less than twenty-four hours after leaving Gibraltar, we ran into a storm. The waves grew, the wind howled—turning the sea white with spray—and I was sick, again and again and again. My memory of the passage is spotty. The storm raged for three or four days. The wind was dead astern, which meant we were being blown on course, but were also in danger of being pooped—having a wave break over our stern, swamping the cockpit and potentially smashing open the cabin doors and swamping the cabin as well. We deployed three one-inch ropes, called warps, each about a hundred feet long, over the stern to reduce the chance that a wave would break over us and also help hold us on course before the running sea. The wind was so strong that at times we made about four knots under bare poles.

During the storm, the skipper spent almost all the time in his bunk. Sylvia was sick and my memory is that she was unable to tell us what to do, but somehow what had to be done was done. I hope I played my part, but I doubt it. Seasickness dulled my will to do anything but lie in my bunk and long for oblivion. What others did, I'm not sure.

The storm eventually subsided. The sun shone, the wind died but remained dead astern at a rate for easy sailing. The skipper, looking drawn and haggard, struggled up on deck. He ordered the sails set, the warps hauled in, and prepared to take a noonday sight with his sextant. After completing his calculations, he reported that we were on course, then returned to his bunk. I was assigned to take the wheel and felt like a real seaman as I steered Dawn Star over a vast blue sea, my seasickness and the horror of the previous four days gradually fading from my mind. The giant swells, so recently crowned with foaming waves, from which the wind whipped a curtain of stinging spray to engulf our world, were now like rolling hills. Exactly how big they were I don't know, but the skipper said the swells in this part of the Atlantic were the biggest in the world. I estimated the crests to be about four hundred yards apart and the height over a hundred feet, but that is just a guess.

Sylvia prepared a good meal, for which I forgave for her all of her previous failings.

As dusk fell, the wind dropped, and we motor-sailed into a moonless night. Suddenly the sails, which had been pressured into shape by boat speed, started to flap violently. I called down for help. I heard the voices from below, but I could not hear what was said. Sylvia appeared at the companionway and looked around, but appeared confused. "What should we do?" she shouted to the skipper down below. After some shouting back and forth, the skipper, gasping for breath, struggled up into the cockpit to take control. He told me to pull in the sheet that was coiled up beside the cockpit. I reached out. My hand squelched through something soft and slimy. For a moment I was confused, then the smell hit me—dog shit. I swore, dropped the rope, and threw up. I leaned over the side to wash the shit off my hands. The skipper grabbed one of the dogs that had come up into the cockpit.

"Filthy bloody animal," he yelled and threw the dog towards the sea. The dog hit the lifeline and bounced back into the cockpit. The skipper made a grab for it, but Sylvia was quicker. "You brute," she yelled, cradling the dog in her arms. The skipper mumbled. Sylvia and the dog disappeared below.

Looking back, the situation was simple to resolve. The new wind, that was comfortable for sailing, had come up on our nose. All that had to be done was to decide which tack to take, bear off, set the sails for a beat, and turn off the engine. It became all too clear that the skipper was not only the only person on the boat who could navigate but also the only one who knew how to sail.

Soon the wind picked up again, the building waves bounced us around and I was seasick again, but it was not so bad this time. A couple of days later we sighted land, the highlight of any voyage. Two humps on the horizon gradually grew into rounded mountains, with steep sides that plunged into the sea. That night, the skipper decided to "heave-to" in sheltered waters between two islands. Heaving-to parks the boat, with minimal drift, by backing the staysail so that it pushes the boat off the wind, then balancing it, by setting the mizzen and lashing the wheel to drive the boat towards the wind, so it stays in approximately the same place in the sea. Easy to say, but it requires considerable skill to find the correct balance to make it work. I spent a peaceful night watch curled up in the cockpit, reading a book for the first time on the voyage.

Shortly after midnight on the following day, we arrived off Las Palmas harbour. Rather than enter in the dark, the skipper decided to wait outside. It was a peaceful moonlit night with a gentle breeze. Kerry and I decided to figure out how to sail. We sailed back and forth and around in circles, gradually learning how to set the sails for the course we wanted to sail, and how to steer so the sails remained set. I was proud that we had taught ourselves the basics of sailing on our own.

Later that morning, soon after we anchored off the Yacht club, a young Spanish doctor came aboard to check on the skipper. He immediately ordered him to hospital. A couple of days later, Sylvia told us the diagnosis: Leukemia, with a very short life expectancy. The skipper and Sylvia moved into a hotel. We also learnt that the "business" trips the skipper and Sylvia had taken in Gibraltar were to doctors' offices. The skipper had seen four different doctors, none of whom could diagnose a problem. The last one, an old navy doctor, had apparently said, "Can't find anything wrong, old chap. The best thing you can do is get back to sea."

Rodney went back to Gibraltar. Kerry, Veronica, and I were in a quandary. We were convinced that the skipper would never sail again, and there was no way that any of us would sail anywhere with Sylvia and her dogs. We had little money, a large quantity of non-perishable food, and were burdened with guilt about the prospect of abandoning a dying man who had brought us safely into port with a crew lacking a single other competent sailor or navigator. What were we to do? After a voyage that, due to seasickness, had often been utter misery, the most logical plan for me would have been to return to England to find a more conventional way to get to Canada. But I saw that not only as quitting a tough adventure but also as the end of a dream. I was determined to beat my seasickness and find another yacht to take us as close as possible to our destination.

As I was becoming increasingly despondent about our prospects, a beautiful seventy-seven-foot schooner, named Seaward, entered the harbour under sail and anchored near us. Yachties in strange ports make quick contact with each other. By the next day we had met the crew and knew a bit of her history. Kris, her owner, was a retired Norwegian merchant marine skipper, who had purchased Seaward to operate as a charter boat out of Antigua. One of the three crew abandoned Seaward to return to England, vowing never to go to sea again. The remaining two were Peter, a twenty-seven-year-old Englishman, and Ivor, in his mid-twenties, who was Dutch. They had sailed into the harbour because Seaward's engine didn't work. Later, I learnt that Seaward was built in Germany in 1936 and had spent the war in a boathouse in Hamburg harbour, which was the only building left standing after intense bombing by the Allies. She stayed in the boathouse until Kris bought her in 1956 and set sail with all her original equipment. Over the next few days, we spent time with Seaward's crew on board and ashore. We asked Peter a lot of questions and soon Kerry, Veronica, and I saw joining her as a possible way to get at least halfway to Canada. As we were mulling over our options, Peter received another offer.

The only other sailing boat in the harbour was a catamaran about twenty-seven feet long. Her owner, an Englishman in his forties, whom Peter had taught to sail several years before, had designed and built her in his back yard. He had two German women for crew. A rather plain, middle-age one lived in one hull, while a young attractive one lived in the other. We were led to believe that he alternated between the two hulls. He was worried about sailing across the Atlantic, and apparently said to Peter that if he would come with him, he could live with the young woman. After one look at the boat, Peter turned him down. The catamaran eventually made it to the West Indies safely, and her skipper became a successful designer of catamarans.

In the meantime, Kris found an additional crew-member. Johnny was a local, who probably paid to be taken to the States, but Kris didn't divulge details of the arrangement. This prompted us to make up our minds, and we asked Kris if he would take us on as crew, with our food. He readily agreed. I think the prospect of us bringing food was the key factor, as we soon discovered that there was not much on board. He said that he would pay us five pounds a week, when we arrived in the West Indies, but we were pleased just to have found a passage.

Our excitement at having found a new passage was only tainted by having to tell the major that we were abandoning him on, what we believed to be, his death bed. We discussed what to say, and I was nominated by the other two to act as spokesperson. The three of us went to the hotel to see the major. He was lying in bed, appearing even paler, thinner, and more haggard than when I had last seen him just a few days before. He greeted us without sitting up. I started my prepared speech, but both Veronica and Kerry quickly joined in to try and justify our decision, without mentioning the real reason: that we thought he was too ill to ever go to sea again. He finally raised himself up on one elbow and said that we must sign statements saying that we left for our own reasons, not because of any problems with him or the boat. We readily agreed and left. I felt relieved, but guilty at having deserted a dying man.

The next day we transferred our food and personal possessions to Seaward. Veronica had a single cabin forward, while Peter, Ivor, Kerry, and I shared a large aft cabin with two bunks tiered on each side. Johnny was assigned to the fo'c's'le [the forward part of the boat]. He did not eat with us on our first night, or thereafter. Kris wanted to keep him separate from the rest of us. He was from a simple, peasant background, with limited education, and did not speak any English. He appeared to have low expectations and, on the surface, to accept his separation into a lower class, a situation that with my background in Africa did not appear unusual. Later in our voyage we did socialize with him on deck, and though the relationship was cordial, he remained an outsider. We also learnt that Kris' idea of a woman's role on a boat was in the galley, a decision that did not displease me, and which Veronica seemed prepared, if not happy, to accept. We had planned to go ashore that evening, but to our surprise, Kris told us at supper that we would be leaving that night. I suspected that he might be avoiding payment of some fees or bills but he did not discuss such matters with us.

Shortly before midnight on December 1st, 1956, with Peter at the helm and Kris standing by the dog house, Veronica and I hauled up the gaff-rigged foresail, while Kerry and Ivor sweated the anchor-winch by hand, as there was no engine to power it. Our running lights either didn't work or were not lit. We set the staysail, followed by the jib, then all four of us heaved up the 1100 square-foot canvas main. Kris called for a tack and, with only a slight heel, we picked up speed and slid silently across the dark harbour towards the mass of lights from the Warwick Castle, a passenger liner moored at the entrance to the harbour. We glided past a silent and deserted Dawn Star, lit only by her mast-head anchor light. I looked back at her, rocking gently in the ripples Seaward left on the silky, black water, with mixed feelings. Our next tack was under the lee of the liner, her lights from high above illuminating Seaward so she appeared to be a ghost ship. We sailed away from the bright lights towards the dark shadow of the shore, tacking when we could hear waves crashing against the rocks. Our next tack took us into the open Atlantic Ocean. Seaward started to rise and fall over the swells, the wind grew and we heeled over, so green water cascaded along the lee deck. Kris ordered the mainsail dropped. Four of us grappled to furl the heavy flogging canvas along the boom, ripping our fingernails as we tried to get a grip on the stiff unforgiving canvas. With the main sail lashed onto the boom,

Seaward's angle of heel eased, though she still charged through the swells, throwing out a curtain of white spray at the bow, which flashed in the dark.

Kris sent Kerry and me below, off watch, to finish stowing our gear. Now came my greatest test—seasickness. I had thought long and hard about it while I was in Las Palmas. It seemed from what I had heard and read in novels, particularly about my fictional hero, Horatio Hornblower, that sea-sickness only lasted for a day or two until a sailor found his sea legs. I had also learnt that, if you don't fight seasickness, it can take control of you, and this was what I came to believe had happened to me on the voyage from Gibraltar to Las Palmas. I had given in. This time, I decided, would be dif-ferent. Kerry said that he felt sick and wanted to lie down. I told him that we had to finish unpacking first. I was sick, but I kept working. I don't recall how many times I was sick, but within twenty-four hours it had passed and the only other time I felt the slightest sensation of queasiness on the voyage was sometime later, when I had to go down into the stern locker where I was bent over double while hand-pumping drinking water from the holding tank into the header tank.

After a couple of days we reached the Trade Winds, which meant that our course to Antigua was before the wind, with following ocean swells. While this might appear easy sailing, it had two main disadvantages. Seaward, as all yachts do, continually rolled from side to side. With the wind dead astern, there was no sideways pressure on the sails to prevent her from rolling. As she had very low freeboard (height of the hull above the water), the sea often washed onto both sides of her decks. Not only was this uncomfortable but also, though I never considered it so at the time, poten-tially dangerous. It was easy to slip, and that could mean falling overboard. The chance of being recovered if you fell overboard in those conditions was minimal. The other difficulty was helming. Following seas can quickly push a boat off course and, if pushed off course, the wind could get behind the sail's leading edge and cause a gybe (sails swinging uncontrollably across to the other side), which can cause serious damage to the rigging or, in strong winds, even bring down a mast. This was a risky situation, as neither Kerry nor I had any experience at the wheel, but with the infallible optimism of youth, I knew we could handle it.

After a couple of days of having two crew on alternating four-hour watches—Ivor with me and Kerry with Peter (Veronica and Johnny did not stand watches)—Kerry and I were able to learn how to keep Seaward on course, and were each assigned three two-hour watches at the wheel. My watches were from midnight to two a.m., eight a.m. to ten a.m., and four p.m. to six p.m., though we were always on call for sail changes or any other necessary work. I quickly learnt to sleep in shorter, but more frequent, intervals and to brace myself in the bunk so I wouldn't roll out.

For better sailing before the wind, Kris made a square sail, out of a spare foresail, with a boom across the top of the sail, which was hoisted up the foremast. After a short while, the sail tore and had to be lowered for repairs. When it was re-hoisted, it twisted the spreader [the horizontal poles on the mast] and had to be dropped again. Kris said he'd go up the mast to repair the damage, but needed a helper. No one volunteered.

"Okay, you draw straws," Kris said. I looked up at the crooked spreader on the foremast, about forty feet above the deck, which swayed back and forth well over the sea at the end of each roll. Every muscle in my body went tense. I drew a straw. It looked long, but my apprehension did not abate until I saw that Ivor's straw was clearly much shorter than mine. As I was scared of heights, my sigh of relief was probably audible to all, but no one said anything. Peter took the wheel. Kerry and I hauled Ivor and a bag of tools up to the spreader in the bosun's chair, a canvas sling hooked onto a halyard. Ivor climbed out and stood on the spreader, holding onto the mast with one hand and onto the rigging with the other, his knees bending with the roll of the boat while we lowered the chair for Kris.

"No," Kris said, "I'll climb up."

Kris was in his fifties, about five foot six, and wiry without an ounce of fat. A heavy smoker, he'd had one lung surgically removed after contacting TB. He walked casually to the forestay, a five-eighths wire rope that was fixed to the bow at the bottom and to the mast just above the spreader, and climbed up it, hand over hand, his legs swaying from side to side as Seaward rolled back and forth in the huge Atlantic swells. There was not one of us crew, all under thirty and all over six feet, who would have considered attempting such a feat.

The spreader was returned to its proper position, Ivor was lowered in the bosun's chair, and Kris came down the forestay, hand over hand.

"Now we have to sail with the foresail," Kris said, "so keep on course. If you gybe, you're off the boat." Sometimes Kris was gruff and made threatening remarks. We always followed his orders when they were necessary, but if he was just playing tough we kidded him, sometimes refusing to do what he demanded. At first he was confused. As a tanker skipper, he had ruled his crew, whom he described as drawn from the scum of the earth, with an iron hand, backed up by a revolver if necessary. We respected his sailing ability, but were not prepared to kowtow. After a while, he relaxed and even laughed at himself. When we made landfall, he told us that it had been the best voyage of his life.

A few years later, I learnt to use a rig called a preventer, which held the boom on the side it was set when running before the wind, to reduce the probability of gybing, but this was not a common technique back when we crossed the Atlantic.

The wind and the sea remained relatively consistent, with only an occasional squall that did not require a sail change. We settled into a relaxed routine that included time for fun as well as completing assigned watches and chores. Ivor and Veronica paired off, while Kerry, Peter, and I became a team. One of my favourite occupations was to lie in the netting beneath the bowsprit that protruded about eight feet in front of the boat, and wait for the bow to plunge me through a wave, often completely submerging me—a fun but risky hobby. As we had limited fresh water, we showered with buckets of salt water on deck, which sometimes ended up in a water fight. Veronica did a great job cooking all our meals, with help from Ivor, but as we had no fridge and little fresh food, meals made with canned food, with limited condiments to spice it up, soon became dreary. To my surprise, I found myself looking longingly at food ads in magazines, in preference to photos of women, and dreaming of the meals I would have when we reached land. After about fifteen days, the pressure stove broke and not even Kris' remarkable ingenuity could fix it. The stove was moved onto the foredeck, where meals had to be heated up over a naked flame rather than over a pressure flame, which would have been very much hotter. Consequently, the quality of food was severely compromised. It was at about the same time that our first water tank ran out. The water in the second tank was brackish and unpleasant to drink. But the sun shone, the wind blew, and we were approaching land, so no one became upset and we continued a harmonious ship.

On day nineteen, Kris said that we would sight a light on land between midnight and two that night, my watch. During our crossing, Kris had taken noonday sights with a sextant, which gave him our latitude. We had trailed a log over the stern, a brass torpedo about four inches long that twirled through the sea to indicate the speed travelled through the water, but we lost three torpedoes to fish, probably sharks, within the first three days. As there was no chronometer, Kris could not take longitude shots. He judged the distance travelled by dead reckoning—checking our speed through the water, by eye, throughout the day and night and adding the estimated drift due to current. I spent the first hour and three quarters of my watch staring at the horizon. I was just about to give up when I thought I saw a flash. I called below for Kerry to take the wheel early so that I could climb up on the main boom to get a better view. I stared ahead, but the only light was the stars. I closed my eyes and then scanned the horizon again. A flash— or was it my imagination? I decided to wait until I had seen at least three consecutive flashes. My patience was rewarded and, after the third flash, I yelled "land ahoy" at the top of my lungs, but my cry was lost in the wind. I jumped down onto the deck, yelled down the companionway, and soon all the crew were on deck staring, full of anticipation, into the dark night. Yells of excitement greeted the first sight of faint, intermittent flashes on the horizon, slightly off our starboard bow.

"We deserve a drink. Someone fetch a bottle," Kris said. Someone rushed below to get a bottle of Scotch, which had come from Dawn Star, and some glasses. As the water was brackish, we each had a neat shot of indeterminable size, our first and only alcoholic drink in twenty days. No one was drunk, but we sang and laughed and joked as if we had been partying all night.

"Go below and rest," Kris said, after about half an hour. "I will take the wheel."

Though that was unusual, I thought nothing of it. I was just about asleep, when I heard a crash, followed by another one. All four of us burst into a raucous cheer. Kris had gybed the boat. Each one of us had gybed the boat once on night watch, and we were ecstatic that Kris, who had been so scornful of our poor helmsman-ship, had made the same mistake. I was just about asleep again when there was another crash. *He's done it again,* I thought. But the crash turned into an ominous grinding. Seaward heeled and swung around. We were aground.

As my bunk was closest to the cabin door, I was first on deck

"Up tri-sail," Kris ordered. I untied the small sail from the main boom, and then, with help from someone else, hauled up it up the mainmast.

"Up jib and haul in all sails tight," Kris commanded. Figures moved quickly in the dark, each somehow finding his right place. Kris handed the wheel over to Peter and went to stand in his favoured spot by the dog house, where he could assess the situation.

All four sails were soon hauled in as flat as they could go. With a strong wind on her beam, Seaward heeled over. The keel ground on the coral. Seaward bounced forward. Another grinding crunch, but lighter this time. Seaward edged forward.

"Helm to windward."

We were floating free.

"Ease sails."

I eased the sheet on the tri-sail.

"That's enough."

I snubbed the sheet. With the sails drawing, Seaward surged forward, like a horse freed from her stable.

A foaming wave appeared directly ahead of us. Kris called: "Helm over." Seaward came head to the wind then bore off so we were heading at about ninety degrees from our previous course, pounding through turbulent water. The moon came out to reveal a mass of foaming waves all around us. As soon as the bowsprit came close to a mass of boiling sea, we tacked again and then, almost as soon as the sails had set, Kris called for us to tack back.

We had no pre-arranged plan for such an emergency. The only time we had tacked Seaward was sailing out of Las Palmas harbour. Kris gave clear orders, each of us responded and, by luck or instinct, no one ran into each other, and each one of us ended up doing what was required.

I shivered with cold. The wind, blowing about twenty-five-plus knots across the deck, was laced with salt spray. Like the others, I was only wearing a T-shirt and a pair of briefs, but there was no going below to put on warm clothes.

I don't know how many more times we tacked, but eventually we left the boiling waves breaking on the reefs astern, and were back in deep water. Kris called for the sheets to be eased, and we headed south, parallel to the shore of the island. Kris stayed at the wheel and we all went below. The others climbed into their bunks, but I was too hyped-up to turn in. I dried myself, dressed in warm, dry clothes and a windproof jacket, and went back on deck to watch the dawn come up and see where we had nearly come to grief.

At the time, I did not realize what a masterful piece of seamanship it was to sail off a lee shore, particularly one that—I learned when I later looked at a chart—was a maze of coral reefs. We had been very close to being ship-wrecked. If Seaward had foundered I would not have had a life jacket, as I did not know where they were. I was a strong swimmer and I believed, at the time, that if we had had abandoned ship I could have survived. Hindsight indicates that I was naively optimistic.

We approached the entrance to English Harbour, a slim gap in the cliffs on the southeast corner of Antigua, guarded by the remains of two eighteenth-century forts, one on each side. The wind was on our nose as we beat into the narrow entrance. The bottom, clearly visible through the spar-kling clear water, came up fast, just before we tacked over and sailed into the centre of the outer bay that was surrounded by brown hills. We doused the main and jib, and then tacked over. Kris headed straight for the dock at an angle of about forty-five degrees.

"Ease sheets on the foresail," he commanded.

The gently flapping sail slowed us as we came near to the dock. At the last moment, Kris ordered Peter to bring her into the wind. Seaward came head to wind, her staysail and foresail flapping in the breeze, and stopped parallel and less than two feet away from the old stone dock, which had been there since Admiral Nelson's day. We threw mooring lines to the small crowd that had come to watch our arrival, and then dropped and furled the sails.

Kris had begged us not to tell anyone about going aground and we respected his wishes until after we left Antigua. His error was due to lack of accurate information. His chart was out of date and he had no navigation guide book that would give him details of navigation aids in the area. The sequence of flashing lights we saw was not recorded on his chart. He was confident that the island was Antigua even though it was only fourteen miles from north to south, from his noonday sights, which gave him Seaward's latitude. He thought the flashing light was on the south end of the island, when in reality it was the light on the north.

Chapter 17

After Seaward was shipshape and securely docked, we went ashore to meet the small group of yachties who had come to welcome us. A tall, suntanned, young man introduced himself as Desmond Nicholson, one of the sons of the operator of the Charter Company for whom Kris was to work. There were no customs or immigration officials—Kris reported to the office in St Johns, the capital city on the other side of the island, some time later. People seemed surprised that we were all still on good terms. After an Atlantic crossing, we were told, many crews (including some families) were not speaking to each other when they arrived. That surprised me as I had assumed that crews learnt how to get along and run a ship, and I was proud that we had worked well as a crew on our twenty days at sea. Perhaps it was the friendly joshing, which led to lots of laughter, that prevented any tension building to trouble.

After chatting for a while about our crossing, I explored the dockyard. The harbour was surrounded by hills covered in scrub bush, which came down to the waters edge and indicated that the flat promontory of land, on which the dockyard had been built, was probably fill. Adjacent to the dock where Seaward was berthed was a grassy area, which could have been used both a parade square as well as space to hold goods and equipment while being loaded on or off ships. Bordering on the grassy area were several stone buildings with slate roofs and wooden-shuttered windows. Most were in a reasonable state of repair, except one, which had no roof, doors, or windows. Only one was occupied, which was the home of one of the Nicholson sons. I later learnt that the stone and slate were brought from England as ballast in ships. The style of the buildings was typical seventeenth-century English: simple, rectangular buildings, of varying sizes, with rows of windows symmetrically placed to give an orderly appearance. At the north end of the dockyard were two rows of stone pillars, about sixteen feet tall and two feet in diameter, which, at first blush, appeared similar to the remains of a Greek temple, but in between them was a slip, into which men-of-war had been hauled up by hand-driven capstans to have barnacles and other sea growth cleaned off the underwater part of their hulls.

The dockyard dated from 1725, when the Royal Navy needed a base in the Leeward Islands to protect British interests in the Caribbean, mainly sugar and slavery, from the French and Americans. The low hills that encircled the harbour provided protection from both the hurricanes that sweep across the Caribbean most years and from hostile attack. We could see the remains of forts at the entrance to the harbour, high on the hills above it. The dockyard, which was named after its most famous commander, Captain (later Admiral) Horatio Nelson, grew to provide the support services required to sustain a large fleet of warships. As many as two hundred and fifty warships visited the Dockyard in 1781. I imagined the mass of rugged sailors from days long past, some press-ganged into service, working on their ships while the smartly uniformed marines stood guard, more to protect the officers, dressed in blue-tailed coats and white breeches, from sailors than from the enemy. English Harbour was never attacked.

The dockyard was closed in 1889 and remained largely unused until the Nicholson family arrived aboard their 66' schooner, Mollihawk, in 1950 and subsequently began one of the first chartering businesses in the Caribbean. Today, English Harbour is a National Park and a major centre for both cruising and racing yachts, with a hotel, offices, and trendy boutiques. When Seaward arrived, there were less than fifteen yachts in the harbour. When I returned to visit Antigua some thirty-five years later, there were over four hundred yachts in English Harbour and adjacent Falmouth Bay.

Carina, a fifty-five-foot schooner, had arrived shortly before us. My pride at having sailed across the Atlantic was quickly put into perspective when I learnt that Ian, the seven-year-old son of Carina's owners, had already sailed across the Atlantic four times.

Peter decided to come to Canada with Kerry and I, rather than return to England as he had originally planned. Our first hope was to continue by sea, but we soon learnt that the prospect of finding a yacht going anywhere on the West Coast was very slight. We looked longingly at a Virtue 27, a small but sturdy ocean cruiser that was moored in the harbour and was for sale, but we had no prospects of raising enough money to buy her. After more enquiries, it appeared that our best option was to go to Miami and then travel overland to BC. In the meantime, Kris asked us if we would work on the boat, for which he said he would pay us. The Nicholsons had been disappointed at Seaward's appearance—too many rust marks on the hull, bright work on the deck that was no longer bright, and brass dulled by sea spray. Charterers expected boats to be in Bristol condition, and a lot of routine maintenance work was required that would keep us busy for some time. Staying in English Harbour while we planned the remainder of our trip suited me.

As Kris wanted to spruce up the interior of Seaward, we moved ashore to sleep in what had once been the officers' mess, on the first floor of one of the buildings. Peter, Kerry, Ivor, and I laid our mattresses from the boat, along with our few worldly possessions, on the bare-planked floor of a barren room, about eighty feet long and thirty wide, with a verandah on the outside. Veronica had a room of her own farther along the verandah. I found the extra space, barren though it was, a luxury after a couple of months of living in close quarters in yachts, especially as the room was cooled by the trade winds that blew through the glassless windows.

Johnny stayed in the fo'c's'le of Seaward. By bringing Johnny to Antigua without proper papers, Kris had created a problem for himself. On the voyage he had suggested we drop Johnny overboard, close to land, so he could swim ashore, but the crew quickly vetoed that idea, and Kris didn't discuss his future with us again. While we were in Antigua, Johnny, whose English remained non-existent, worked alongside of us, but he did not join in our social activities and, as far as I know, did not stray far from Seaward, possibly for fear of being arrested for illegal entry. I wonder if Kris ever declared him as crew, as no official ever came to check out the boat.

We spent six weeks scraping, sanding, painting, and varnishing Seaward. I volunteered to sand the mainmast, to try to overcome the fear I had felt when I was faced with the possibility of having to go up the mast at sea. I was hauled up in a bosun's chair with a bucket containing some tools, plenty of sandpaper, and my camera. The higher I went, the faster my heart beat. When I reached the top of the mast, eighty feet above the deck, I hugged the mast like a terrified child hugging his mother. I told myself not to be such a wimp and get on with my job. While still gripping the mast tightly with one arm, I opened my camera and took several shots. When they were printed, the first three or four photos were a blur, as I was shaking so much. Telling myself to behave like a man, I began my tasks. First I checked the rigging attached to the masthead for signs of wear or corrosion, as Kris had instructed. I hope I did a proper inspection, but as I was still very nervous, I could easily have missed something. I started sanding, yelling down to be lowered when I had sanded all within my reach. After sanding the top twelve feet or so, I finally relaxed, began to enjoy looking around the harbour at the yachts moored around us. When I went up the second time, to varnish the mast, I felt almost comfortable and more confident in checking for wear and tear on the rigging.

Our working life was not onerous and we had time to explore the island. We visited a few of its many beautiful beaches, which were then wild and deserted, but were surrounded by houses and hotels when I returned thirty-five years later. Our biggest night out was New Year's Eve. We went to the Bucket o' Blood, a small resort in the northern end of the island that was run by an alcoholic American who, we were told, may or may not have organized the party depending on the state of his hangover. Luckily, when we arrived there was a party in full swing, with the wild and exotic beat of a steel band playing under palm trees, which appeared to dance in the breeze to the music far below them. Our one worry was girls, or rather the lack thereof. The island was segregated then, at least socially, and the only blacks at the party were staff. I had a crush on Lisa, a tall, long-legged brunette from Connecticut, but unfortunately she was Desmond's fiancée, and she had no interest in me. Our fellow guests at the party were a few couples, older than us, and a small group of American sailors. We were the only yachties. Somewhat despondent, we sat down and ordered the ubiquitous rum punch, when two attractive girls came in with an older man, who appeared to be their father. I figured I better move quickly or be left on the shelf and, as soon as she sat down, I asked the elder of the two to dance. We got on well and I learnt that she lived on a ranch in Oregon, was planning to attend an ivy league university, and that she and her sister were spending the holidays with their father, who was the officer-in-charge of the US Radar Base on the northern tip of the island. Unfortunately, they were going back to Oregon the next day, but she invited us to visit the ranch on our way to BC. Peter ended up sitting at the bar with the younger sister who, to his embarrassment, turned out to be under sixteen. Her father didn't appear concerned, but when they left, shortly after midnight, the American sailors took exception to the scruffy yachties commandeering two American girls. We suddenly found ourselves threatened with a fight, in which we were outnumbered three to one. Somehow we talked our way out of it and ended up drinking with them. Like us, they felt that Antigua, for all its beautiful beaches, swaying palm trees, sun, and cooling trade winds, couldn't be paradise without girls. We commiserated together and became great buddies as we consumed a lot more rum.

The local rum, from Barbados rather than Jamaica, was both a very smooth drink that we all enjoyed, particularly Kris, and about twenty percent of the price of a similar product in Europe. One day Kris approached us with a proposal: we pool our resources and fill Seaward with as much rum as we could buy, sail to Norway, around the north of the British Isles, where we would be met by Norwegian fisherman outside the three-mile Norwegian limit and sell the rum over the rail for cash. As the Norwegian kroner were not easily exchanged, we would then sail down to Casablanca where, through the money black market, we would buy young Arab girls with the kroner. We would then sail to Venezuela to sell the girls for a tidy profit. Neither I, nor any of my crew-mates, were tempted to become booze smugglers, let alone slave traders.

Kris was never short of ideas. His next one was that he would train Merchant Marine cadets, and asked if I would act as his purser. At least this idea was legal, but hardly sound, if he thought I was a good choice to handle the business side. I thanked him but declined.

By the end of January 1957, our plans to head for BC were in place. Seaward was in Bristol condition, freshly painted topsides, a rich varnish gloss over all her woodwork, and polished brass that reflected the bright, tropical light under a new, white awning. Kris had cleaned, tinkered, and then started the engine without trouble, for the first time since 1939. The generators provided ample electric power, not only for lighting but also for the winches that raised the mainsail and the anchor. Kris hired an experienced cook and a deckhand/steward to work with Johnny, who was now kitted out in white shirt, shorts, and shoes. The first charterers, three American couples, arrived the day before we were due to leave, but I did not meet them. I heard that one couple was very disappointed in the small cabin, which Kris had used during the voyage.

Ivor had found passage to the Eastern US on a thirty foot sloop. Veronica stayed in English Harbour, to look after young Ian and help his parents. Sadly, I lost contact with both of them, mainly because I did not take the trouble to write. Kris had no money, or none that he was prepared to admit to, so none of us was paid for crewing or refurbishing Seaward. We were not surprised. The last I heard of Kris was that, after a couple of charters with the Nicholsons, he and Seaward worked for an American film crew.

We booked passage on a local freighter bound for Jamaica, where we had to obtain a visa to enter the US, with stops at a couple of islands en route. One of the few other passengers was a young British Army corporal heading back to barracks in Jamaica. We asked him about cheap lodgings in Kingston. To our surprise and delight, he suggested that, as they had empty beds in the barracks, we could stay there for free as long as we did not come in before nine in the evening and left before six-thirty the next morning. After we cleared immigration at Kingston, little more than a formality with British passports, we arranged to meet our new friend that night, so he could show us our lodgings. In the meantime, we went to the US Embassy to fill out the forms and have our fingerprints taken to apply for a visitor's visa. We paid extra so that they could phone England to check if we had a criminal record. All being well, our visa would be approved in about ten days. We checked in periodically, mainly to make sure we were not forgotten, but also because the air-conditioned Embassy building was one of the few places to escape the hundred-plus-degree heat.

That evening we met our army friend in a bar and, after buying him a drink, he showed us how to climb through the fence to enter the barracks out of sight of the guard at the gate. The barracks was a Nissen hut, a tunnel-like building with a semi-circular, corrugated iron roof, with about eight beds—only three of them occupied. We had no bedding, but the nights were warm enough that we didn't need covers. An alarm woke us in the morning and we slipped out through the fence undetected, before inspection at 6:30. After three nights as guests of Her Majesty, our welcome wore out as the risk of detection increased.

While walking around Kingston, we came across a British seamen's mission and went in to enquire about a place to stay. They had accommodation, but only for people with seamen's papers.

"But we're professional yacht crew, waiting for our next assignment," we said. The manger was somewhat taken aback, but after more persuasive talk, much of it a gross exaggeration of our nautical life, past and future, he agreed to let us stay. He took us to the back of the main building, which led into an enclosed courtyard—with bougainvillea growing over a trellis—where seven small, single, clean, and comfortable rooms overlooked a swimming pool; the cost of each was one dollar a night. We stayed there for about ten days and had the place to ourselves, except for one day when a British ship was in port and some of the crew spent the day at the mission. None of them appeared to have washed for a long time as when they left, the swimming pool, which was usually crystal clear, had turned a murky grey. It was scrubbed clean the next day.

We also used our yachting experience to gain an invitation to the Royal Jamaica Yacht Club. Impressed with our crewing experience, the Secretary invited us to come on any race day to be available to crew, and use the club facilities after the racing. We only spent one Sunday there before we left. I crewed on an eight metre, my first experience of racing, and then we spent the rest of the day in the bar regaling members with tales of our voyage. Off-shore sailing was rare in 1957.

Jamaica was still a British Colony and segregation was still evident, but I don't think it was legal. As my colour prejudice was crumbling, I was not surprised to see that the Yacht Club had some coloured members, including the owner of the yacht on which I had crewed. There was political unrest in the country and we were warned to be careful in Kingston, but I didn't feel threatened as we explored the town or when we took an excursion in the country on a local bus. Occasionally a few locals were rude, but relaxed when we joked in response—most were friendly.

My only other notable memory of Kingston was an introduction to tourist marketing. I was sitting at a bar when the white manager came in with some animals made out of cigarette packets. He put them up on a shelf and told the black barman, "A dollar for locals, five dollars for the English, and twenty dollars for Americans." I wondered what price I was paying for my beer.

Our visas came through after two weeks. Our plan was to buy a car and drive to BC, but US Immigration regulations required that we have a ticket to leave the country. They were satisfied with us buying a bus ticket from Bellingham, a town just south of the Canadian border, to Vancouver. Fortunately, they did not ask us to show that we had enough money to travel over 4000 miles from Miami to our port of exit. The next day we flew to Miami.

Chapter 18

Our first destination in Miami was a series of used car lots. As I have little memory of them, I suspect I was humiliated by some fast-talking slime balls who were overjoyed at seeing at least one sucker, if not three, pretending they knew the score. Our hope of finding a VW van was quickly dashed— Floridians didn't buy European cars in those days. We ended up buying a 1948 straight-eight, Buick Coupe for $150. Peter, often the most ingenious of us, figured out that by removing the back of the front seats, storing them on the roof, and filling the small gap between the front and back seats with our kit bags, we could sleep three abreast, head to toe.

Our first trip in the car was across the lagoon from downtown Miami, to see the famous resort community of Miami Beach. After parking, we walked between two high-rise hotels and onto a windswept beach, over-looked by what seemed to be an endless row of tall, white, high-rise build-ings. While the beach was nearly deserted, we saw older women parading along the sidewalk behind the hotels, made up to the nines and wearing fur coats, even though the temperature was in the seventies. Their accents indicated they were probably from New York. After the relaxed lifestyle of Antigua, it was a depressing sight. When we returned to the car, a police cruiser was parked nearby. The cop in the passenger seat, wearing the ubiq-uitous shades, and chewing gum, beckoned us over.

"What you boys up to?"

As we were soon to learn, police checks were to become an almost daily occurrence. Our old car, scruffy dress, and youth made us suspicious. Our strange accents—few Brits visited the US in those days—and the fact that we were courteous seemed to allay much suspicion.

As we had already spent a couple of nights in a cheap motel, and did not find much to like about Miami, we decided to head out of town so we could save rent and sleep in the car. Prices were high compared to London, and we could not afford to pay for accommodation. Our destination was the University of Florida in Gainesville, where two ex-DLD boys, Bob Trigg and Arwas, were studying, on the recommendation of Finn.

As soon as we were in the country, we stopped at a roadside stand, in an orchard, where we bought a large bag of oranges, a gallon of honey, and a large jar of peanut butter, the first cheap food we had found in America. They lasted for our entire trip and, with the addition of a loaf of bread, became our fall back diet for the next four weeks.

Our first night was spent parked in an orchard. Still half asleep the next morning, I drove off and came face to face with a large truck flashing its lights. I was driving on the wrong side of the road. I woke up fast enough to avoid a head-on collision. That was the only time any of us drove on the left side of the road.

After arriving in Gainesville, we asked several students for directions. They were as bemused and confused by our accents as we were by theirs. We found Bob's house, which was adjacent to the campus. A beautiful blonde opened the door. After explaining who we were—I had not met Bob's wife, Joy, before—she said that Bob was not there, but told us where to find him. Later, Bob invited us to dinner at his house, with Joy and their two small children. It was the best meal we'd had for some time, but the atmosphere was distinctly tense. It was not until later the next day that Bob, clearly very embarrassed, told us that he and Joy were separated. He appeared surprised that we were not shocked, but relieved that he didn't have to keep up appearances any longer.

Over the next few days, Bob and Arwas introduced us to student social life. We drove out into the pine woods, where we went swimming in a natural pool, about a hundred feet in diameter, whose crystal-clear water bubbled up through rocks far deeper than any of us could dive and stayed at a constant temperature of about 75 degrees. After swimming, we were introduced to what, for us, was a strange American custom: roasting marshmallows over a fire while drinking beer. Back in town, we went to our first drive-in, the "Whatta Burger", where a whatta burger and a whatta chocolate milkshake cost 36 cents—a meal that both filled me and one that I could afford.

One evening we attended a party where, at about two in the morning, a slightly inebriated man poked me in the chest with his finger.

"You attending this school?" he asked.

I told him that I wasn't.

"I'll give you two thousand bucks a year to come here," he continued.

"Why would you do that?"

"I'm the basketball coach."

"But you've never seen me play."

"I'll teach you," he said, in such an aggressive manner that I shuddered.

I never followed up on his offer, partly because I naively believed then that universities were for academics, not sports, but more realistically because I knew that I was no athlete.

Through Bob's girlfriend, I met Alice, a true Floridian girl who had never been more than fifty miles from Gainesville. She was the first in her family to finish high school, let alone go on to university. She invited a group of us to her parent's home for supper. We drove through the woods on a narrow, dirt track to an unpainted clapboard house on stilts, where we were greeted warmly but formally by her father, a grey-haired, bearded man, wearing a stained work shirt, and rough work trousers that were held up by suspenders. He appeared intrigued, if slightly suspicious of three young men from "over the pond." There were about fifteen people there for supper, including her mother and three younger siblings, Arwas, Bob and his new girlfriend, and a couple of others. We sat on benches around a rough-hewn pine table, in a room that included the kitchen and took up most of the ground floor. What I mainly remember about that meal was sitting with my head bowed while the patriarch recited a lengthy prayer. Though I was scornful of their religion, I hope I was respectful and courteous, for though they were poor and uneducated, they had a natural dignity and were kind, thoughtful people, and fed us a tasty chicken stew. We returned to Arwas' small house, where we had been staying, to continue to party in a more relaxed environment. When the party broke up, instead of going back to her residence, Alice followed me to my room as if that was what was expected of her. She was so nervous that we slept on top of the bed in our clothes.

When we mentioned that we wanted to go to Mardi Gras in New Orleans, one of our new friends told us that it was scheduled to close the following day. We drove overnight, taking turns to drive while the other two tried to sleep. We arrived in the afternoon in a sleazy part of town, where the street gutters were overflowing with empty beer cans. We looked for Basin Street, as it was in the title of a popular jazz song, but it had been transformed into a series of office buildings, with no sound of music or sign of life. Tired and disappointed, we drove around town until we saw a nightclub. Inside, the few patrons appeared even more weary and disillusioned than I. There was no jazz, just pop music, to which a well-worn stripper gyrated dejectedly as she stripped down to pasties, which were covering her nipples, and a G-string. The big parades we had hoped to see, we were told, had had taken place a few days earlier.

We left town well before midnight, to find a place to park the car and sleep. After driving around several back roads, we drove into a field where the car became stuck in some mud. Too tired to dig it out, we decided to kip down for the night, but within a few minutes, we were besieged by the biggest mosquitoes I had ever seen. In spite of the heat, we shut all the windows. For a few moments, there was blissful silence. Then a high pitched whine hovered close to my ear. I lashed out. Silence. Then another mosquito and another, until we were under siege again. They had found gaps where the brake and clutch pedals went through the floorboards, of which we hadn't been aware. Urged on by swarms of buzzing mosquitoes, we dug and pushed the car out of the mud and drove back into town, to spend an undisturbed night in a parking lot.

Disillusioned with New Orleans, which had not lived up to my expectations as the world capital of jazz, we headed for Texas—a state that stood tall in my mind, due to the number of western movies I had seen about Texas cowboys. En route, as we drove through the back country of Louisiana, the generator packed up. Luckily, we were able to get to a small garage with one gas pump and what looked like a repair shop. It was closed, but there was a light at the back of the building. One of us knocked on the door. A man, I'll call him Bill, who must have weighed over 300 pounds, answered the door. At first Bill was suspicious, but as soon as we explained our predicament, a broad smile spread across his face.

"Where you boys from?" he asked.

Bill had never met anyone other than locals before and, fortunately for us, he must have felt that strangers with strange accents—at times we had trouble explaining ourselves in words he understood and we had trouble understanding his responses—deserved to be looked after. He gave us a beer while he finished his supper, checked the car, called a friend to see if he had a spare part, and then we climbed into his car and drove about ten miles to a wrecker's yard. Another large man, I'll call him Jake, met us at the gate. We wandered through a maze of wrecked cars, some stacked several high, until Jake found a similar model Buick to ours. He opened the hood—Jake and Bill both roared with laughter when one of us referred to it as the bonnet—and prepared to remove the generator.

"Now why would you boys want to go to Canada, when all they got up there is snow and ice?" Jake asked, as he worked under a flashlight. The mechanical work was delayed by many other questions, punctuated with much laughter. The replacement generator cost ten dollars. By the time our car was running again, it was after midnight. Bill charged us twenty dollars, an unbelievably low price.

We arrived on the outskirts of Dallas the following evening. Up until then, it had always been warm enough to sleep in a sweater covered by a jacket, but that evening it was a lot cooler. We thought about staying in a motel, but funds were low. As we were driving around, looking for a place to park for the night, we saw a stand full of newspapers. *If a hobo can sleep on the street, covered only with newspapers,* I thought, *why can't we?* Each of us had two weekend editions with which to cover ourselves. It was the coldest night of my life.

As we drove towards town early the next morning, we passed a park with some large, pseudo-Greek-style buildings, which were signed as an Art Centre. It was our need for a bathroom, rather than an interest in art, that led us to drive in. The parking lot was empty, but the main door was open with no security. Following signs, we found a magnificent and empty men's room with a row of about twelve sinks, set in marble with ornate faucets. As we had not had a bath or shower since leaving Gainesville some days before, two of us stripped down to wash all over, while the third one kept watch. No one disturbed us.

Heading into town, we turned off the main road and ended up in a seedy looking area. Seeing a pawn shop, Kerry and I thought that we might be able to increase our limited cash if we pawned the cameras we had each bought duty-free in Gibraltar. Peter stayed in the car while Kerry and I went to investigate. As I entered the shop, it appeared that about the only thing they sold were handguns of all shapes and sizes. I was mesmerized. A salesman asked if we wanted to buy a gun.

"Could I buy any one off these without a license?' I asked. I think I sounded incredulous, because I was.

"Sure," he replied, "which ones would you like to look at?"

I told him I wasn't interested in buying a gun, but he took one out of the display case anyway and handed it to me. When I told him I wanted to sell my camera, he suggested I might be able to trade it for a gun, despite having been told I wasn't interested. About then two cops walked in and asked us why we wanted to buy a gun. They did not believe our story and accused us of stealing the cameras. They marched us back to the car and woke Peter, who was sleeping in the back seat. By now we were surrounded by an ever increasing audience, predominantly black. We were frisked, then one of the cops searched the car. He found a knife with a six-inch blade and a cord wrapped around where a bone handle had once been. We did not know it was there. The cops moved quickly. Kerry and I were handcuffed right hand to right hand, and placed in the back of a squad car. Peter was handcuffed behind his back and placed in the passenger seat of our car. One cop drove our car, while we followed in the squad car. At the police station, we were held in separate rooms. I was eventually led into an office. A man was sitting behind a desk in shirt sleeves, his collar button undone with his tie pulled down, a fedora perched on the back of his head, and a cigarette hanging from the corner of his mouth. The butt of a handgun stuck out from a shoulder holster. Another man, similarly dressed, was standing by the window staring at me. When I sat down, the man placed his feet on the desk, crossed them at his ankles, and looked at me through the V of his two shoes. I nearly burst out laughing. His pose was a dead ringer for one in a scene from a movie (and a poor one at that) that I had seen recently. The questions were straight forward, and it was easy to identify when he was testing to see if I would contradict the others. After a while, the detective decided that we were harmless and became quite friendly. He called a uniformed officer to take us down to our car, commenting, almost as an afterthought, that he should check our passports. I don't think the officer had ever seen a passport before. He carefully read the flowing script on the inside of the front cover, which read something to the effect of:

"Her Britannic Majesty's government hereby requests and requires that ... you allow the bearer to pass freely and without hindrance ... etc. etc."

He never checked to see if we had a visa.

As we drove away from the police station, we erupted in laughter, joking about our interrogation and what we considered the ineptitude of the cops. Whatever the situation, humour got us through any difficulties we had, and kept the bond between us tight but easy.

We were determined to see a bit more of Dallas and drove around, choosing our direction by intuition. I may have been an adventurous traveller, but I was not a good tourist. It never occurred to me to go to a tourist centre for maps and guide books. The only place of note I remember was a sports-car dealership. As Kerry and I were sports-car nuts, we went to look at the Jaguars and Ferraris on display. A salesman approached us. When he heard our accents, he said we must meet his boss—who was also English. He was a small man with red hair and a broad Lancashire accent.

"I don't know much about these damn cars and I'm afraid to drive them," he told us. "They hired me because of my English accent."

He had married an American girl and had previously worked as a bank clerk in England.

Texas was not the romantic state I had imagined. It was flat, dusty, and boring to drive through, with not a genuine cowboy in sight. But though some parts of the country were dull, there was always the excitement of being on the move and wondering what lay over the horizon. And if that was dull as well, there was always something new not far ahead. As we approached New Mexico, the land became more rugged and even drier than flat dusty Texas. Mesas grew from lumps on the horizon to huge majestic pillars of rock, which stood sentinel over a desert that changed colours as the sun dropped towards the western horizon. This was the cowboy country I had seen in so many western movies, though how cows could have survived in this desert country was never explained. But my imagination ran wild. I could see myself galloping through the country with a band of Indians hot on my tail—naturally, I outran them.

After we had passed a couple of mesas, a sign invited us to see an ancient Indian village on top of one. We turned off the highway, and continued down a dusty track until we came to a car park at the foot of the mesa, filled with pickups. There was an entry fee.

"Let's walk around and see if there is another way up," I said to the others. Sure enough, on the far side I saw a climbing route. I led, and Kerry and Peter followed. Though not difficult, the climb of about three hundred feet became almost vertical near the top, but with hand and footholds. Determined to overcome my fear of heights, I continued to the top, where I was greeted by four Indians with their hands out for money. I looked down the route I had just climbed and swallowed. Coming up was bad enough, but going down, looking for footholds below me, was a different matter. The others agreed. We paid up, something we could ill afford. The village of small dwellings, built of mud, was interesting, but additional fees were demanded to enter a house or take photos. My decision to try and find a free back door was not popular. We left when the Indians closed the village at dusk, and went down by the regular path. When the Indians came down after us, they had changed from traditional Indian costume, and were dressed like cowboys. They drove away in pickups, with rifles on racks in the back windows.

A couple of nights later, we drove off the main road after dark to park for the night. The next morning, I climbed the small hill behind where we had camped, and looked down to see a jagged crack snaking its way across the desert, with sides so steep and sharp that it seemed as if it had just been ripped apart by an earthquake. By chance, we had camped on the east end of the Grand Canyon. This time, we did spend time as tourists. We drove to the state park viewing area, where I was blown away by the grandeur and beauty of what is one of the most spectacular sights in the world. I knew I could not capture it on my camera, so I spent some of my dwindling cash on a few postcards.

My cash reserves were getting dangerously low, but I had a plan for replenishing them—at the roulette tables in Las Vegas! All it would take was discipline. Wait until red or black had come up five times in a row, then bet one dollar on the other colour. If it didn't come up, double my bet, and keep doubling until it did. One colour could not come up more than eight times in a row, could it? We checked into the cheapest looking motel we could find and headed for a casino. At first my system worked, and I doubled my stake, but then … did my success result in my becoming less disciplined? Did one colour come up more than eight times in a row? I don't remember. But thankfully Peter was watching. He came over and said, "I'll buy you supper," in a tone that indicated he would brook no argument. I had lost about a quarter of the money I had, but I learned my lesson. I have never gambled in a casino since, and when I went back to Las Vegas about thirty years later, I saw three excellent shows but didn't bet a penny.

En route to Los Angeles, we visited the Hoover Dam. I was awed by its sheer power and splendour. How could so much water be contained by such a slim curve of concrete standing well over 500 feet tall? It was the most impressive engineering feat that I had ever seen, and made me wonder if I should reconsider and see if I could become an engineer with one kidney.

Our lack of tourist skills resulted in Hollywood being a flop. First it was the freeways—seemingly endless streams of cars that gave no quarter to a dusty, old Buick that was struggling to figure out where it was going. As I tried to ground myself, it seemed as if we were flying over the city, with exit ramps that circled over and under each other so it was impossible to tell where they led to. Finally, we saw a sign for Hollywood and left the freeway to look for a town centre, as there would have been in a European town, but the wide streets had no focal point, and after driving around block after block of sameness, we decided to abandon the sprawling, and inhospitable, metropolis of Los Angeles for the peace of the country.

All of us were now low on funds, so we decided to head for Canada as quickly as possible.

We drove through San Francisco without seeing much. Even the Golden Gate Bridge didn't live up to my preconceived romanticized notion. We headed inland to the east side of Oregon, where the parents of the two girls we had met in Antigua had a Ranch near Lone Rock—population 27. The girls were not there, but their mother, a sophisticated East Coaster, gave us lunch and a tour of the working ranch with her manager. We drove past a bunkhouse for cowhands, cattle corrals, and feed sheds, and rolling brown hills spotted with reddish-brown cattle, and even saw real working cowboys on horseback. I would love to have stayed and ridden over the hills, and maybe help round up some cattle, as I had so often dreamed about as I rode over the plains below our house in Kenya. But it was not to be. By late afternoon she sent us packing. We parked for the night off a back road, where I shivered under my one blanket, bought in Dallas, as snow covered the car—the second coldest night of our trip.

We arrived at the Canadian border in the early afternoon on March 20, 1957. The Canadian immigration official was unarmed, conservatively dressed in a blue, traditional British-style uniform, was courteous and friendly in a formal way, and gave me no indication that he thought I was unusual, let alone up to no good, even though I must have appeared unkempt and scruffy. This was such a contrast to the many American police officers who had checked us, when we were sleeping in the car or just walking around a town, during our four-week odyssey across their country. They had all given me the impression that they knew we were up to no good, that they were willing to use force—backed up by their ubiquitous and always obtrusive handguns, which hung on their hips, and expected subservience. But many did become friendly after they had checked us out, particularly if it was the middle of the night.

We were interviewed individually by the immigration officer. As my immigration visa was in order, his only concern was how much money I had.

"Three hundred and thirty-six dollars," I told him.

"May I see it?"

I showed him the thirty-six US dollars.

"There's only $36 here."

"I sent $300 from England to a bank in Vancouver, as I wanted to make sure I had some money when I arrived."

Fortunately, he believed me, as there was no money in a Canadian bank, though my monthly allowance—from the money my grandfather had left me—would be available once I was settled. I could have supported myself then for about four months on $336.

But we were not allowed to bring the car into Canada. We drove back into Blaine, immediately south of the border, asked at a gas station if they knew anyone who might buy our car, and were directed to a garage down the road. We parked the car with the engine still running, as the starter motor had packed up, and asked to see the owner. After a quick look at the car, he offered us $35. Taking a tough negotiating stance, we forced him to up the price to $36, so we could split the proceeds three ways!

I stuffed my few belongings, including the blanket I had bought in Dallas, into my kit bag, and said a sad farewell to the sleek, green monster that had brought us safely across America, about 4000 miles, as well as providing cheap (if cramped) accommodation. I was even more sad later, when I learnt that the car would have been worth somewhere between $300 and $400 in Vancouver.

The three of us walked to the bus stop, just short of the border. As I waited for the bus, wondering about my future in a country about which I knew so little, my reveries were disturbed by the squealing tires of a police cruiser, which did a U-turn across the road and stopped a few yards ahead of us. A short cop in a dark blue uniform, with a large silver badge on his chest and wearing reflecting silver shades, climbed out of the driver's door. As he sauntered up to us, he hitched up his belt onto his small pot belly, and hooked his left thumb into his belt, while his right hand swung by the pearl-handled handgun hanging low on his hip.

"Okay, what's the story boys?" he asked, as he paused in masticating his gum.

We looked at each other and smiled, but said nothing.

"I asked you a question." His tone was tinged with anger.

At that moment, the Greyhound bus for Vancouver, BC came around the corner, drew up in front of us and opened its door. Without saying a word to the cop, we climbed in; the doors closed behind us and the bus headed for the border. My last look at the US was a surprised-looking cop standing beside the road.

By the time all the passengers had been cleared by immigration, it was dark. My first sight of my land of opportunity, Canada, was fleeting glimpses of ghostly trees, flashing past the side window of the bus.

Epilogue

Canada was kind to me. I found a job as a construction labourer three days after I arrived, which paid me the exorbitant rate of $1.69 an hour—over three times as much as I would have earned in England. In September, I enrolled at the University of British Columbia to study engineering, which, to my surprise, taught me that engineering was not for me. In my second year, without the benefit of any counselling, I took six courses whose descriptions were appealing, and decided to major in the two that I liked the best.

One evening in March 1958, I was studying for mid-term exams when a friend phoned and persuaded me to abandon the books and come to a party. As I walked into the crowded house, I saw a girl drinking Lucky Larger out of a bottle. When she smiled at me, tingles ran up and down my spine. Suddenly it seemed as if all the others at the party were but fleeting shadows in the background. I didn't realize it then, but I was hooked, and my plan to play the field before settling down, until I was about thirty, went out the window. Stephanie and I married in the spring of 1960, and set off for a three-month honeymoon bumming around Europe.

I graduated a year later with a BA in English and Psychology, but still did not have a clear career goal. My options dwindled after I read *The Man in the Grey Flannel Suit,* by Sloan Wilson, a book that painted such a bleak picture of burgeoning business corporations that I decided I did not belong in business. I remained convinced, however, that somewhere there was a good career for me. A year after I graduated, I saw an ad for a probation officer. It looked intriguing, but I had no idea what the job entailed. After researching probation in the library, I applied and got the job.

For the next thirty-three years, I worked for the British Columbia government as a probation officer, in prisons, in training, and in three assistant deputy minister positions in: Corrections, Court Services and Aboriginal Affairs. When I left the government, I was appointed to the National Parole Board, from which I retired in 2001. How I became so fascinated with criminal behaviour, and how to correct it, is still not clear to me, but it was an exciting career that gave me the feeling that I was working to make the world a better place. Looking back, I have few regrets.

That magical spark that sent shivers down my spine fifty-five years ago is still there. Stephanie taught me how to relax my stiff upper lip, and share more of who I really am. Over the years, we have grown from passionate lovebirds to loving best friends. She read and reread the drafts of this story, and her support and criticism did much to smooth out the rough edges and jettison irrelevancies. She is my true soul mate and my rock.

CPSIA information can be obtained at www.ICGtesting.com
Printed in the USA
LVOW11s0917110314

376802LV00001B/41/P